S
W
E
E
T

&

S
O
U
R

SWEET & SOUR

One Woman's Chinese Adventure, One Man's Chinese Torture

By Brooks Robards & Jim Kaplan

Foreword by

Andrew J. Nathan

Director
East Asian Institute
Columbia University

FOR STEPHEN & VIVIAN —
READ THIS. DON'T BOTHER —

BEST,
Jim
7/17/23

Published by Summerset Press
First printing 1995
Second printing 1995
Third printing 1995
Copyright 1995 by Brooks Robards and Jim Kaplan
ISBN # 0-9645250-0-3
Library of Congress Catalogue Card # 95-067939

Portions of this book previously appeared in The Atlantic Monthly,
The Boston Globe, Daily Hampshire Gazette and Hampshire Life.

for

HAIYAN

friend & lifeline

TABLE OF CONTENTS

FOREWORD

By Andrew J. Nathan
Director, East Asian Institute
Columbia University

U.S.-China relations sometimes seem like an endless wrangle at the official level. But fortunately private citizens on both sides have quietly built a more enduring bridge, one that starts in inquisitiveness, amusement and tolerance, and can lead to mutual learning and even friendship.

Brooks Robards' and Jim Kaplan's five-month experience in Beijing was an example of such bridge-building. Whether in Brooks's work teaching journalism and Jim's work polishing broadcast news scripts and newspaper copy, or in their joint and separate adventures in and beyond China's capital city, or in their culinary and social adventures, the two brought to their experience a common sense of curiosity and a determination to be at once observant and accepting. Thus they report the good that they saw with unfeigned affection, the not-so-good with good humor and an absence of the acid criticism that often contaminates attempts at cross-cultural understanding.

Many books have been written about China, but the variety of human nature and of the Chinese way of life give each one something special to report. Brooks and Jim bring us the sounds and smells of life in Beijing today, the travails of Chinese transportation, the different stages of culture shock and bright portraits of Chinese and American newspeople, Chinese film directors, and other characters who are making their lives for the long or short term in an increasingly complex China.

Along the way the co-authors supply serious insight into Chinese society, the unit system, the pains of economic growth, the perils of the Chinese news business and even the world of Sino-foreign card playing.

The book is also a tribute to a marriage. In this institution forbearance of mutual differences is as important as it is between nations. Love and a sense of humor are the catalysts that precipitate enjoyment out of contrasts in character and experience. Respectively curmudgeon and enthusiast, Jim and Brooks were clearly the Spencer Tracy and Katharine Hepburn of their class of foreign experts in Beijing.

As a China specialist, I enjoyed taking a vicarious trip to the land I study and savored the chance to experience its wonders with fresh eyes. As an old friend of Brooks's and a new friend of Jim's, through the medium of print I relished visiting with two people who are energetic and entertaining. Finally, as a sometimes-weary traveler, I came away from their memoir celebrating the fact that there is still a place in this shrinking world far enough away and different enough to engender excitement, wonder and a sense of new challenge.

Andrew J. Nathan
New York
April 1995

READERS' NOTE

We intend this breezy, informal account of our five-month sojourn in China for other Americans heading to China for an extended stay, as well as friends and family. If you are expecting an authoritative history of China past and the "word" on China present, you won't find it. We leave that imposing job to the historians and foreign correspondents. We did go as citizens spending five months abroad, and we guarantee that no one can describe our experiences as well as we can. We hope the insights and events will entertain you, as they did the readers of dispatches we sent to national and local newspapers and magazines.

ACKNOWLEDGEMENTS

It's tempting to credit first-person accounts to oneselves and be done with it. The truth is, even journals are not always one-writer accounts by the time they reach publication. We never would have had the experiences we did without our capable *waiban* Zhang Haiyan. Among the many Chinese who helped us feel comfortable were Hu Yusheng, Chen Hui and Zhang Dan. Nellie Wang enabled us to travel through China with the minimum discomfort possible. American colleagues and friends like Marilyn Goldstein, Bob Slagter, Eldon Elder, Mike and Rachel Connelly and David and Cecilia Jenkins were sources of everything from quotes and insights to moral support. Our Fulbright family—Bill Shine, Mary Ernst, Gene Nojek and Liz Kauffman—kept us headed in the right direction.

Our gratitude goes to Andy Nathan and Paul Ryan for taking the time to scrutinize the text for factual errors, misspellings and misguided generalizations. To Donna Phillips for her cover graphics and ever valuable advice. To Teddy Milne who gave us the benefit of her self-publishing experience. To Cheryl Corey of McNaughton & Gunn lithographers, who shepherded us through the production process. And as ever, to Felicia Lamport Kaplan who gave the manuscript a bracing gut check for style and clarity. Thanks to all.

I

WHY CHINA? WHY ME?

"Suzhou is known as the Venice of China because of its many canals. They feed into the Grand Canal, believed to be the longest inland waterway in the world, stretching from Suzhou to Beijing."

1

HERS: OCCIDENTAL TOURIST

If you trace the longitudinal lines on a globe from the eastern United States over the top of the Arctic to the other side, you'll end up in China. This most populous country on the planet is the U.S.'s antipodes—literally on the other side of the world. The distance is not merely physical, and traveling to China—let alone living there—continues to be one of the great adventures of the Western world.

My husband Jim and I spent five months living, working and traveling in China during 1993 and 1994. I went as an academic on exchange; he came as my dependent spouse. The experience changed our lives. For five months, we were like fish out of water. The simplest, most basic things—eating, talking, working, traveling—provided so many challenges that the extraneous worries of daily life vanished. As we struggled to adapt to the customs, habits and language of a culture so entirely alien to us, our own culture began to take shape in much sharper definition.

I found the experience exhilarating. For me it was pure adventure—exotic, exciting, frustrating, rewarding. In retrospect China seems like a dream—a magical place where life, though hardly perfect, was simpler and somehow purer. It's the view of a romantic and may explain why I still feel we left much too soon, why I long to go back. In five months we barely scratched the surface. For my husband Jim, living in China was more like a bad dream. He found as many reasons not to like it as I did to love it. When you put together our two views, you find the yin and yang, the sweet and sour that make up the whole picture of China seen through Western eyes.

\#   \#   \#

It was not just chance that took us to China. My fascination with this country on the other side of the world began in childhood with stories my father told me about his relatives. They grew up together in the rural Kentucky of my father's boyhood, a place that was as foreign as China to a little girl living in suburban New York in the 1950s. Cousin Malcolm Moss seemed especially fascinating.

After attending Wesleyan University in Connecticut, Malcolm took a job with an export company and traveled to China. Even as a little girl, I knew that was the kind of adventurous thing I wanted to do some day.

While en route to China in the early 1920s, Malcolm met a young Mississippian named Fredonia. She was on her way to visit an aunt working in China as a medical missionary. In those days the trip to the Far East by boat was one of several months, and by the time the couple got to Manila, Malcolm had popped the question. Malcolm and Fredonia were married in Shanghai at Fredonia's Aunt Annie Fearn's house and lived in the Far East for the next five years.

Although Malcolm died long before I ever had the chance to meet him, I did come to know his sister Kathryn, and our lives became entwined in a way that further whetted my appetite for going to China. Kathryn had followed her brother north and attended Connecticut College for Women, where she served as Alumnae Secretary for many years. I became legally responsible for Kathryn at the end of her life, and when she died I inherited the many Chinese artifacts in her apartment.

There were Chinese tables, chairs and cabinets; Chinese pottery, rugs and drawings. I especially cherished a hammered silver tea set with its own wooden traveling box. Kathryn's chinoiserie, passed on during many years of living and traveling in the Far East by her brother Malcolm and his wife, became a valued part of my home and fed my sense of what it might be like to visit and live in China.

My first visit to China was, in fact, a day trip. It came inadvertently in 1988, during a trip to Japan. Jim and I were on our honeymoon, visiting former major league third baseman Doug DeCinces, who was spending a season in Tokyo playing for the Yakult Swallows. On the way back we stopped in Hong Kong for a few days. Although China had been open to the West for more than 10 years, for casual travelers like us it still seemed a difficult if not impossible place to enter. "Why don't you take a day trip into China?" Lord Lawrence Kadoorie, a family friend from Hong Kong, suggested when we paid him a visit. It had never occurred to us. The next morning, visas in hand, we climbed aboard a hydrofoil and sped past the breathtaking vistas of Hong Kong Harbor to Macao.

In Macao we transferred to a bus and spent the day on a tour through Guangdong Province in southern China, what used to be known as Canton. I felt an immediate attraction to this country and its people. By contrast Japan seemed crowded, expensive and Westernized in the least attractive ways. In China we entered another era and another kind of world. It was a distinctly non-Western one. We passed water buffalo in fields, duck farms, rice spread out in the streets to dry. The young woman who was our guide talked about living in dormitories in this Special Economic Zone and the need for "cutting" (abortion) as a means of controlling China's swollen population. We visited the childhood home of Sun Yat-sen, the founder of modern China, and a medical clinic complete with a pedal-operated dental drill. We ate our lunch in a collective. It was not hard to pick up from the Chinese people we came into contact with the sense of idealism that I continue to believe is basic to the Chinese character.

Four years later when I decided to apply for a Fulbright Scholarship to teach abroad, it didn't take much deliberation to pick China. Established in 1947 under the guidance of Senator J. William Fulbright, the Fulbright Program provides opportunities for American academics and professionals to teach and do research in a wide variety of international settings. The Fulbright Program has sent more than 28,000 American academics abroad to teach and do research. Funded by Congress and administered through the U.S. Information Agency, it has provided the opportunity for more than 31,000 foreign scholars to come to the United States.

With the Fulbright application materials arrived a thick pamphlet listing the many countries who participate, what disciplines they needed expertise in, and what kind of exchanges they were interested in. The requirements listed under the People's Republic of China included full professor status, which I had, and ability to teach news writing and reporting, which I also had. Fluency in Chinese was not required, and the award could be for five months, beginning in late August, the equivalent of one academic semester. The latter

5

was particularly important, since I had to take into account Jim's needs. To ask him to spend a year out of the U.S. would have been an excessive burden for someone who makes his living as a freelance writer and is at best a reluctant traveler.

I spent several weeks in the summer of 1992 preparing my application, which included a lengthy personal statement, course syllabi, and recommendations, for an August 1 deadline. Some time in December I was notified I had received preliminary approval from the Council for International Exchange of Scholars, a private organization that helps USIA administer the Fulbright Program. That was no guarantee of acceptance, however, since final approval lay in the hands of the Chinese government. I didn't get my hopes up yet. Then in March, 1993, Jim, who writes a bridge column, was hosting his bi-weekly men's bridge club at our home in Northampton, Massachusetts, when he fielded a telephone call from the China School of Journalism in Beijing. The school was officially inviting me to teach there beginning in early September. I quickly made arrangements with Westfield State College, where I teach Mass Communication, to take a leave of absence.

In June Jim and I went to Washington, D.C., for three days of orientation. We met the program officers who had been voices at the other end of a telephone line for the past year. We learned about the history of the Fulbright Program and what to expect when we got to China. We were briefed by former Fulbrighters in China, and we met the more than 30 others who would accompany us to China as 1993-4 Fulbright Scholars. Some of them would ultimately become cherished friends.

The summer months whizzed by as we made the preparations necessary for being out of the country five months. We purchased carrying cases for our computers and a printer. In one of the more comical decisions about how to travel to the opposite side of the world, we acquired giant, sailor-style canvas duffle bags. Once loaded, they were so heavy it took two people to carry them. The strain was too much for mine, which arrived in Hong Kong at the end of our stay with its metal closure broken and its contents spilling out. As a communication professor, I had felt duty bound to purchase a super-8 camcorder, but decided to get by using my old Pentax 35 mm camera, with a couple of additional lenses.

We had our passports renewed and applied for visas. We took medical exams and got ourselves properly inoculated. We made arrangements to rent our home in Northampton, as well as our summer house on Martha's Vineyard, since we were leaving before the end of the season and Bill Clinton was arriving with his entourage the day we departed. We had our mail forwarded, our cars stored. On Friday, August 20, the day before my 51st birthday, we said goodbye to friends and family. After a brief stopover in Northampton, we arrived at Kennedy International Airport in New York and left for Beijing.

The first leg of our trip was a 13-hour flight to Tokyo. Going directly from New York to Tokyo rather than stopping in Los Angeles or Seattle simplified things. All we did was eat, sleep when we could and watch movies. When we arrived at Narita Airport for a three-hour layover and spotted some of the other Fulbrighters we'd met the previous June during our Washington orientation, we greeted them with hugs like long-lost relatives. Then we left on the last leg of our journey, a four-hour flight to Beijing.

We arrived in China's capital on what was now Monday, August 23 at 9:15 p.m., since we had crossed the international dateline and picked up a 12-hour time difference. The airport was awash with people and confusion, but a Cultural Affairs officer from the U.S. Embassy and our liaison from the China School of Journalism quickly found us and spirited us through the crowds, wondering no doubt what on earth had possessed us to stuff all our belongings into such oversized duffle bags.

Amidst the din and chaos of Beijing's airport, our *waiban*, or CSJ liaison, stood out as startlingly familiar. Zhang Haiyan, who was to become our most intimate Chinese friend and associate, was as American as a Valley girl. Thirty one years old, fluent in English and amazingly articulate, she peppered her conversation with "hell" and "in your dreams, homeboy." As we drove through the dark along the old, tree-lined route from the airport, it was hard to get a sense of the giant, sprawling city that would be our home for the next five months.

We hurried through broad, empty streets lined with what looked like warehouses. Almost no people were out and traffic was sparse. A few heavy trucks and an occasional taxi. Eventually, the giant, brightly painted facade of the Friendship Hotel, loomed before us. The van drove us directly up to the entryway of our new home, 62833 Yi Yuan—sixth building, 28th entry, #3 on the third floor. We spent the next day sleeping in bizarre blocks of time as our internal clocks tried to reset themselves.

2

HIS: ACCIDENTAL TOURIST

Brooks was going to China to teach journalism. I was going to China to...what was I doing there, anyway? Many husbands would make some pathetic excuse for staying home, like a job. As a freelance writer, I had nothing to fall back on, except maybe checking into a mental hospital.

Not all of us anticipated five months in China to be a transcendent experience. Let me describe my own world view. To me China always represented memorizing an interminable list of emperors with weird names. The only figures I knew were Mao Zedong, Sun Yat-sen and Joyce Chen. You may not recognize the last name, but you should. She is a well-known restaurateur from my boyhood. Speaking of which, I was also familiar with Chinese food, which seemed good enough in America.

What other associations? Oh, little things like the Cultural Revolution that cannibalized culture and the Great Leap Forward that wasn't. When I thought of an antipodal country, I pictured not so much a place on the other side of the world as a culture and philosophy as similar to mine as that miserable little rodent Mickey Mouse is to my main fowl, Donald Duck.

Obviously, I had a lot to learn. Or so I tried to convince myself.

The record must also show that my version of the summer's events was somewhat different from my wife's.

Living in China looked as if it would be a snap compared to preparing to live in China. All you had to do was take a physical and so many shots you'd be too sore to shake hands; book round-trip, round-the-clock flights; apply for a visa; read nine or 10 books on the country; speak with everyone who has ever been there, get a State Department briefing and learn how to squat. I'll explain later about squatting.

The first three months were actually fun. Sure, medical forms kept getting lost and our faxes from Northampton to China weren't always answered, but there was a certain exhilaration to the

9

proceedings. "It will be a life-changing experience," we were told every day, and I kept repeating the line like a mantra.

Then came the June briefing in Washington. Finally, I would learn about the weather, the dress, the food, the monetary exchange—everything a traveler needs to know. Not.

We should have figured something was up when we were booked by our dutifully cost-conscious government hosts into the neighborhood-challenged Dupont Plaza Hotel, where even the televisions didn't work (Don't think the feds give *everyone* a free lunch). The opening session was interrupted by a loudspeaker that pumped in a lecture from another conference, possibly the friendly Baltic States affair from next door. "This happens every time I talk about foreign policy," said one of our speakers.

Once the intruding P.A. system was turned off, two of the scholars' kids took over. One babbled, the other hollered. Our hosts, still living in the Reagan era, had neglected to supply day care. When the children quieted down, one of the opening speakers had the presence of mind to begin, "In conclusion...."

The session was quickly taken over by an interminable series of bureaucrats from a mind-numbing list of agencies: the U.S. Embassy in Beijing, the United States Information Agency, the Council for the International Exchange of Scholars, the Council for International Programs, the Office of East Asian & Pacific Affairs, the Division for the Study of the U.S., World B. Free, Air Jordan. I wasn't sure what their purpose was. "There are three pillars to American foreign policy," one speaker droned, "the economic prosperity of the United States, our security and defense and the democratization of the world." Very interesting but, uh, what do we pack? "You will be carrying the name Fulbright, and defining it by your experience," said a double-breasted "facilitator."

Yes, we have commissars just like the Chinese. But where else do cadres disagree so publicly? One embassy official told us that our greatest accomplishment could be to undermine Communism. Another official later told some of us these political asides made his blood boil.

10

Let's hear it for dissent. Hey, we running dogs of imperialism are tough!

The afternoon session began with an IRS official and an accounting professor telling us foreign barbarians and outlanders (among other terms the Chinese use for us) the whys and wherefores of our tax situation. No one understood a word, a fact not lost on the panelists. "My greatest asset in this job is that I have a sense of humor," said one of the tax experts.

I don't want to suggest the day was a dead loss. We saw a video featuring commentary from former Fulbright Scholars. For the record, Chinese students were used to taking notes from lecturers; getting them to talk would be the Fulbrighters' first major challenge. The second would be finding a Chinese ally to guide you though the jungle of departmental chaos.

We heard lots of hints about cultural differences. China is not one of those idiotic countries where efficiency is prized above all else. We were given a nifty little adage to take with us: the three P's of China are patience, politeness and perseverance.

Of course, the speakers intoned, the standard of living is different in a Third World country. So are the attitudes. We see bathrooms as places in which to clean up. The Chinese see them as places for dirty and disgusting acts. That's why their bathrooms are dirty and disgusting places, where you are expected to assume a squatting position over a seatless hole in the ground. Made perfect sense to me.

In other respects the Chinese are somewhat like us, we were told. They're gradually turning to a free-market economy and discovering whole new levels of corruption. The machinations in the universities would make many a Capitol Hill elbow-twister feel right at home. The difference is that in China that struggle isn't as much among university officials as between university officials and their friendly Communist overseers and class monitors. "Once you get by the bureaucrats, the people couldn't be more friendly," one of the better speakers told us. That got the biggest laugh of the day.

After taking several pounds of reprints, position papers and other jabberwocky to our rooms, we dined on a delicious mixture of

11

fruits, vegetables and meats at the City Lights of China restaurant and got to know some of our fellow Fulbrighters. In the crowd were professors of everything from economics to pre-Columbian art, some of whom couldn't wait to take a vacation from U.S. values. Even a Vietnam veteran looked forward to another stay in the Far East.

Some of the professorial types were back for their second Fulbrights. A few had Chinese spouses. Other husbands and wives included freeloaders like me and a woman eager to study the Chinese approach to wellness. The kids were very young, which augured well for their chances of happiness abroad. Teenagers can only be counted on to complain.

On the last day of the briefing, we were divided into four groups to discuss living and teaching in China. Aha! Now we would learn what to pack. Not so. We traded generalizations and helpful hints like "I'm scared." Then, goody-goody, we gave reports like a bunch of high-school students returning from summer vacation.

At the living-in-China panels, people were asked to state what they hoped to accomplish. Establishing friendships ranked high, along with taking exotic trips, learning about a new culture and working on research projects. Everybody laughed when I said I wanted to learn the Chinese precision-bidding system of bridge. Did they think I was kidding?

The trip ended with a luncheon at the Chinese embassy, a large, unpretentious brick building on Connecticut Avenue. I decided I was looking forward to five months of Chinese food. According to one of our sources, American men in China lose an average of 12 pounds per semester. The women don't. Apparently, they already eat a healthy diet.

Eating also seems to be a good way to conduct foreign policy. Never mind ping-pong politics; we were headed for dumpling diplomacy. When an American official tactfully alluded to eight of our members who hadn't received their teaching assignments, the Chinese man in charge said he'd get right to work on the matter.

We left Washington a whole lot wiser. But they never did pack our bags for us.

Then came my worst summer in memory. Martha's Vineyard had never looked more enchanting to me. I was transported by the sight of the icebox-cake ferries in the bay. I looked at a neighbor's porch with its orange night lights on and swore I could see a Hopper painting. The idea of falling asleep to the sound of the foghorn outside Oak Bluffs harbor seemed almost too good to be true. Moreover, we didn't lose a single day to the weather. If it rained in the morning, it was clear enough to play golf or tennis in the afternoon. If the sun roared all day, by night were walking around comfortably in shirt-sleeves. This here couch potato took many a midnight stroll by Waban Park.

That was the problem: I didn't want to leave.

Our date of departure was August 19, fully two weeks before we normally decamped. Not a day passed without some preparation for China. I especially enjoyed learning how to kowtow. To Brooks the trip was excitement, to me a shroud. I resented the loss of every passing day.

Two friends arrived for a weekend, and we went to dinner at the home of Taipei-based friends. Bill is a consultant on international issues, and native-Taiwanese Yvonne is an interior decorator. Brooks kept telling people how ambivalent I was about the approaching trip, and people kept assaulting me with "What a wonderful opportunity" and other pieties.

Terrific. It would be a great trip if I learned Chinese, wrote a wonderful book, experienced some magical transcendence. Boy, if I don't take advantage of all those opportunities...

We had a lavish Chinese dinner. I could handle the many courses and the chopsticks, but a guest's comment gave me pause. "When you're at a dinner, someone across the table will toast you one-on-one. You have to empty your glass and turn it upside-down to show how appreciative you are." Apparently, this ritual can occur many times in the course of a meal.

I asked Yvonne about the tonal quality of the language. Depending on which tones you use, she said, the word "ma" can mean mother, horse, numb or scold. "You better be careful," said one of our friends, "or they'll scold your mother numb and put her out to pasture."

We took Chinese lessons from a Chinese-born housekeeper in Chilmark. (I would use her name, but she can't return home for political reasons). Many old China hands, including the author Ross Terrill, have proclaimed the language next to impossible for Westerners to learn and even urged people not to bother. For one thing, the sounds made by "z," "c," and "s" are almost identical. So what's the problem? I say czsszccsz all the time.

O.K., but surely I could learn some simple words and phrases? Not so fast. After an early lesson, I repeated *"Ni hao?"* (how are you?) and *"Wo hen hao"* (I am fine) about 50 times each, then promptly forgot them. I finally developed some mnemonic devices like "Knee how?" to help me.

The preparations continued daily. By mid-summer all I had to do was lock in tenants for our New York apartment; get someone to close up the Vineyard house for us; write a bridge book proposal and two magazine stories; peddle a proposal I'd already written but couldn't sell; write my weekly bridge column "Dummy" for the Daily Hampshire Gazette back home in Northampton, Massachusetts, and the Vineyard Gazette on the island; pack; deal with whatever crises emerged on a given day and learn an impossible language.

Before long I couldn't get to sleep before 4 a.m. and then couldn't get back to sleep after I awakened a few hours later. Thus refreshed, I screamed at Brooks and any driver or pedestrian who caused me even a minute's hesitation on the road. Don't let anyone tell you being a Type A personality isn't fun.

It doesn't help that I was getting very little aerobic exercise. Normally I would swim or racewalk about four times a week. Instead, I was playing golf. That spring we had been accepted at the Vineyard's Farm Neck Golf Club after six years on the waiting list. Naturally, I had to play every other day to take advantage of the handicap service, the preferred tee times, the tournaments, and mainly to justify the yearly fee. Naturally, I played my worst golf in 10 years.

What did I fear about five months in China? Loss of creature comforts, for one. Live like a Republican, think like a Democrat, I always say. Getting mired in some Kafkaesque machination from the folks who produced Orwell's worst nightmare. Acquiring one of the myriad strange diseases people catch over there and absorbing the strange cures available. I tried acupuncture once and never felt the friendly jolt called a "chee" everyone said would be forthcoming; what I felt was "ouch." If you enjoy getting stuck with needles, that's your own business.

Here was the up side as I saw it. I needed to be entertained night and day. TV, movies, friends, sports—anything to keep me from having to do something by myself. I'm a writer and writers need to read, but I wasn't perusing much beyond the baseball box scores and the bridge column. Without the movies and magazines I was used to and the choices in English-language TV, perhaps I would be forced to read some actual books and otherwise change my own diapers.

Then there was a little life crisis I seemed to be experiencing. I'll let Arthur Ashe's monumental memoir, "Days of Grace," which I actually read, speak for me here. Ashe quoted from "The Seasons of a Man's Life" by Daniel J. Levinson and four colleagues at the Yale University School of Medicine:

In the Second Polarity—Destruction/Creation—a man is aware as never before of the pain and affliction that other people have wrought on him and also the pain and affliction he has wrought on others, including his family. At this point, aware of his own mortality as never before, he also has a strong and assertive desire to become more creative.

That's where I was at age 49. Actually 49 1/2, which was one of the toughest (un)birthdays. Not that I hadn't accomplished anything in my lifetime. After graduating from Yale College, where I majored in procrastination, I learned how to write serious news leads—talk about a duck out of water—while getting a Master's at Northwestern's Medill School of Journalism. Then I built up an impressive-looking resume by spending three years at the Minneapolis Star and 16 at Sports Illustrated asking athletes what

15

they ate for lunch. I turned to freelancing in 1986, and four years later I had an epiphany. It was time to stop sportswriting and turn to something more relevant, something more socially significant. So I became a bridge columnist.

I could also boast of two fine and accomplished sons from my first marriage. Every other generation we get some brains in my family.

I was a good burgher, a member of Rotary International for crying out loud. Yet I regretted. Not a day passed without bemoaning old mistakes: opportunities lost, people hurt, personal and professional shortcomings. You know, really important things, like the day I was too chickenhearted to ask Beth Noble on a date.

Fortunately, the Ashe passage ends with these comforting words:

Dr. Levinson puts it this way: "In middle adulthood, a man can come to know, more than ever before, that powerful forces of destructiveness and of creativity exist in the human soul—in my soul!—and can integrate them in new ways.

Maybe this unprecedented venture would be a way out of the tunnel for me. "It will be a character-building experience." Brooks reassured me in her inimitable way. "After China, you will no longer be a candy-assed crybaby."

"Don't hold your breath," I thought.

II

AROUND & ABOUT BEIJING

"Before leaving Tianjin, we went shopping on the lively
ancient culture street and bought two kites, a deck of cards,
a little fake-jade horse, a fake-jade pig, some wrapping paper
and a Mao button."

## 3

HERS: CULTURE SHOCK, CHINESE STYLE

Living abroad is a series of shocks and gradual adjustments that with luck turn out to be rather trivial and much funnier in retrospect than while they're happening. It's all part of that wonderful psychological process known as Culture Shock, as we discovered on our first day in the Friendship Hotel.

The *Youyi Binguan*, reputed to be the largest residential hotel in Asia, was one of Beijing's oldest foreigners' compounds, where those of us who came to Beijing as foreign experts were made as comfortable as possible. Could it also have been to keep us from wandering around too much elsewhere? The building design combined utilitarian rectangles with pagoda-ed porticoes and roofs in garden settings.

A third-floor walk-up, our apartment was in the rear of a four-building square doughnut surrounding a grassy, tree-lined courtyard. Chinese grass, which like birds has made a comeback in Beijing since the early days of the Communist regime, was appealingly long and wavy. Our apartment was comfortable if somewhat shabby by American standards: a tiny hall, a living room, a bedroom, a kitchen and a Western bath. Early modern Asian in dingy shades of beige and mahogany. Air conditioning...hooray! Cable tv...whoopee!

Jim and I spent our first day in a jet-lag daze. Sleeping past breakfast, we decided to explore a bit before lunch. Next door we found two swimming pools—indoor and outdoor—two tennis courts and a small golf driving range. Across the street was the equivalent of an American mini-mall, a rat's maze of indoor shops deceptively labeled Pierre Cardin, with souvenirs, booze, groceries, baked goods and, yes, Cardin clothing that looked as if it were left over from the Sixties.

As the protests from our stomachs increased, our pace quickened, and we concentrated on the search for food. A sign at the entrance to our building sub-complex told us it was supposed to have its own restaurant. In Beijing, though, form doesn't necessarily follow function à la Western architecture. A sign for a restaurant may point to a particular building, but when you enter, you still can't find what you're looking for.

We circled the courtyard several times, arguing over which building might house the restaurant. The back of the indoor swimming pool? Not likely. The building that housed our apartment? Not unless it was hidden in the non-existent basement. That left two options, one of which was clearly another apartment building like ours. When we entered the other one, we saw nothing but a large lobby with rest rooms on either side and walked out. Next time we came back and went upstairs, where we discovered a large, empty dining hall with a bunch of young Chinese glued to a tv set. They turned and gaped. Apparently we beat even the tv for entertainment. Noting the dishes and cooking implements in piles on the floor, we concluded that lunch would not be served. Just because a sign says there's a restaurant doesn't mean it has to be functioning. At least not in China.

We marched double time the quarter mile past Building #1— the grandest part of the complex—and found another restaurant sign. In we went, but no restaurant. No second floor either. Since this was the foreigner's compound, I had imagined we would be surrounded by other foreign devils who would show us the ropes. Not yet. We waited patiently at what looked like a hotel counter. Finally a clerk came out who could manage some primitive English. It was better than our Chinese, despite six weeks of tutoring. He pointed us outside and around the building. "*Xie xie* (Thank you)," we said, clutching at the few words of Chinese we could remember. We retraced our steps without luck, until it registered that here in China, where you want to go is not where you think you should.

Zigzagging around the lobby, we found the advertised restaurant. It was set in the middle of a lovely garden with a pool and a garden house. We sat down anxiously at a table on the terrace in front of the restaurant building. Then we took bets on whether the menu would be in English. Surprise: it was. Not that it helped with our menu selections. When our order arrived, we discovered we had chosen two kinds of soup and two kinds of noodles. A

20

strange combo, but we devoured it. Exhausted, we then headed back to our apartment for more sleep. Setting up housekeeping halfway around the world from home reduces you to the most basic of needs: food and sleep.

Despite our virtually unliftable duffle bags and three large carry-on bags for computer paraphernalia, we had forgotten numerous basic necessities. Each day brought a new quotidian challenge. The first major crisis, though, was that none of the plug adapters we brought fit, so we had no working computers. Our *waiban* Haiyan—her name stands for sea swallow—found us a Chinese power strip with multiple plug styles, so we thought we were in business. Plug in the computers to the converters and let your fingers fly? Not exactly. We had brought the wrong kind of converters.

China, like most of the world, uses 220 volts rather than the U.S.'s 110—as international travelers know—so we needed an electrical device that would reduce voltage. Hertz and amperes are also involved, but I don't have a clue how. One explanation for why other countries use 220 is that it's more efficient, but Americans remain as habituated to 110 as they are to fahrenheit. Neither Jim nor I had read the fine print on the converters we brought. They all said use only for short periods of time—and certainly not for computers. What we really needed was a step-down transformer, said one returning Fulbrighter upon consultation. Another veteran suggested a power stabilizer.

I'd already run the battery for my lap-top down to near death. Close to desperate, I experienced a breakthrough one night around three in the morning. Since thanks to jetlag I was still up, I started reading the manual for my computer. Dimly I remembered that other Fulbright colleagues had told me their laptops converted to 220 all by themselves. Maybe mine did, too. Sure enough, that was the case. The truth hit like a bolt of lightning.

Ready for action, I removed the converter we'd brought and got ready to plug in my laptop AC adapter. Wait, I thought. I'd better put it on the surge protector. No one in their right mind uses a computer without a surge protector. In it went. Poof! The apartment plunged into darkness.

"I've shorted out the whole building," I groaned to myself. Groping around, I found a flashlight. Thanking myself profusely for remembering to pack that little device, I looked through the peephole in the front door and found to my relief the hall lights were still on. Where on earth was I going to find someone awake, though? I pulled out my Chinese-English dictionary and looked up the word for electricity. I already knew the word for no. Then I began pushing buttons on the telephone. Finally a woman answered. "*Bu dianliu* (No electricity)," I said. I tried it several ways, to cover all the possible tonal changes. It was hopeless, and after a long, awkward pause, she hung up.

Giving up, I went to bed, convinced I'd destroyed the power strip and the surge protector—which was designed for 110 volts—and almost melted down my computer. In the morning, a young hotel worker knocked on the door, took off her shoes, walked briskly over to the fuse box in front of my nose and reset the circuit breaker. It was something I would have done at home almost without thinking. Not in Beijing. At least not during our jet-lag ridden, disoriented first week, when quotidian matters loomed larger than the Great Wall itself.

4

HIS: ORIENTATION II

Our on-site orientation began at the United States Information Service, which is the same as the USIA except that it's overseas. After coffee, tea and doughnuts, we sat in a briefing room and listened to welcoming remarks from USIS press and cultural affairs officials, as well as Chinese officials in charge of education. All this wasn't as dull as it may sound. For one thing, there were no kids in the room for *this* orientation. They had been taken to the home of Liz Kauffman, the assistant cultural affairs officer in charge of educational exchanges. I was deeply grateful.

I took reams of notes, which won't be recounted here but will be woven into the text every time I feel like sounding pompous and official. No attribution necessary.

At the noon break we walked to a Chinese restaurant in the International Club and had a meal waiting for us. It was the usual fare of 12 to 15 courses. I don't think we ate dog.

Back at the USIS, Thomas Huan, the regional medical officer, briefed us. "For the first six months, you get depressed," he said. That was comforting for those of us in China five months.

"You make big things of little things. You turn introspective. You need to adjust. Things that seem overwhelming—reserve your judgment." I wrote in my journal, "My expectations are bad, so it can't be any worse."

We were warned about the multiplicity of diseases offered to us courtesy of the host country—hepatitis, rabies, Japanese B encephalitis, TB, AIDS, malaria—with the assurance, "The actual condition is never as bad as we say." We needed MedEvac insurance, though, because if we had to be flown out of Beijing on some medical emergency, we'd be paying $75,000 without insurance.

Let's see: water must be boiled five minutes, don't eat anything that hasn't been cooked first, peeling vegetables gives you false confidence, dairy products are problematic.

Following the afternoon session, we had dinner with three colleagues at an Italian restaurant in the Palace Hotel downtown. The place had a four-piece ensemble playing "Swanee" and "My Way." If I'd had my way, I'd have been on the next flight home.

Second day. Following another slew of instructionals—the economy, U.S.-China trade, American citizen services, living and teaching in China—we walked to the residence of U.S. Ambassador J. Stapleton Roy for a reception.

That morning the U.S. had levied sanctions on China for allegedly selling missiles illegally to Pakistan. You wouldn't have known there was any problem. The ambassadorial reception went on as planned, with as many Asian as Western faces in the crowd. So many cards were exchanged I thought I was at a bridge tournament. Of course, these were business cards. We ate enough chicken, shrimp, vegetable and fruit hors d'oeuvres to make up dinner.

I got into a conversation with a young American political attaché. His business card said "second secretary." Coming off a Master's in Asian Studies from Berkeley, he landed a job that 20,000 apply for and 2,000 get. He told me that assignments averaged two or three years, depending on whether it's a hardship post.

"What constitutes a hardship post?" I asked.

"Well, if you're going to freeze to death or bake to death. This is a hardship post, because it's a Communist country, people don't always want to help you and it's halfway around the world."

"I hear Washington is considered a hardship post. How come?"

"Here you get free housing. In Washington you pay. I can bike to work in 20 minutes. In Washington it can be an hour's drive."

"How does this line of work affect you?"

"Well, you have to want to see the world to get involved in this line of work, that's for sure. It can be tough on the spouses. They just have to tag along. Until recently—very recently—a woman had to leave the foreign service if she got married."

I persisted with nosy questions. What do spouses do for work? "Get a crummy job in the consulate. We have quite a few of those, since we can't give jobs to [local] people who may report on us."

Your wife? "She has a crummy job in the consulate."

24

5

HERS: HOME AWAY FROM HOME

Our home for five months in China, the *Youyi Binguan* (Friendship Hotel), was located in the northwest district of Beijing. The *Youyi*, as residents affectionately called it, was built by the Soviets to house their advisors and families in the Fifties, when they were still friends with the Chinese. Despite the fact that it is 40 minutes from downtown Beijing, this enclave, with its fascinating mix of foreign experts, expatriates and members of the Chinese creative community, is considered among foreigners to be one of the most desirable places to live in Beijing.

The *Youyi* was a world unto itself, a cross between a ghetto and a third-world version of the luxurious Miami resort, Fisher Island. Constructed in the Soviet style of the time, it was an attempt to provide all the amenities the Chinese think their Western guests will expect. The complex retained a heavy, utilitarian look despite numerous renovations and face-lifts. Like many Chinese residential complexes, it was surrounded by a wall with entrances that had soldiers on guard. The main building, #1, was faced with an imposing red, blue and gold pagoda roof. Everything in Building #1 was designed to impress, from the slippery marble floor we used to skate across on our way to the coffee shop/bar, to the pianist perched on an island in the middle of a water fountain, playing classical music from 7 to 9 every night

Arranged around and behind Building #1—roughly in the shape of a classical Chinese garden—was a variety of other buildings providing more modest hotel accommodations, shopping, restaurants, residential apartments, conference facilities, and a grandiose special events center called the Friendship Palace. Our courtyard, Yi Yuan, was designed as a replica of the Summer Palace, where members of the imperial family stayed during the hottest part of the year. Right next to us was the recreation facility, which included indoor and outdoor swimming pools, a small golf driving range, a combination video and dance hall and two tennis courts. I would often see hardy

Chinese tennis players braving the cold at 7:30 a.m. or batting the ball at night under lights.

To the endless amusement of taxi drivers loitering around the various hotel buildings and anyone else walking by, Jim and I used to race-walk along the driveways inside the complex. Our favorite landmarks were the deer park in the center of the complex, where we'd stop to feed "Buster" and his herd, and the Suzhou-style garden in the northwest corner, complete with rock caves, pools and tiny artificial hills.

Relatively free from the air pollution, traffic, dirt and noise that characterize most of Beijing, the *Youyi* was a wonderful, protective enclave. Best of all was the heady brew of people who lived there with us and became our friends. They included Bulgarians, Scottish, Japanese, Russians, Australians, French, British and Chinese, as well as other Americans.

We would meet over lunch or dinner at the Foreign Experts' Dining Room, where you could buy everything from mashed potatoes to Middle Eastern lamb for the equivalent of a dollar or two. Sometimes it tasted delicious; other times it was inedible. We would travel together on *Youyi*-sponsored outings to places like Dragon Falls or the Fragrant Hills. Together we would attend movies or Ed Sullivan-style variety shows. We entertained each other in our apartments and traded tips about where to buy or see or do what.

All of our *Youyi* friends seem to have led fascinating lives. Our Bulgarian friend traveled all over Europe with her rock-and-roll-star first husband, before marrying an American academic. My Australian colleague was teaching at CSJ in 1989 and had to be evacuated with his wife in a truck during the Tiananmen crisis. A Chinese-British friend, born in Shanghai and raised in London, returned to China to join the revolution in 1949, when she was a girl of 18.

I've concluded that living in China attracts a very special breed of individual. China's appeal comes from the difficulty in getting into China and living there, the challenge of learning to speak the language, as well as the pure fascination of China's ancient and complex culture.

You never knew whom you might find tucked away in one of the *Youyi* 's cozy little apartments. The most exciting encounter for me was with Chen Kaige, the celebrated Fifth Generation filmmaker, known in this country for his Oscar-nominated epic "Farewell, My Concubine," as well as the classic "Yellow Earth." I stopped by his apartment to drop off some books and found him in front of the tv with his assistants, hard at work on his next project or just relaxing— I'm not sure which. In either case, he had obviously loosened his pants to be more comfortable. When I arrived, there was an awkward scramble to buckle up yet still be cordial while I stared straight into his face in an embarrassed attempt to seem unrattled. Although I had hoped to interview him, this was the only chance I got to meet the great director, who spent most of the time we were in Beijing working on the script for his latest film, "To Live," in southern China.

6

HIS: A DAY IN BEIJING

At the *Youyi*, the day's drama could start before you got out of bed. Getting asleep, then staying asleep was always an interesting challenge. There were two unattached bedsheets on the mattress, rather than the fitted bottom sheet that we had back home. They were only a couple of inches longer than the mattress, they didn't tuck in and they did bunch up.

Maybe we shouldn't have slept at all. Chinese mosquitoes were silent but deadly spirits of the night. Giving no warning and stinging painlessly, they merely attacked and left an unbelievable rash that would linger if it wasn't treated right away. Two days into our stay I had a circular rash six inches in diameter just below my right buttock, and it itched like crazy. It took two weeks of hydrocortisone cream to cure the damn thing.

With or without sleep, we had to rise and dress before 9 a.m., when a little woman with a pageboy haircut came to clean the apartment. She whipped through the place like a dust storm. We liked her, though, because, unlike some *Youyi* staffers, she was cheery. One morning I was on my back in the living room, doing exercises. I had it wrong, she told me in Chinese and sign language. Whereupon, she got down on the floor herself and did a routine Mary Lou Retton would have been proud of.

Every morning two delightful treats were waiting for us outside the door. The thermos of hot water—one of China's greatest joys and available to virtually everyone—was absolutely essential. We didn't dare drink the faucet water, but anything hot was safe. The second treat was the English-language China Daily, which had a crossword even I could complete.

Yet another delight was minutes away. Since we didn't care to eat cabbage or whatever they served for breakfast at the Foreign Experts Dining Room, I'd head across the street to the bakery for some of the most wonderful rolls I've ever tasted: not too sweet but with a chocolate surprise inside. We'd dine on them, orange juice and Celestial Seasoning herbal tea we brought from America.

If Brooks was teaching, I might spend the morning reading. *Faute de mieux,* I usually had lunch at the Foreign Experts Dining Room. The waitresses were poorly paid for boring jobs and had dispositions to match. These professional grouses, who threw menus at us and then stood by our table expecting us to make an instant decision, were bad in the best of times. The worst of times came during my son Matthew's visit in December. There we were—Brooks, Matthew and I—eating lunch. Brooks and I routinely expected to pay half-price, because we had foreign-experts cards. No matter that Brooks forgot to bring hers: she'd eaten at the not-so-great hall many times, and the waitresses should have recognized her. They tried to charge Brooks full price. We protested. A whole bunch of waitresses gathered around the bill like a flock of magpies. Our imprecations were in vain. Brooks marched back to the apartment, got the card and returned to confront them. She received half price but no apology.

I used the outdoor pool regularly before the cold weather came and it closed down. It was Olympic-sized—50 meters—with three levels of diving boards. I did my patented individual medley—breaststroke, backstroke, sidestroke, freestyle—one lap each. Four laps total. Brooks found this laughable for some reason. I say 250-odd yards ain't bad. I swam for eight whole minutes: what did she want? In the winter I probably swam at least 18 minutes a session in the indoor pool.

After dinner cooked by our *ayi* (housekeeper), there was always something to do. Assuming it wasn't one of the two days per week that I copy-edited at the China Daily, we would walk or bike to the main building for tea and the just-arrived Herald Tribune. The evening might also include a bridge game at the apartment of David and Cecilia Jenkins, our favorite American-Bulgarian couple. David, a polisher at Xinhua, the national news agency, had insights on umpteen subjects. Cecelia, who taught English, was of particular solace to me, because she may have been the only person more miserable in Beijing than I was. As a friend said, "She has good minutes."

She always had good conversation. Take this one over bridge. "There's a Bulgarian expression," said Cecelia. "'It's not important for me to be O.K. It's important for my neighbor to be miserable.'"

"I like that," I said. "I like that a lot."

"Bulgaria was sardonic before there was Sardinia," said David.

So far, so good. In fact, I would venture to say the *Youyi* was the best foreign plantation in Beijing, and Beijing was the best place to live in China.

So what am I about to complain about? Well, it simply wasn't possible to spend all day, every day at the *Youyi*. Short trips were no problem, because biking was sheer joy and merited a chapter of its own. Longer-distance travel? Read on.

We took just one subway, which was well-lit, on time but not air-conditioned—putting it roughly on a par with New York. When we tried to get out, a flying wedge of incoming people almost knocked us off our feet. I asked Haiyan if this was typical. After a long pause she said, "Yes, unfortunately."

On buses we were cheek-by-jowl with other customers. So on virtually every substantial trip across town we were stuck with taxis. We always took the breadloaf-shaped *miandis*, because they were the cheapest, at 10 RMB for the first 10 kilometers. Brooks will describe these vehicles at greater length. Let me just detail my impressions. The things were box-shaped and rickety. If you were unfortunate enough to be in back, as I usually was, the experience was roughly comparable to sitting on a bench in a pickup truck. If you sat in front—as at least one passenger was supposed to do in order to ensure that the driver took the proper route—you held on for dear life. Cab drivers are the same in large cities everywhere: crazed by carbon monoxide.

The Chinese hacks seemed to view their job as one part transportation and two parts Grand Prix. Few of them spoke or understood English, many didn't follow our instructions even when we pointed out our destination on the map, and plenty were outright hustlers. When they deliberately took long routes, I often raged out

30

of control, exhausting every obscenity I knew. It was kind of fun, because they didn't have a clue what I was saying. At other times I began having revenge fantasies. "Nothing is too good for these guys," I told myself, "including capital punishment." And I don't believe in capital punishment. I'm sure I lost a lot of friends for America.

Communication problems dogged me daily, and not just when I was speaking Chinese. I'd get my haircut at a *Youyi* barbershop: all female barbers and a cost of maybe $2. Late in my stay I told the supposedly English-speaking barber, "Short beard, long hair," demonstrating with my hands. She cut my hair so short it too two months to grow any curls. A balding man's pride and joy are the curls on the back of his head. I was devastated.

Homesickness was always lingering in the wings. Another time at the barbershop, I heard Whitney Houston singing "I Will Always Love You" on the radio. I don't like Houston's work—as far as I'm concerned, she screams more than she sings—but the sound of a familiar voice singing familiar music in a familiar language tore me apart.

Late in our stay we went to the Holiday Inn/Lido Hotel to collect on a free brunch I won at a bridge game. The food was delicious, of course. I ate too many desserts, of course.

Afterward, we sat in the lobby and listened to what looked for all the world like a Mexican trio playing songs like "Take Me Home, Country Road," "La Bamba" and "Fun on the Bayou." Homesickness set in so heavily that I had again trouble maintaining my composure.

We wandered off to inspect the Lido stores and passed the trio on a break. "That doesn't sound like Spanish to me," I said, after overhearing them.

"I think it's Chinese," said Brooks.

We wandered back, and they started singing again in English, Spanish and a language I couldn't identify—presumably Chinese. One of their numbers was "Blowing in the Wind," which I've always considered the unofficial international peace song. Home. Peace. I was almost beside myself. I looked around, wondering if the hotel employees were picking up on the words. No sign of recognition.

When the trio finished, I drew myself together and asked the leader, "Where are you guys from?"

"Indonesia," he said. At that moment any place sounded better than China.

Maybe it was being in a relatively Westernized Chinese city that did me in. If we'd been completely cut off from Western culture, I might have coped. As it was, there were daily reminders of what I'd always taken for granted and suddenly missed desperately. I'll never know for sure. In the spirit of my host country, I stopped trying to understand. Yin, yang, up, down. Buddha said the best way to find something is not to look for it. I got sick of thinking, sick of trying, sick of even wondering whying.

In retrospect, it's obvious to me that certain people can handle an alien culture, and certain others can't. A perfect example coming up. Around 8:45 a.m. the doorbell rang. A hotel employee presented me with a phone bill. No big deal, we paid the hotel five RMB per outgoing call even though we billed them to a charge card. Why was this one was for 197.80 RMB? Plainly, they were charging us wrongly. I went slightly berserk. Brooks got out of bed, explained the error ever so calmly, and sent the woman on her way to check the hotel's mistake. My chest started pounding, undoubtedly on its way to cardiac arrest. My Type-A personality was a royal pain day and night.

By the last week, I was not counting the days at all. I was counting the hours. As the Maoists themselves might have said, it was entirely my fault and a matter deserving of much self-criticism.

#   #   #

There were days when I actually had a modestly good time. Here's the chronology of one.

The next sentence is going to sound like an Alfred Sheinwold pun-and-fun bridge column, but it really happened as I'm writing it. One sunny day in October a certain Mr. Sun arrived at our apartment two hours early, at 8:30 a.m., carrying two paintings we bought from him and his son. One of the paintings was a very subtle sunset in various shades of brown and yellow. The other had wind-blown reeds and marsh in black and white. With them on the walls of our apartment, the place looked like the Met. I guarantee it.

We had lunch with fellow Fulbrighters Bob Slagter and Marilyn Goldstein at the same *Youyi* restaurant where we ate during our first full day in China. Good food, good company—who could ask for more? This time we had two varieties of chicken. What the hell, they're the noble fowl: schmoos come to life.

After lunch, Bob, Brooks and I walked to a nearby park. Kiddie rides, foot-pedaled swan boats and rowboats, soft-drink stands and piped-in music—who could ask for more? "Muzak," Brooks said, pointing to the loudspeakers. I would describe it as Muzak even when it wasn't Muzak.

We had to pass a lotus pond to reach the lake in the middle of the park. I don't like lotus pads. They just get in the way. Rip 'em up and throw 'em out, I say. Ugly, rotten old things anyway. We watched a couple of ducks make their way through the pads: two tough quackers. Let's face it, nature belongs on a golf course. Why miss the chance to trash it?

Elsewhere, there was a section for angling. The fisherpeople had their trademark long poles sitting on supports, hanging way over the water. I didn't see anyone get a bite, and just as well. Chinese fish were tough, kind of like the New York worm-eaters who look up at you and say, *"Whaddaya doin' with a hook in my mouth!!!"* Or so says comedian Robert Kline. The difference is that the Chinese fish I saw were really ugly. When you're named carp, things don't get better very quickly.

By night the Fulbright four reassembled and headed to the Peking Opera. From our cab the downtown buildings looked terrific bathed in green and purple light. In fact, the use of light was superb in Beijing. I also found myself enjoying the ingenious English translations of street signs and posters. One of them read, "Take care of the fire in the important place." Your guess about what that meant is as good as mine.

The ride took longer than we expected, and we arrived for the 7:30 p.m. performance almost half an hour late—too late to sit in the front section where they serve food. We didn't see many Chinese in the theater, just tourists. They were eating dinner in front of the stage and shooting off flash cameras. The performance was somewhat less tacky than theirs. The Monkey God beat off the Supernaturals with a variety of wily stratagems. The costumes were elegant, the music enchanting, the acrobatics and swordplay enough to suit this sports fan. Best of all, we were out of there in 45 minutes. Just about right.

Famished and far from any familiar restaurant, we hailed a cab and headed over to Frank's Place, a hamburger bar near the embassies. For joy: cheeseburgers. Oh, heaven: french fries. Oh, rapture: the house drink. Made of Grenadine, Southern Comfort, rum, pineapple juice and lemon juice, it was called "The Memory of You Tonight." The Chinese create poetry even when they're not creating poetry. Crewcut young men—Marine guards from the Embassy, we guessed—were playing darts with their dates. There was a football game on the television and American pop on the P.A. that even the Chinese waitresses were dancing to. "I never thought I'd miss 100-decibel rock music," said Brooks.

Paintings, ponds, short opera, Frank's Place: a perfect day in Beijing.

## 7

HERS: CULTURE SHOCK, THE SEQUEL

If Jim and I had elected to stay behind the protective walls of the *Youyi Binguan* most of the time during our stay, we might have kept our level of culture shock down to an occasional tremor. Everyday life, however, necessitated at least an occasional foray into the rest of the city. Aside from being unable to comprehend the language, one of the biggest challenges was understanding Chinese money.

Foreign currency typically involves some of the more complicated adjustments to living in another culture. It isn't just the difference in the name of the currency and the rate of exchange into your own that you have to keep in your head. It also becomes a matter of values. Things you take for granted at home may be exorbitantly priced—if available at all. We soon resigned ourselves to spending the equivalent of $6 or $8 for a half-gallon of orange juice. The compensating factor was that other goods were incredibly cheap. A wool sweater could be bought for $4.

At the time we were living in China, two official monetary currencies existed. The FEC, or foreign exchange certificate, allowed the government to charge foreigners a higher price for the same goods that native Chinese bought with native currency, called RMB, or renminbi. I'm sure the Chinese government argued that, poorer than a lot of the world, their people should get a better deal in their own country. A clue to the inequity of the system, however, was the fact that the FEC was abolished in January, 1994, so that China could participate on a more equal footing in the world economy.

While we were in Beijing, a thriving black market existed to counter the government's attempts to inflate the the currency used by foreigners. A tactic used in many socialist countries, it was the same system I saw in the Eighties when visiting Nicaragua.

Seasoned travelers that we were, we bought plenty of traveler's checks in the U.S. before we left. We arrived only to discover that what we should have done was bring dollars. Nobody would take our traveler's checks except banks or big hotels. We routinely kept thousands of dollars in an unlocked cupboard drawer at our apartment. Merchants were mostly happy to take your FECs, but they did so at the rate of around five to one per dollar. RMB, which you could only acquire with dollars, exchanged at roughly eight to one per dollar while we were there. Officially, the rates were supposed to be the same. That explained the black market.

Factor into all this high-low finance the service charge a bank or hotel hit you with every time you cashed a traveler's check, and you see the problem. The losses started to add up. In the meantime, some establishments accepted only FECs—places like the stores and restaurants in the Friendship Hotel complex. You might see a souvenir or necessity there that you thought was a bargain, only to forget that the price tag was in FECs, not RMB.

Since each type of money had a lower value than the dollar, you always found yourself stuffing what felt like awkwardly large wads of bills in your pockets. Plus there were all those funny little coins, mini-bills and micro-mini bills worth next to nothing. You'd get so much into understanding the money thing that you lost all sight of how much you were actually spending. None of it corresponded to what you were used to shelling out at home.

Changing FECs for RMB on the black market was the only way you could convert your money, but it meant breaking the law. The first time I did it, I sneaked into a little shop and traded 300 FECs for 420 RMB. If I'd felt a little less like a criminal, I might have had the courage to bargain for a better rate. After a while, Jim started changing money at a candy store near the China Daily offices. He routinely saw hundreds of thousands of dollars cross hands in a matter of seconds. As long as the police hadn't targeted the place for a crackdown, everybody left a satisfied customer.

When the government announced it would eliminate FECs on January 1, 1994, all hell broke loose. One Chinese friend of ours who did business with foreigners got caught with her life savings in FECs. Even though her reasons were legitimate—she was planning to start her own business—she would have had some uncomfortable explaining to do. Fortunately, we had saved most of our official money transaction receipts. We accompanied her to a bank with her supply of FECs and cashed them in, no questions asked.

Our first major money transaction occurred when we bought our bicycles. My Australian colleague at the China School of Journalism, John Morgan, was an old hand at used bicycle negotiations, since he and his wife Freda were on their second tour of duty at the School. We planned our bargaining strategy beforehand. John told us what he had paid for his and Freda's bikes. The catch was, he had paid in RMB. Freshly arrived, we had none. Since John was a foreign expert rather than a Fulbrighter, his salary was paid by the China School of Journalism in RMB, rather than—like me—by the U.S. government in dollars into my bank account in the U.S. After negotiating a price, the trick was to ask what the peddler would take in FECs and try to get him to knock the price down some more. I came out a lot better than Jim in the bargaining. My hunter green Flying Pigeon was a equipped with a bell, a lock and a rack over the back wheel. Jim's lacked any of those amenities. After we biked home, Jim discovered a small cut on his hand. "I got gouged," he wailed.

Before long, it was time to venture into the larger world of downtown Beijing. My first downtown shopping excursion occurred on a day when Jim was playing bridge. I accompanied him to the Holiday Inn Lido Hotel, a large, joint-venture apartment-hotel complex near the airport, where he had heard the bridge game was scheduled for 9:30 a.m. Since Beijing is a gigantic city, 12 million strong, with no real superhighway system, we allowed an hour to get to the Lido Hotel, arriving at 9 a.m. Once there, we discovered to our dismay that the game didn't start until 2:30 p.m. We had plenty of time to kill. I suggested heading back into the center city to visit the Friendship Store, the famous, state-run department store for tourists. It was a big, multiple-story affair, carrying everything from cosmetics, furs, and souvenir porcelain to cigarettes and chicken parts.

The display of goods was by Western standards drab, confusing and unsystematic. Try finding the right aisle for tahini paste in an unfamiliar American supermarket, and you get the idea. At least in the U.S., you can ask a clerk in English where the item is. Some even have computer directories you can punch into. The only thing remotely Western about the downtown Friendship Store was its escalators—that is, if you can visualize escalators from the late Fifties. I never did manage to decipher the logic of goods arrangement. Making a purchase was an ordeal. The first clerk, if you could catch her attention, retrieved the item you wanted to look at. The second wrote up the bill. Yet another took your money. Then you returned with the receipt to pick up the merchandise. Overwhelmed, we walked out without buying anything.

We moved up the street to Silk Alley, which was a lot more fun. A narrow, little side street off Jianguomenwai Dajie, one of the main east-west thoroughfares downtown, it opened up into multiple alleys with row upon row of individual stalls. These stalls were chock full of shirts, pants, skirts, dresses, sweaters, jackets, lingerie, ties, quilts. It was easier to part with our money here. The merchants practically grabbed you by the collar and begged you to name your price. Many of them even spoke a little English, giving me the confidence to spout back some of my halting Chinese. After we had wandered up and down a while to compare goods and prices, Jim bought a bright purple shirt, a bathing suit and a tie. I picked out a paisley silk vest.

After lunch, Jim got into a taxi and set off for his bridge game. Alone in the middle of Beijing, I headed for China World, yet another giant hotel complex within walking distance on Jianguomenwai Dajie. The ground floor at China World consisted of a three-level shopping arcade, much more modern than the Friendship Store. I sauntered confidently past the cashmere sweater shops, the shoe stores and designer boutiques, and headed straight downstairs to the Western supermarket. I knew exactly what I wanted: peanut butter. What better food to have around for emergencies? Not only did I find it, but I also found dinner knives and, joy of joys, a butterfly-handled can opener to replace the gouge-your-hand model we had foolishly brought with us from the U.S. This supermarket was so efficient it had separate check-out lines for FECs and RMB. It even bagged your groceries for you. Mission accomplished, I was ready to head home. Wait a minute. How was I going to do that?

I thought I remembered which way I'd come in. Ten minutes later, I had to admit I still didn't have a clue. It turns out China World is not just a hotel cum shopping arcade. It's also a trade center. And that day, it was the scene of a rehearsal for the opening ceremony of the Chinese National Games. With China competing hard to become the site for the next Olympics, the government had organized a nationwide sports event to impress the visiting Olympics Committee. Squadrons of soldiers were marching around in formation. Battalions of little girls dressed in identical costumes practiced acrobatic feats. Black Mercedes filled with businessmen or dignitaries crawled up and down the ramps and driveways outside.

Every entrance I headed to was blocked off for the rehearsal. I had a phrase book with me, but how was I supposed to ask directions? By now I had learned enough Chinese to know that even if I got the words out right, I didn't have a chance of understanding the answer that came back. I was carrying a map, but downtown Beijing is laid out Soviet style, with chasm-like boulevards as treacherous to cross as the Grand Canyon and blocks as endless as football fields. Besides, English names on Chinese maps didn't always translate into what you expect. What I knew as the China World Hotel was officially called the International Trade Center on my map.

I repeated a mantra the U.S. Embassy staff had taught us during orientation—patience, politeness and perseverance. Then I added my own admonition. Don't panic. Eventually, I made my way around the parade formations and far enough down the street to find a taxi. "*Youyi Binguan*," I said, with a sigh of relief. The driver promptly took me three blocks west to the Friendship Store. Much mangled Chinese and a flurry of map gesturing later, we straightened out the confusion. In 40 minutes I was back at the Friendship Hotel in northwest Beijing. The ride cost me $7. I was convinced the driver had cheated me, but retracing our route on my map, I had to admit it really took that long. It was like going from Rockefeller Center to Queens in New York, except the signs were in Chinese.

8

HIS: BIKING IN BEIJING

A week into our stay, Brooks's Welsh-born colleague John Morgan and his wife Freda, who lived in Melbourne, Australia, took us bike shopping. They walked their own bikes beside us for the full hour it took to get there. Along the way John gave me a running commentary about Chinese life.

It was fun hearing English spoken by an Australian. I couldn't get enough of Morgan's blokes, buggers and blighters. "Make sure you take toilet paper when you go out," he said. "There isn't any in the public restrooms....See how the kids' pants slit down the middle? They can stop wherever they want and pee or defecate." The mess was hardly overwhelming, because there were virtually no dogs or cats on the street as per an old Maoist decree that was starting to erode. The decree was a typical example of Mao thought: dogs and cats don't build socialism, so let's get rid of them.

"The Chinese adults are very clean," John continued. "People think they're lazy, because you see them napping at midday. They just don't have the energy we do. It's their diet." All manner of foods were now available, but I assumed they couldn't afford the calories they needed.

The outdoor bike shop looked like a parking lot filled with used merchandise. Though the Chinese are hardly touchy-feely people, men started poking me in the ribs to try their wares. I hadn't owned a bike since I was a kid, and I felt completely lost evaluating them. With the Morgans' considerable help—Freda spoke enough Chinese to haggle—we bought two used Flying Pigeons for about $75, each gearless because Beijing is almost completely flat. It never occurred to me to check for a bell, rack or basket. I had none of them. This pawn was rooked.

The trip back to *Youyi* took only about 20 minutes, and I will never forget it. For the first time, we were in the swing, literally, flowing along on a river of bikes with businessmen and women in suits, peasants, tourists, workers, students. I felt as if I were participating in Chinese history, with no beginning or end in sight.

Bikes weren't the only wheeled vehicles on the road. In a scene out of a Red Grooms painting, there were bread-loaf taxis; accordion buses; motorcycles with sidecars; motor*tricles*; pediwagons, or bike-wagons, carrying 10-foot-high loads of everything from cabbage to black vinyl sofas piled on top of each other; cars; limos; pickup trucks, tractors with naked engines.

Non-bike traffic remained relatively new to Chinese bikers, and they were struggling to cope. Concrete strips separated large bike lanes from major boulevards. "The bikers are not supposed to cross over," said Brooks's *waiban* Zhang Haiyan. "If there's an accident, they usually get most of the blame."

What happened when there weren't bike lanes? Bikers constantly cut in front of motorized vehicles without even looking. Once, taking a cab home from the China Daily, where I worked as a "polisher," or copy editor for Chinese writers typing in English, I came across a bunch of police cars and a small crowd. They were standing on the side of the road, waiting. I quickly realized what for when I saw a bike lying on the road and its driver a few feet away, face down in a pool of blood.

Fortunately, nothing remotely similar happened to Brooks or me. Not that cycling wasn't a contact sport. When we were biking to a bazaar to find a pair of sunglasses, Brooks got cut off by a pediwagon and collided with another biker. She had a cut knee and elbow to show for the accident, not to mention a wrecked front-end fork. It was inevitable: the only question was which one of us would be felled first. Late in our stay I pedalled into a small pothole, which flipped me over. I did a nice roll-fall with my shoulder. "Were you hurt?" someone asked W.C. Fields after one of his cinematic pratfalls. "Not physically," he said.

Our shortest trips were to our complex's main building or to the supermarket, where we packed our stuff on the basket and in our knapsacks and headed home.

Biking around Beijing, we saw a sea change from the bad old days. No wall signs, no loudspeakers blaring Red Guard messages, no lines, little drabness, virtually no Mao jackets. Freelance vendors were competing with state-run stalls to sell a multiplicity of goods and foodstuffs. You could buy fruits and vegetables, both of which used to be scarce.

Biking was the key that unlocked adventure for us. One afternoon Brooks went horseback riding with Haiyan while I stayed at the *Youyi*. About 6 p.m. she called and asked if I'd like to meet them for dinner.

They weren't far away, so I biked along with the crowd for 20 minutes at a stately 10 kilometers per hour and met the women and Hiayan's friend Mike, an American who was studying Chinese, at an intersection. We all biked down an alley—most Beijingers seemed to live behind high walls in alleys—to a Moslem restaurant and had lamb, beer, noodles and string beans for a grand total of about $4. The peppers accompanying the noodles made my tongue burn and my eyes water.

Not all the lamb was chewable. "The Chinese custom is to spit it out," said Mike, using his napkin to demonstrate. He was taking four hours of Chinese per day. "Some of the words are really expressive," he said. Right now I *chi bao le*, which means that I have achieved happiness in the food sense. There's no word quite like it in English."

Mike biked all over. "It's the most unobtrusive way to see the city," he said. "You look like you're just passing through, but you see a lot."

"Mike's really a nice guy, don't you think?" Brooks said later.

"He's a fresh-faced, idealistic youngster," I agreed.

"Disgusting," she added.

"Just makes you sick," I said. I was pleased to see that Brooks was becoming as sarcastic as I was.

A week later I whipped over to the bike shop to buy a bell and decided to continue on to the physical-training school where I'd be playing my first bridge game at a Chinese duplicate club the next day. It looked easy enough on the map, and I was so confident I stopped on the first leg to buy a pair of blue jeans. I actually remembered some Chinese numbers Haiyan taught us: *san* (three) *shi*

(10) *liu* (six), which, stated in that order, indicated to me the 36-inch waist size I was asking for. They had no place for me to try the jeans on, though. I had to stand inside the shop, and do a little striptease right there. There's no easy way to express privacy in the Chinese language, and evidently no need for one. But the damn pants fit perfectly, and I forked over 42 RMB on the spot, completely forgetting to bargain.

Back on the road, I attempted to follow the simple map signs: Take Beisanhuan East to Changping South, then a left onto Gulou and a right onto Zhangzhung Lu a hundred yards or so from the school. Except that the signs were written in characters. I got lost, but as happens on the rare occasions when I drop my guard in a foreign land, delightfully lost. I drove down high-rise-flanked boulevards full of vehicles and narrow, tree-overhung streets with carts, people playing board games on the sidewalks and retirees in red armbands that signified they were on the neighborhood crime-watch detail. I enjoyed passing beautiful Hoishai Lake, with its fishermen throwing four lines at a time and bathers apparently immune to the parasites we'd been warned about. In a serious step backward, I was enjoying a day in China.

Eventually I realized I had passed the bridge-playing site some time ago, there being no signs in *pinyin*, or English transliteration of Chinese. I pulled in at the museum home of Song Qing-ling, Sun Yat-sen's late widow. From the picture captions, you got the impression there might not have been a modern China without her. Speaking of modern China, I never had the feeling I was being followed.

Back on the road, I found I was too exhausted to peddle and began hailing cabs. After a few rejections by drivers who saw I had a bike in tow, a breadloaf taxi, or *miandi*, picked me up. The driver, who helped me load the bike in back, wore white gloves and politely insisted that I use the working seat belt. As I've said from the start, Chinese cab drivers were really fine fellows.

China being China and yin being yang, not every bike trip was joyous. One fine September day we went to the Summer Palace, the spectacular summer home of emperors. Actually, "zigzagged" is a better word for it. Trying to bike there by the map, we got lost, spent an hour walking around at the Palace because we had an appointment at home, and got lost again on the way back. Same map problems as I had a few days earlier, except this time "delightfully lost" didn't apply. We wandered through one sterile high-rise zone after another; the buildings looked like props from the movie "Bye Bye Brazil." Just as exhaustion was setting in, Brooks figured out the way home.

Some misadventures were not so innocuous. We'd been hearing stories about anti-foreigner incidents in Beijing. One day our friend David Jenkins was bicycling along when he was surrounded at an intersection by five or six young people on bikes. One of them claimed David had bumped into her, causing an abrasion on her hand. Only after she and her friends dragged David into a police station did he realize what they were really after with this con job: they demanded a bribe of 100 RMB. He bought them off at 30.

Some Chinese were angry that foreigners got so much money and supposedly gave back so little, David explained to us. The last accusation was nonsense: working foreigners in Beijing routinely provided services like teaching English. The monetary rewards were definitely skewered—not by overpaying foreigners, but by underpaying Chinese. The 100 RMB I made every night at the Daily didn't sound like much, but many Chinese were making 200 a *month*. The low prices we were paying for everything were low only to us.

But I digress. Mishaps not withstanding, my bike became so precious to me that I would have shipped it home if the effort hadn't entailed taking the thing apart and paying maybe $200 for passage. Perhaps it's enough that my Flying Pigeon left me with one of my happiest memories abroad. There ain't no thrill in China like biking around Beijing.

9

HERS: BEIJING, YOU'RE DRIVING ME WILD

Nothing epitomized China's economic boom more visibly than Beijing's traffic. According to the English-language China Daily, 700,000 cars clogged the city in 1993, their number increasing 15% annually.

Beijing had extensive mass-transit systems. The closest subway stop for us, however, was not within walking distance of the Friendship Hotel. While buses would take you virtually anywhere for a pittance, you needed a pretty precise idea of which bus you wanted and what stop. Unable to read Chinese characters or ask directions easily, neither Jim nor I could negotiate bus trips with much confidence. Not to mention coping during rush hour with the sardine-can insides of a tandem bus. These giant vehicles with their accordion-jointed middles looked like caterpillars.

For us, taxis were the fastest, and with luck, surest way to travel. If bicycles transported us around our neighborhood, taxis were our lifeline to the rest of the city. Armed with a map, we would rehearse the Chinese for where we wanted to go, climb aboard and hope for the best.

Miandis, the little yellow microvans so-named because they looked like loaves of bread, were our chosen form of transportation. They hadn't been in existence much more than a year and already were swarming the streets like killer bees. Part of the wave of entrepreneurship washing over China, they might make their drivers rich by Chinese standards, if the vehicle managed to last longer than the debt incurred to acquire it.

We learned quickly enough to climb into the front seat next to the driver. In the event of an accident, of course, your body parts might end up draped across another vehicle, since the engine was not in front to protect you. Most drivers took it as an insult to their driving if you wanted to use the seat belt. They usually disabled them. Seated next to the driver, your map in your lap while you peered out at the indecipherable street signs whizzing by, you stood the best chance of actually ending up where you wanted to go without being cheated.

If there was more than one of you, someone had to clamber into the back. The standard *miandi* had two rear seats. They were designed for midgets, which meant you had to fold up like a praying mantis to fit in one. Usually the middle seat had been removed. If you felt your life was in danger sitting up front, the back-seat alternative provided no consolation. You could at least stretch your legs out when the middle seat was gone, but every time the *miandi* went around a corner, you rolled around like dice in a crap game.

Jim swore every taxi driver was a demon in disguise, ready to take him out of his way and charge double. I enjoyed most of my taxi-driver encounters. I usually had my longest Chinese conversations on the way to some remote part of the city. I would take out flash cards and practice on the drivers. As my fluency improved, I learned what part of the country the drivers came from, how many children or brothers and sisters they had. We discussed the weather, my work as a teacher at the China School of Journalism and what life in the U.S. was like. Sometimes they felt inspired to point out some of the city's landmarks. Other times they would correct my pronunciation or improve my vocabulary. They invariably offered me cigarettes, which I politely declined.

Taxi drivers being taxi drivers wherever you go, I had my share of misadventures. One rainy fall afternoon I set out for the Academy of Dramatic Arts, where Fulbright colleague Eldon Elder was lecturing on set design. Because I had never been to the Academy, I allowed an hour's travel time. None of the *miandis* parked in front of the Friendship Hotel wanted my business. They claimed to be out of gas or else wanted a more profitable customer. Since *miandis* collected their 10-RMB minimum charge for the first ten kilometers of travel no matter how short the ride, they often held out for a customer who was just going up the street.

One of the medium-sized taxis, which charged a 1.4 RMB minimum for each of the first 10 kilometers, offered to take me to the Academy for 30 RMB. It seemed like a fair deal, so I agreed. We got downtown to Changan Jie reasonably quickly. Then disaster struck.   My directions were carefully written out in Chinese characters. The driver took one look at them and let loose a stream of questions in Chinese. She clearly didn't have a clue where the Academy of Dramatic Arts was. First we went to the Beijing Children's Theatre. Then a Peking Opera House. In desperation, a movie theater. We tried asking other taxi drivers and pedestrians. No one had ever heard of the Academy of Dramatic Arts. Nothing is more frustrating than driving in circles while tongue-tied. Since I couldn't read Chinese characters, I was helpless to offer any advice. The appointed hour for the lecture's start came and went.

Just when I was ready to give up and go back to the Friendship Hotel, we rolled up to the Academy of Dramatic Arts. Two hours had passed since we left. I pulled out my 30 RMB, the driver looked at me, and I looked back. I was determined not to relent. After all, she was the one who said she could take me for 30 RMB. Eventually I broke down and added another five RMB. It only took another 15 minutes of wandering around the campus on foot to find the auditorium, where I arrived in time to hear the end of the lecture.

Some 57,000 taxis vied with the city's seven million bicycles, as well as pedestrians, pediwagons, motorcycles, mule trains, trucks, tractors and buses—all acting as if they still ruled the concrete. Watching the traffic from inside the safety of a *miandi* provided an education in how much Americans take for granted about cars. In Beijing repairs began wherever a vehicle broke down. Cars involved in crashes remained in locus flagrante until the police arrived, long after the participants disappeared. I once passed a truck with a bicycle lying beside it, the vegetables its owner had been carrying scattered on the pavement. No clue as to the fate of the poor cycler.

In the U.S., getting your driver's license at 16 is a rite of passage soon forgotten. In Beijing, driving remained a novelty. Drivers ambled across lanes when they needed to dodge delivery wagons or construction sites. They drove through red lights when convenient, turning right on red with relish. They drove at half or twice the posted speed. They gave new meaning to the term gridlock. And kept up steady staccatos of honking. If you needed a cab, you waved your arm and one stopped no matter where you stood, blocking traffic, ignoring safety, haggling over fares.

Mercedes, Audis and occasional Jaguars or BMWs used to have the run of Beijing's roads. By the time we got there, these cadre cars had been outnumbered. They would still try to pull rank by turning on emergency flashers or clapping blue lights to the rooftop like cops from an American tv show. The frequency with which we saw them abandoned, fenders crunched into the side of a too sluggish bus or truck, struck a note of righteous satisfaction in our democratic hearts—and no doubt those of the perk-less Chinese populace.

The authorities knew how bad it was; in the fall of 1993 they called in 200 foreign experts for consultation. Work on the airport highway was completed practically in the blink of an eye, turning what used to be a nightmare trip through the city into an almost pleasant experience. By the end of 1993, work crews were busy removing every tree and shrub near us along the Third Ring Road, one of the city's main arteries, for an expansion project. We read in the newspaper that more suitable homes would be found for the vegetation, a welcome cry from the chain-saw ethic in the U.S. Remembering many a leisurely, shady trip up the street on my bicycle from the Friendship Hotel and along the Third Ring Road, though, I was more than a little sad to see the trees go.

My only real taxi ride from hell came at the end of our five-month stay. After spending the afternoon at the Italian news agency ANSA doing some research, I was going to meet Jim and some friends for dinner at a dumpling restaurant downtown. By then, I could speak Chinese reasonably well, even if I couldn't read characters. The directions to the restaurant seemed simple enough. Deceptively so. Take a taxi to the Minzu Hotel on Changan Jie; walk up the street to the China Air building; go to the restaurant across from it. I hailed a cab, told him to go to the Minzu Hotel and pointed on the map, just to make sure there was no misunderstanding.

It was dark out, but not so dark that I couldn't tell we had turned onto the Second Ring Road. We were heading north, almost in the opposite direction from the Minzu Hotel. "He must be going this way to avoid rush hour traffic," I rationalized. In the meantime, the taxi meter was blinking away. Politely at first, I began to ask, "Isn't this out of the way?" No answer. The more insistent I was, the more he looked at me as if to say, "What strange tongue are you mumbling in, lady?" When you don't speak a language well, it's very easy to believe you're mixing things up. Particularly in the case of a four-toned language like Chinese. There's no mistake about "*bu*," though. It means "no." As we got closer and closer to of all places the Friendship Hotel—at the opposite end of the city from where we had started—my protests turned into shouts. Finally, after a lot of yelling and violent jabs at the map, I persuaded the driver to head in the right direction. So far I was only a half hour late, but I could hear my long-suffering husband complaining to our friends, "She's never on time!"

At last the driver turned onto Changan Jie, and I saw the Minzu Hotel loom up—across the street from us. Not just a hop, skip and jump across the street but a Gobi Desert across the street. The driver pulled over and waited expectantly for me to get out. No way was I going to risk life and limb to cross Changan Jie mid-block at rush hour. "*Bu*," I said firmly for the hundredth time. "Go to the hotel." With great reluctance, he maneuvered onto a side street, across to the north side of Changan Jie and up to the entrance of the hotel.

I looked in my wallet and saw I had no bills smaller than a 50-RMB note. "*Bu*," I said to myself. There was no way I was going to pay this crook the full rate on the meter. I went into the lobby of the hotel to get change. He followed me, waiting somewhat smugly for his fare. When I gave him half the amount on the meter, he complained vociferously, so I marched back out to the taxi, grabbed his taxi license off the visor and returned. In English I explained to the desk clerk in the hotel that I wanted to file a complaint against this man. Would they please help?

"Are you a guest here?" the clerk asked.

"No." I answered, and I knew my goose was cooked.

"Let me get the assistant manager," the clerk said, disappearing into an office behind the counter.

In a minute she came out with another young woman, who took a quick look at me and the taxi driver before going back into her office and closing the door. It was an instant lesson in international diplomacy.

"I'm sorry," the clerk said, "I'm afraid we can't help."

By now my level of anger and frustration was so high I had lost the ability to speak Chinese. I handed the driver some money. "That's all you get," I said in English.

He stuffed the cash back in my hand, sputtering something I couldn't understand. Throwing the money at him, I stalked out. I had made the one mistake you never want to commit in China. I had completely lost my temper. Would he follow me into the parking lot and punch me in the nose? I didn't stick around to find out but melted into the crowd on Changan Jie. I needn't have worried. Once you lose your temper in China, you've lost face, and the other guy wins. I'm sure my taxi driver gloated all the way home.

Now I was an hour late, and the problem remained of finding the China Air Building. It was dark, and nothing looked familiar. I wasn't even sure anymore which side of the cavernous street the building was on. I was hanging desperately onto what little Chinese I could still remember. After a few blocks, I went into a jewelry store and asked for directions. On the third try, the clerk finally understood what I was trying to say and offered to write it down. "But I don't understand characters," I said. She snickered. A Westerner with a speech defect who's illiterate, she must have thought.

Screwing up my courage, I walked into another store. Drawing a picture of an airplane, I asked, "*Zai na'er* (where is)?" "Up the street," the two clerks said in English, writing down a number and address in Chinese. There were no visible numbers on the buildings, so after another block or so, I decided to wing it and try the other side of the street. Plunged into despair, I wandered past legions of anonymous restaurants and was about to do what I least wanted to in the world: hail another taxi. Then Jim came walking up.

"Where have you been?" he asked.

"You don't want to know," I said. It was the only time during our five-month stay I really lost my composure.

10

HIS: EXCESS OF ENTHUSIASM

Our sightseeing began in and around Beijing. First stop: the Forbidden City. This place is merely the Eighth Wonder of the World. The Home of Chinese emperors, it comes complete with a 20-ton marble staircase; stone lions; bronze dragons, cranes and turtles, and a veritable panorama of Chinese history. Here's where yin and yang came from. Here's where the practice of kowtowing started. And what scope. It took fully two hours to walk through the Forbidden City: the place looked as unreal as a sci-fi movie set.

Now here's the kicker. The best way to see the Forbidden City was the tourista way. One didn't just walk around and emote. Every Man Jack and Woman Jill in our party of Fulbright Scholars and significant others used headsets and listened to a tape narrated by Roger Moore. "We'll pick up again at Station Five," Moore would say, and we'd walk over to a red-and white sign at the next highlight. Tourista-bashers will gag, but it was the best possible way to proceed. You didn't want to be reading while looking at sights. Our eyes were on the prize while we listened to something even more entertaining than the guidebook. Moore confided that one emperor dropped dead after doing the wild thing with too many of his concubines.

The tour and tape cost under $10.

Next stop, next day: the Great Wall of China. Show me another country where you get a double play like the Forbidden City and the Great Wall.

The best thing about the Great Wall of China is that you can say you've been there. I know, I know. It spans fully 3,000 miles or kilometers or something. Took 300,000 men 10 years to build. Visible from the moon. Wide enough at some points to fit five horses side by side. One of the Seven Wonders of the World. Trust me, there's less to the Great Wall of China than meets the eye.

After a two-hour bus ride from Beijing, we were let out at the Mutianyu entrance. One of the first things we saw was a sign with the words "quiet and tasteful" describing the tourist area. You be the judge. First, we had to climb about 10,000 steps through a gaggle of at least 100 chattering souvenir hawkers. "It's not the soldiers we have to worry about," said a member of our party. "If the hawkers ever attack, we're in trouble."

So we ran the gauntlet and took the cable car to the top. What did we see? Exactly what we'd already seen in pictures and books: a wall. Our designated segment was open for one kilometer in each direction. We went left. A couple that started right turned back and caught up to us. "What did you see?" we asked them. "Same thing," they said. Exactly: a bunch of rocks thrown together. After 15 minutes, I hit the Wall.

What they don't tell you about the Great Wall is that it didn't work. The place was supposed to protect the Chinese from their enemies, but they were colonials before the thing was built and after. The problem was something called the concentration principle, a political scientist told me. If you have too many soldiers at one point, your enemies pick another spot. If you spread 'em too thin, the attackers pick you apart. The Great Wall didn't protect the Chinese from the barbarians, or the librarians, either.

I really loved the graffiti on the Great Wall of China, and I can't wait to see the Burger King at the Taj Mahal. As I write, I'm salivating over the water slide at Victoria Falls.

The record should show that Brooks was transformed by the Wall. She clattered around with her still camera, monopod and video camcorder slung over her shoulders like a peddler with tin cans. She ordered us to pose before the big fence and its mountain background. The little bustler was so delighted by her loony venture that she insisted on walking all 10,000 steps down. Her calves screamed at her for days. "Excess of enthusiasm," she admitted, earning herself a nickname that will last forever.

That's also a fit description for the Chinese slogan at the scene: "Climb the Great Wall to be a hero at least once in a lifetime." Somehow I don't think they're going to use that expression to describe me.

## 11

HERS: BEYOND THE CITY WALLS

If living in China was an adventure, traveling was the next step beyond. We quickly discovered it was foolhardy to try making our own arrangements. Air and train reservations could only be booked one way, so what happened after you left was anybody's guess. Particularly, if like us, you weren't fluent in Chinese.

Our first excursions were easy because they didn't require any planning on our part. They were trips to the Forbidden City and the Great Wall organized by the U.S. Information Service at the American Embassy in Beijing as part of our Fulbright orientation. The entrance to Beijing's famous Forbidden City is located downtown, directly across from Tiananmen Square and behind the Tiananmen Gate with its giant picture of Mao. Home to China's emperors from the 15th century on, the Forbidden City is an opulent enclave surrounded by a moat and massive, 35-foot walls.

When Italian director Bernardo Bertolucci filmed his epic "The Last Emperor" in 1987, he had a fresh coat of red paint put on the buildings of the Forbidden City. It was fading fast by the time we got there. Once we entered through the inner gate, we found ourselves in a seemingly endless maze of temples and courtyards, one behind another. Tourists milled everywhere. Entrance to most of the buildings was prohibited. Jockeying with the crowds to get a good view, we peered in at thrones, sedans and ornate furniture, trying to imagine what it must have been like to live in such an exotic place. With few signs of animal or vegetable life, it seemed a pretty barren spot. No wonder the last Chinese Emperor Pu Yi made friends with a mouse and a cricket he kept hidden behind the imperial throne. The most inviting part of the place was the Imperial Garden, tucked behind the myriad of palaces.

Our trip to the Mutianyu section of the Great Wall was more up my alley. This part of the wall, less frequented by tourists, was two hours outside of Beijing by bus. We left the flat urban landscape behind and moved into hilly countryside. Once there, we wandered on top of the wall as far as we liked, through guard towers, down stone stairways. The views of the hills, with the wall snaking across them, were breathtaking. So was the thought of horses galloping five abreast between the parapets to fight off the Mongols. When it was time to leave, a group of us decided to hike back down rather than take the cable car. We arrived at our bus with spaghetti legs.

After our Fulbright orientation, we soon began making tentative forays into the city on our own. One of our first independent excursions was to the Great Bell Museum, not far from the Friendship Hotel. We went by bicycle and nearly rode right past it. Like so many Chinese buildings, it looked deceptively humble in front. In fact, we had a hard time even figuring out where the ticket office was. We decided we were merely supposed to give the giant bell in the courtyard a few bongs with the big wooden baton hanging next to it and go on our way.

Then we discovered a little shed nearby that contained the ticket office, paid a few RMB and happened upon the main entrance almost by chance. Beyond it were a courtyard and many other buildings. One exhibition hall unfolded behind another, and the entirety was ringed by long, narrow buildings filled with other displays. We meandered through each building, looking at every possible variety of cast-iron bells from the Song, Yuan, Ming and Qing dynasties, moving without a sense of destination or order. It was pleasantly confusing and aimless.

The biggest bell of all, Zhong-le, rose two stories and was housed in its own separate building. One of the oldest large bells in the world, it was inscribed with over 17 sutras, the scriptural texts attributed to Buddha. We paid an additional fee to climb up to the second story and look down at mighty Zhong-le, which resonates for over a minute when it is struck and can be heard for 25 miles. If you toss a coin through the hole in the center of the bell during the first 15 days of the new year, you will have good fortune for the coming year. That was the Chinese tradition, but we tourists didn't wait for the New Year. It was no mean feat to keep your coin from bouncing off the rim.

The Summer Palace, a bicycle ride of less than an hour from the Friendship Hotel, became one of my favorite outings. Serving as the summer residence for Qing dynasty emperors, it was where they went to escape the city's heat. The Palace grounds were much bigger than I anticipated, their centerpiece a large, artificial lake with pedal boats and larger, imperial-style barges for rent. We were far enough from the center of the city to see a line of mountains on the horizon. Crowded with people, temples, walks, climbs, pagodas, concession stands and dusty buildings, the grounds also included several islands, attached to the mainland with bridges.

Another afternoon excursion to the Beijing Art Museum, just north of Zizhuan Park, turned into an art-buying expedition for us. Located in an alley next to a canal, this charming place belied its imposingly formal name. You wouldn't know it was there or even how to find it without help. We learned about it by reading in the China Daily about a father-son exhibit in progress there. Since the museum was no more than 15 or 20 minutes from our apartment, we decided to look for it on our bikes.

Like the Great Bell Museum, the Beijing Art Museum was a rectangular complex far larger than its modest entrance indicated. Once you paid the admission and walked in, you came to a handsome Buddhist temple in the center. Rock gardens and walkways unfolded between it and the outside rim of buildings, one of which contained an exceptionally good exhibit of early porcelain. Behind the temple was another building where the museum proper was located. Inside was not only a spectacular array of brush paintings, but their creators, Sun Chuanzi and Sun Dewu.

Sun Chuanzi, the 56-year-old father, came from the northern province of Shandong and belonged to the Chinese Painting Institute of Beijing. His 29-year-old son Dewu was a member of the Qingyun Painting and Calligraphy Society. They were eager to show us their work, mostly landscapes and nature scenes. After their personalized tour, we began an elaborate negotiation to buy a painting. Since they didn't speak English and our Chinese was minimal, we decided to come back with Haiyan to act as negotiator.

Haiyan gave us an on-the-spot lesson in bargaining. First she explained to the Suns that we weren't tourists but were living in Beijing, working "for the good of China." Next she softened them up by telling them Jim wasn't working and we had to live on my salary. Before she was done, Haiyan got us two paintings for the price of one. In a act of fortuitous diplomacy, we happened to pick out one each by Chuangzi and Dewu.

For travel outside the Beijing metropolitan area, the Friendship Hotel's Foreign Experts Office provided us with day trips. One Sunday the Hotel organized a particularly pleasant excursion to Yun Ju Temple, about two hours or 75 kilometers south of Beijing.

The main building was a six-sectioned tower one tier rising up after another. Literally thousands of ancient stone tablets inscribed with Buddhist sutras were found underneath one of the other buildings during the restoration. We viewed them in what was essentially a barracks full of grimy old pieces of stone. Everything was covered with dust, so you had to use your imagination. I had learned on our honeymoon in Japan that Jim was not a temple man. He got fed up with visiting temple sites about as fast as I did going to Japanese baseball games. This time was the exception. Once we started walking around this stone library and the temple grounds, they grew on us. We watched restorers laboring over freshly minted pieces of stone sculpture or making rubbings from older ones. The sound of a giant bell being rung in a nearby courtyard was echoed by the distant whistle of a train passing through the valley below. The quiet, the country setting and the relics from an earlier era worked their magic.

On the same excursion, we went to Shi Jing Mountain and hiked to a nine-cave Buddhist site. There were two levels of caves. The upper, Lei Yin, had Buddhist icons carved on the the cave's four pillars. Altogether, the caves contained more than 10,000 stone slabs inscribed with Buddhist sutras during the Liao and Jin Dynasties. A long way from the computer age. After inspecting them, we climbed to the very top of the mountain to eat our peanut butter sandwiches in the shade of a small Buddhist shrine and enjoy the valley and hills stretching out below.

## 12

HIS: IN CHINA EVERY DAY IS AN ADVENTURE

"When you take one of these tours in China," said an American who had been in Beijing six months, "you'll get little advance notice of where you're going or what you're going to do."

She wasn't talking about the dog-and-pony shows to the Great Wall, Forbidden City or some other landmark. This was a horse show of another color. About 40 of us had coughed up just under $5 apiece for a bus trip to "Fall of Dragon." No one had the least idea what that meant.

The Huanghai bus arrived at the *Youyi* at eight one Saturday morning. A nice bus it was, with air conditioning, curtains, a clock and such a smooth ride we could read. But what was Fall of Dragon? "I translated directly from the Chinese," the driver-organizer said. "I'm not sure there's a black dragon, but I know there's a fall. It's a mountainous region near China's biggest boulevard—I mean reservoir." That last verbal blooper inspired great confidence.

Once we left Beijing, we turned onto a highway with three lanes on each side and no breakdown lane. The road was flanked by trees whitewashed at the base to prevent insect infestation. After two hours of flat country—I had a Mike Lupica murder mystery to keep me from terminal boredom—we began climbing. We passed fields of corn and farmhouses made of baked mud, stone or brick. At 10:15 we saw some watchtowers on the mountains. It couldn't be...it wasn't...Yes, it was the Great Wall of China. "If this is what we came for, I'll behave like a three-year-old," I told Brooks.

"Then I will have to abandon you," she said.

Happily, the Wall was just a flash in the window pane. At 10:30 we descended through an opening in the sedimentary rock, crossed a bridge and reached the reservoir. "Here we are at last, and we'll stay here until 1:30," said the driver. "You have your own choice, and take care of yourself."

Three hours to look at a reservoir? I would have stayed on the bus if they hadn't switched off the air conditioning. Following the crowd, we walked back across the bridge, picked up drinks supplied for us at a hut, and started climbing steps on a metal platform next to a little brook trickling down a crevice in the hills. "Oh, goody," I thought. "We'll walk a few hundred feet and then break for lunch."

Except the metal steps turned into ever-steeper stone steps, the little brook into a big brook, the crevice into a gorge and the hill into a mountain. Along the way people were selling nuts, fruit, a squirrel and some small nets for catching fresh-water shrimp. *"Bu yao,"* I said more than once—"Don't want." I wasn't just talking about the wares. I don't do mountains.

The party spread out, my wife racing well ahead of me with a full knapsack, me spluttering and stammering in the rear, with a bottle of water in one hand and a Pepsi in the other. I finally caught up to her at a cave. I was convinced we had climbed right back to the Bronze Age.

Actually, it was a good place to stop. The breeze blew in and bounced off the back, creating some ad-hoc air conditioning. We looked out over a 70-foot straight drop, with water pouring over it. At last: Dragon Falls. "It's a nice view," said Brooks.

"Especially when you're sitting down," I added.

But when I looked at the cave more carefully, I saw an opening in the back, with more steps leading through it. We hadn't found Dragon Falls at all. At least not the top.

We climbed a really steep rise and headed down a precipitous grade to the next level of water. I saw the Chinese characters for men's room on a large rock and climbed up behind it. Nothing was there but a trench. I breathed through my mouth and left the place as quickly as nature allowed.

Around 11:45 we found some boulders and shade by the brook and broke for lunch. Out came the peanut-butter sandwiches, orangeade and cookies. Sugar barons everywhere were grateful. We spread our feast before us and gorged by the gorge.

At 12:15 we started up the mountain once more. We found some Americans speaking with a Chinese woman. "Ask her how far to the top," I said. "Three kilometers." That didn't translate to up and down by 1:30, so we started back. Some people never climb past the tree line. We hadn't reached the vendor line.

I always wind up alone on mountains. After a few minutes my bustling wife announced she was detouring to a pagoda high above the trail, and we parted company. I reached the bottom at 1 p.m. When other climbers straggled into base camp, I asked them how high they'd gone. Someone said the trail ended at a picturesque pool of water next to a roaring waterfall: a regular Shangri-La. Someone else said he'd met a mountain woman who grows corn for an income of 600 RMB, or about $75 a year.

I sat down on a wall at the base of the mountain instead of walking back across the bridge. Others joined me. I like to think I personally created a kind of impromptu strike. We played eyeball-to-eyeball, and the driver blinked. At 1:30 sharp he drove around to pick us up.

On the way home we motored along a two-lane section of highway with a grassy median strip about three feet across. Coming around a curve, we had to stop quickly in front of a two-truck collision that blocked our side of the road. With no tow trucks in sight, our driver simply turned around, heading against all approaching traffic, until he found an opening in the median strip. He crossed it, drove gingerly through more approaching traffic on the opposite side, passed the scene of the accident and returned to the right side of the road, leaving me under the seat. I remembered at this point that we had been told every day in China would be an adventure.

As advertised, we reached the Friendship Hotel at 4 p.m. "I do hope you enjoyed the Fall of Black Dragon," said the driver, re-translating his earlier description. "We have dragon everywhere. How did you like the trip?"

"Too short," said some macho climber who never made it to the top.

"Too short is compact," said the driver. "I hope you join us on the next trip, which is not planned yet."

Bu yao.

#   #   #

Not every Sunday outing from the *Youyi* was a study in misery. On one occasion the bus arrived at 7:30 a.m. for a two-hour drive to Yun Ju Temple. It only took one and a half hours. "Ah, tangerines," Fulbright friend Marilyn Goldstein said when we got off the bus and saw a few vendors. We drew a little closer. "This must be a magical country," she said, "when the tangerines turn into persimmons."

We passed a rest room labelled "Women' Slavatory." A must for all the cameras. Next we headed into a room with 1,000-year-old stone slabs on which sutras, or Buddhist prayers, were carved. After gleaning that tidbit, we had trouble understanding the rest of the guide's English. Apparently, English is a tonal language. If you don't get the tones right...

Built during the Tang Dynasty, the temple was bombed by the Japanese in 1942 and now was being restored. There were half a dozen compounds, two pagodas and many Buddhas but, like so much in China, no central focus. We were zigzagging around the lot, creating order out of chaos. When we viewed one corpulent female statue, the guide explained that fatness connoted wealth. You know, buy 'em and fatten 'em up. The Goddess of Fertility had many heads and hands, with dolls and apples laid out by worshippers as offerings at her base. Many of the male Buddhas were adorned with swastikas, which in this culture connote longevity. "That's what Buddha believed," said a *Youyi* amigo. "You live forever. No beginning, no end."

The place was high up in the mountains—great stone faces with enough green on them to resemble a two-week growth on a man's cheeks. On this particular day it was quiet enough to make the sounds very distinct. A bell gonged. A moment later a train whistle sounded. Somewhere a dog barked. I made up the last part.

"You can see how Americans get into Buddhism," Brooks said. "It's an escape from hyper-reality."

I liked the little touches. There was a trash receptacle between the four legs of an elephant. A stone pagoda was structured with stone beams, the same way as if it had been wooden. "You saw the same thing when plastic first came out," said Marilyn, the art professor. "Only after it was accepted did it evolve into something unique in its forms."

Turtles and dragons made their usual appearance. I was finally starting to understand their significance in the culture. The turtle is a stoic figure, carrying the world on its back. In this case it carried a sutra slab. The dragon starts in the underworld, ascends to the earth, then to the heavens. It connotes the universe in its many forms.

Returning to the bus, I saw a British friend, Esther Sampson, munching on crab apples attached to a stick. "Won't that make you sick?" I asked her.

"Not me," she said. I've built up immunity. I first came here in 1949."

We bused over to Shi Jing Mountain, the site of nine caves for storing Buddhist classics. "You will climb the mountain," the guide said. "Be back by 1:30." Oh, God: another mountain-climbing surprise.

This one wasn't so bad. We climbed the stone steps, then the more rough-hewn stone trail. For once, my wind wasn't so bad, and my legs were holding up. We passed the first pagoda with scarcely a pause for breath—O.K., Brooks did burn some incense—and headed right up to the next level. There was only one cave open, featuring yet more slabs. This was apparently where the trail ended, but Brooks found another one going higher still. Like a little cat snooping its way into trouble, she headed up, with me following and nipping at her heels. We reached another pagoda, then headed for the top of the mountain. Some Chinese youths singing songs and waving a red flag passed us as we plodded forward. "Did you ever imagine you'd be sitting on top of a Chinese mountain," Brooks said, "eating a peanut-butter sandwich?" On the way down we chatted with some young climbers, whose English was better than our Chinese. My calves started to go. My spirits were actually holding strong.

The day was complete as far as I was concerned, but the bus driver insisted on taking us to the Marco Polo Bridge. Yes, it's a great stone structure with lions' heads. Yes, the Chinese-Japanese conflict started there. I'd had enough. I just looked for the bathroom.

III

WORKING FOR THE GOOD OF CHINA

"All 15 of my students squeezed into our living room and devoured most of five large Pizza Hut pizzas. The men drank beer, but the women stuck to soda."

13

HERS: TEACHING IN CHINA

"You're teaching first-amendment rights to the Chinese?" friends and colleagues responded incredulously, when they learned about my Fulbright at the China School of Journalism. I wondered myself how much freedom I would have and how closely I would be monitored.

The school responded reassuringly to my queries, saying that there were no specific requirements other than to teach newswriting and reporting. I could do pretty much what I pleased. The two orientation sessions sponsored by the Fulbright organization—one in Washington before we left and another in Beijing at the beginning of our stay—yielded more information.

I would find a monitor in my class. This person was a student elected or chosen—the process was never clear—to act as my liaison with the students and the school. In addition to arranging for photocopies or audio-visual equipment, the class monitor would make reports on my conduct.

"Use common sense," we were told. "Don't denounce the Communist system in class. If you want to make criticisms, be diplomatic."

The school was at that time located in northwest Beijing (it has since moved to a new site closer to downtown). The campus was not far from the Summer Palace, on what was supposed to be the site of a former military training barracks. Certainly it was Spartan enough. The four-story building where my office and classroom were situated was built in the mid-Eighties. The walls were already peeling, windows were broken and some of the lighting fixtures dangled by their wiring. Buildings go up very fast in China, but maintenance is not a high priority. Heating was minimal. I always had piping hot water for tea, though.

My class of 15 students all had Bachelor's degrees in American Literature, and many of them had worked as teachers. They ranged in age from their early to late twenties but seemed a lot younger.

Winning their places at the school by competitive examination, they came from all over China. I found out very quickly why they wanted to be journalists: 1) because they didn't want to be teachers, the alternative their prowess in English offered them; 2) because they wanted to get rich.

I puzzled over the riches part until someone explained to me that bribery flourishes in the field. How else did one of the myriad of new factories garner a feature story touting its successes? It was hard to match up such calculating greed with my bright-eyed, ebullient and conscientious students. But then I also found it hard to envision Woody, my considerate and very helpful class monitor, reporting to school officials what I talked about in class. *Guanxi* —we would call it bribery—was a fact of life in China, although it didn't have quite the same puritanical overtones there. It was closer to an elaborate form of etiquette. And informing of the kind my class monitor most likely did was more like a government-sanctioned grapevine. At least at the school such a practice seemed somewhat more benign than it might appear to Western eyes. It depended on the people and the circumstances—just as it would anywhere.

The only time the ethics of my students gave me pause was when I assigned them early in the semester to cover a newspaper exhibit at the Military Museum in downtown Beijing. The quotes they came back with were manufactured out of thin air. When one of the students blew the whistle, I tore up their stories and gave them a verbal pounding on the importance of absolute accuracy in quotation. It was hard to tell if they were guilty of deviousness or of trying too hard to please the teacher. They learned their lesson, though, and considering the difficulties involved in interviewing and writing in two separate languages, it wasn't a simple one.

Every Monday and Wednesday at 7:40 a.m., I was picked up in front of the Friendship Hotel by a school car and driven to the school 15 minutes away. At the end of classes, I was whisked back home again. By Western standards, it felt luxurious and indulgent, although transportation was one of the routine perks provided by your work unit if you didn't live in situ. It was part of the VIP treatment we saw "foreign experts" get in China. The rest of the faculty and staff, except for the most senior officials, had to settle for a bus.

If this system seemed decadent and elitist, the drivers wielded a surprising amount of power. I never could be sure what type of vehicle I would be traveling in or who was going with me. After the driver delivered a reprimand once through Haiyan, I made a point of not keeping him waiting. Most important, transportation effectively limited my contact with other faculty, as well as with my students. I wasn't sure whether this was intentional or not. Chances are, it was a little of both. Considering the freedom I had in the classroom to say and do what I wanted, I didn't put up an argument.

My assignment at the China School of Journalism seemed idyllic to me. Most of my teaching career had been spent at a college where the primary mission, unlike a university's, was teaching. That meant I taught four courses a semester, eight a year. It was a heavy load, leaving little time for research and writing. With just one class of graduate students, I could concentrate intensively on preparation of my lectures and work closely with students on an individual basis. Because my class met only twice a week, I had plenty of opportunity for research and writing. The prospect of meeting the same class of students from 8 a.m. to 3 p.m. was more than a little daunting, but I soon discovered the hours were not what they seemed.

The academic day was broken down into 45-minute units, with 10-minute breaks in between. This system enabled me to organize my lectures into segments of reasonable length instead of trying to fill a single, overwhelmingly large block of three or four hours. Plus I had 10 minutes between periods to catch my breath. What looked like a seemingly endless day of teaching whizzed by. At 11 a.m. everybody stopped for a half-hour study period before lunch. In fact, all my students went straight to their mid-day meal, explaining to me that if I kept them in class, there wouldn't be any food left.

One of the perks for "senior" professors like me and my colleague John Morgan, who taught the other English-language class, was dining privileges in the faculty dining room. At 11:30 a.m. the two of us trooped across the courtyard from the school's classroom building to the dining hall, dodging stray volleyballs from the exercise class already in progress. We went through the students' mess hall, which looked like a set for "Animal House." Most of the students had finished eating at the rows of long plank tables with benches. Left behind were puddles of soup, heaps of bone, gristle and other debris unfamiliar to Americans weaned on McDonald-style no-fuss food in disposable paper, cardboard and plastic wrapping.

Upstairs we entered a smaller, sunny and invariably empty faculty dining room with three or four large round tables. Several of our Chinese colleagues—rarely more than two—wandered in and joined us at our table. The food would begin to arrive, bit by bit. Serving bowls of vegetables, rice, soup, meat or tofu made the rounds on a lazy susan in the center of the table. The most memorable entrée was mystery ribs covered with short bristles. Barbecued dog, I was convinced, although John's theory was piglet. I often sneaked glances at our Chinese colleagues for clues on how to manage, since it was almost impossible to eat such an entrée with chopsticks. The problem was compounded by the fact that napkins were never provided. I learned to carry my own, unless I wanted to return to class with my lunch decorating my wardrobe.

Often nary a word would pass between us and our Chinese companions, except the obligatory "*ni hao*," or "hello," when one of us arrived. John spoke virtually no Chinese, and if I was lucky I might catch an occasional sentence. The basic phrases I was learning, like what time it was or what the weather was like, did not make for extensive small talk. It was as if each group, Western and Chinese, existed in its own separate bubble. I often wondered why it didn't occur to the administration to ask Haiyan or some other English-speaking staff member to join us and make conversation possible. Perhaps it would have been too great a breach of protocol, since most of the faculty had to brown-bag it.

The pedagogical method practiced at the school depended heavily on lecturing, with very little interaction between professor and student. According to my students, some of their professors simply read directly from notes. Students spent much more time in the classroom listening to their professors lecture than their American counterparts. It was no wonder that occasionally I found a student with his head down in class, looking half asleep. They spent all day in classes and often had to squeeze their studying time into the wee hours of the night.

I puzzled over why John and I, unlike my Fulbright friends, had almost no contact with other faculty at the school. The easy answer was the language barrier and the fact that many of the faculty did double duty, working in some capacity for *Xinhua*, the New China News Agency. In addition to being a wire service, *Xinhua* oversaw the school, which was not connected to the university system run by the State Department of Education. I have since wondered if maybe the critical factor was that the school discouraged fraternization with the "enemy" in as politically sensitive an area as journalism.

Nap time came after lunch. Most of the faculty had cots in their offices for that purpose, but John and I were not provided with such amenities. Maybe you had to supply your own. Our students went back to their dormitories and crashed. Sometimes I sat in my office and graded student papers, held student conferences or scheduled a film screening. Occasionally I was tired enough to fall asleep at my desk, but most of the time John and I took walks. We would stroll through the fields west of the school or wander into the market just north of it. The school's campus was poised on the outskirts of Beijing—literally at the point where city turned into country, with dirt roads and fields of crops stretching out beyond.

On Mondays, classes began again at 2 p.m. and ended at 3:40 p.m., although the bell to mark the beginnings and endings of class periods sometimes seemed to ring at random. On Wednesdays, I finished teaching in the morning. On both days, I was driven home within 10 or 15 minutes of the end of class. It meant almost no contact with students outside of class. Used to a more flexible academic schedule, I tried rearranging thing—staying late on Wednesdays, holding office hours during the lunch break—but the students were locked into a routine and unaccustomed to having open-ended access to their professors.

Fulbright colleagues who were quartered on the campuses where they taught reported very different experiences. They might be pulled out of bed first thing in the morning by a knock on the door from an inquiring student, and a steady stream of visitors, both students and faculty, arrived the rest of the day and evening with both personal and professional queries. One friend said a student even asked for an opinion on a prospective spouse. I debated whether my students didn't feel comfortable talking to me. It seemed more likely that while the school wanted its students to learn the techniques of Western journalism, it preferred to keep to a minimum their exposure to Western journalistic values.

I tried increasing student contact in a number of other ways, some successful, some not. Although they were as fluent in English as could be expected of people who had never visited an English-speaking country, my students had a long way go in writing clear, technically correct English. Just as I found the task of learning Chinese in a mere five months impossible—and I didn't even attempt to learn the written language—their years of English study were not enough to let them avoid the perennial problems that Chinese speakers run into with English. They added or left out definite and indefinite articles ("a," "the"). They singularized or pluralized nouns in the wrong places. They ran aground with subordinate clauses. On top of it, they had to learn an entirely different and to them unnatural method of writing, as journalism is for most beginners. At least my study of Chinese helped me understand the kind of mistakes they were prone to make.

I quickly decided that they would learn a great deal more from meeting with me individually and going over their writing word by word, sentence by sentence, than from my droning at them about principles and precepts. I limited lecturing to a minimum necessary to convey the necessary concepts. The rest of the time I spent with them in individual conferences. These appointments inched into the lunch hour, nap time and the post-class period, but they seemed to relish the individual attention.

My experiments using film were less successful. I had brought with me a series of feature films about journalism, ranging from "His Girl Friday" to "Broadcast News." The idea was to give them a cultural context for their understanding of Western journalism, an introduction to some of the relevant social issues and an opportunity to practice their English. Initially I arranged screenings during the two-and-a-half hour lunch break. No one showed up. Figuring they needed their naps, I moved the screenings into class time and subjected the films to detailed analysis. Even then, they didn't seem to understand that movies were not merely entertainment, but texts they could learn from.

One of the difficulties with the school's reliance on a lecture-based pedagogy was that my students had very little opportunity to report on real news. In the Chinese system, journalists act as mouthpieces for the government. Their job is less to uncover the news than to give an official report on what the government decides is news. It is a profoundly different philosophy than the one on which Western news values are based, where journalists are considered the Fourth Estate, independent of the government and, if anything, its adversary. In all their other classes, my students were encouraged to understand news in an entirely different sense than the Western one. There was little reason for the school to create an environment that made it easy for students to gather news independently, because that was not how the Chinese system worked. What seemed amazing was the fact that they incorporated Western techniques of journalism into their curriculum at all.

One of the basic tenets in effective teaching of journalism, Western style, is that students learn by doing. Since the school was so far out of town, I couldn't exactly give them an assignment to interview a government official about the announcement of an increase in inflation. They were in class all day, every weekday, and besides, they couldn't afford taxi fare downtown. A new campus closer to the center of Beijing was under construction while we were there and may have already alleviated that problem. In the meantime, I could assign only so many newsgathering opportunities with local farmers and merchants.

Field trips were the solution to the dilemma of how to provide news stories. John and I would arrange for a bus, pack our two classes in and deliver them to the news sources. One Monday we took our two classes downtown to *Xinhua*. Jim came with us. The

New China News Agency was the largest wire service in the world, a giant complex west of Mao's mausoleum. It was as fascinating for Jim and me as my students, and all the presentations, except the final briefing, were conducted in English.

We began in the morning in a large auditorium where a senior correspondent described his experiences. Then we moved upstairs to the main newsroom, a big open space filled with computers where international news was processed, along with domestic news for international markets. The students were able to look over the shoulders of writers and editors as they edited the news.

For lunch, we went downstairs to the cafeteria, a scene out of bedlam. You can appreciate the overcrowding that goes with the high population of China when you see how aggressively people in a food line will cut in front of anyone who lets them. Not knowing the system and not knowing how to ask, we were babes in the woods. After finally getting our food and downing it at a scummy, white-plastic-covered table in a room where the noise level was on a par with a tournament basketball game, we moved into a darkly lit lounge for tea with a group of my students. It was one of the few times we were able to answer questions and learn a little about the students in an informal atmosphere.

An exhibit of newspapers from 1979 to the present at the Military Museum turned out to be a trade fair with newspapers, magazines, and all forms of publications hawking their wares. When I plopped myself down into a chair, exhausted from wandering through the endless exhibits, a stream of visitors walked up and asked if they could have their picture taken with me, all in sign language once they discovered I didn't speak Chinese. I nodded my head, happy to oblige, and a friend or relative would snap the picture. It was a little like being one of the exhibits.

Our students loved their field trip to a new data-processing firm, started by a Chinese-American doctor taking advantage of the wave of entrepreneurial growth in his native country. The prospect of working for that kind of company seemed to appeal to them more than *Xinhua* or English-language publications like the China Daily, probably because they thought it would be more lucrative.

I brought the semester to a close with a pizza party at our apartment. All 15 of my students squeezed into our living room and devoured most of five large Pizza Hut pizzas. The men drank beer, but the women stuck to soda. The women also asked questions about what it was like to have a family and manage a career. I told them not to expect to find it easy. They all talked about their plans for the long break between semesters. School did not start up again for them until the beginning of March, after the Chinese New Year.

I remembered hearing how a Scot we met at a tree-trimming party before Christmas claimed that *Xinhua* gave the students a two-week "deconditioning" program after graduation to clear their heads of any Western contamination we foreigners had introduced. He had been enticed by *Xinhua* to leave his job with a London newspaper with promises that in China he would be an editor. Disillusioned by the polishing work he ended up doing instead, he called it "correcting schoolchildren's homework." We never discovered if his charge was true. I wondered how my students would fare when they started their careers and how many of them I had made an impression on.

A week before our departure, the School held a farewell banquet for Jim and me in the Faculty Dining Room. Dean Liu Binjiang's opening toast, translated by Haiyan, announced we should conduct ourselves like family. When I thought back to what our welcoming banquet was like in September, I saw how appropriate that had become. We were a family of sorts. We dined lavishly on Mongolian hot pot, with generous portions of Great Wall wine and a potent sorghum grain alcohol known as "the great white dry."

After a few toasts by others, Jim got into the spirit of things and made one of his own, for the first time getting to drain his glass and turn it upside-down Chinese-style. I was presented with a porcelain coffee and tea set, but the best gift was having two of my students, who had learned I was on campus, show up afterwards to say goodbye.

14

HIS: POLISHING THE NEWS

Popular Chinese joke: a man takes his son to the "crazy doctor," the term Chinese use in referring to therapists. "What's the matter with him?" the doctor asks.
"My son watches the news on television and reads the People's Daily," says the man. "He believes everything. Therefore, he must be crazy."

How does a foreigner living in Beijing pass the time? It was obvious I needed something to do, other than bitch and moan.

Plenty of work was available. Chinese authorities would anoint any English-speaking person as an English teacher, even a recent high-school graduate. Almost as common were "polishers," or copy editors whose job was to improve, or "polish," the English scribblings by Chinese writers. What the locals wrote was commonly, and seriously, referred to as "Chinglish."

I had my doubts about polishing: since everything we polished was ordained by the Chinese government, weren't we lowly workers for the powers that be, sort of like Winston Smith in "1984"?

No, no, no, said embassy and consular people I took my worries to. Their arguments came in three categories: 1) The more the Chinese are exposed to outsiders, the more they're likely to change. You can teach them something about Western news values. 2) Whenever these publications and electronic outlets are the least bit professional, it's because of polishers. 3) The Chinese are more sophisticated than you'd think and know when they see propaganda.

At the time, I was still unconvinced I should do anything but gather information for a Chinese-bridge story I had contracted to write for the Atlantic Monthly. Nonetheless, I had a preview of the Chinese news process when Brooks's and John Morgan's classes were guests at the national news agency *Xinhua*, which not only runs the China School of Journalism but serves as a government P.R. outlet in countries where it has bureaus. I came along as Brooks's spouse and, as the Chinese might phrase it, second journalist.

We met the *Xinhua* van outside Building #1 of the Friendship Hotel at 8 a.m. A lot of *Youyi* residents worked as *Xinhua* polishers, and the bus was chock-full. Outside, winds were blowing with temperatures down in the 60s—the first real day of fall. Once the weather turned in Beijing, it didn't turn back very often (or so I was told). Unprepared, I was freezing in my sport jacket, dress shirt and the paper-thin slacks I bought on the street. The slacks, incidentally, were worth every bit of my $4.50. To the penny. Exactly.

Xinhua is a city within a city: a massive, guarded, self-contained complex in downtown Beijing. One of the English-language polishers told us that most of the employees actually live inside or very close to the complex—a typical setup in China. Brooks wouldn't let me use the word "Orwellian."

The day's official business began in the downstairs theater, where a *Xinhua* correspondent of some 20 years gave the students the first of several briefings. Associated Press, Reuters and other Western agencies were decentralized wire services that got their stories from the hinterlands, he said. Financially strapped *Xinhua*, centralized in Beijing and somewhat less than independent of the government, was getting only 30% of its funds from the government, a fee that was decreasing 7% each year. Chen Tagtao, the engaging 52-hear-old chief of China Features, outlined other problems. Each of his 30 writers was supposed to turn out 25 features a year and got a bonus for extras. "We produce about 500 features a year, which is not a good thing," he said. Why such a small output? He gave three reasons:

1) Writing a feature takes time. Anyone turning out a 10,000-word story would be lucky to do two in a year.

2) Writing features in English, as China Features personnel do, is a difficult, time-consuming job for a native Chinese.

3) "Some people are not too highly motivated." Now he was at the heart of the matter. *Xinhua* employees had 100% job security and got paid even if they fell short of the 25-story quota. "In the language of the Communist Party, we use persuasion [laughter from the students], we do ideological work [more laughter]. Sometimes it doesn't work."

In addition, many employees got picked to go abroad and had little to do with China Features when they were overseas. "You are very interested in going abroad," Chen told the students. They howled.

Xinhua produces copy in English, French, Spanish, Arabic and Russian as well as Chinese. The newsroom, a massive area with computers and desks everywhere, was a regular House of Babel.

Despite the intriguing *Xinhua* tour, I still wasn't sold on polishing. For one thing, I had visions of travel writing. Before I left the states, I called the travel editor of the St. Petersburg (Florida, not Russia) Times. I had written some pieces for him before and wondered if he'd like some stories from China. "One of our staffers, Hal Lipper, will be working for the English-language daily in Beijing," he said. "I think I'll rely on him." Figures. You go halfway around the world, and somebody else is already there and writing about it.

Soon after the *Xinhua* meeting, I called up Lipper at the China Daily and asked if he'd like to have lunch. We set up an appointment for a week later, and Lipper offhandedly mentioned that the Daily was looking for an "editor/polisher."

Thanking him for the tip, I said I had too many commitments to be a nine-to-fiver. At most I could work three days a week. No sweat, said Lipper, we already have a polisher working two days a week and you two could dovetail. I still didn't feel interested, until Brooks mentioned that time on my hands was becoming depression on my brain. How could she possibly think that? Was it my kicking and screaming every morning after I got up? Was it my tantrums when the International Herald Tribune was late? I had no answer to her insight: I faxed in an application.

Then things happened quickly. Not only was I accepted by the China Daily, but Brooks and I were asked to substitute polish for CCTV, the national tv station. Mike Connelly, the regular polisher, was taking some leave to become a father for the third time. Brooks, a couple of other foreign experts and I would replace him over a three-week period.

The CCTV polishing came before I started at the China Daily. Naturally, Brooks and I wanted a preview. On my arranged day a

76

van picked me and Mike up at 3:10 p.m., and we headed over to CCTV. The lobby had flowers, seven-foot urns, a fountain, a pool with goldfish, and an armed guard. We walked up a spiral staircase, took a few turns, passed a soldier and a room with lots of tvs and found ourselves in a windowless room maybe 15' by 15' with a tv monitor and a bunch of computers.

First Mike and I watched the foreign-news selections with the producer, Fang Jiqing. Fang and Mike picked four of the stories for the news: Yeltsin's victory in the mini-Russian war at Russia's White House (shots of fighting), the U.S. stepping up its deployment in Somalia (a graphic picture of crowds pulling a dead American soldier through the streets), more on the Indian earthquake, and a suspected IRA bombing in London (potential departure from the usual horror story: this time they didn't issue a warning). "We tend to be an American-oriented news show," said Mike, "because we get most of our footage from WTN, which is headquartered in the States."

Mike sat down and wrote two- or three-sentence lead-ins to each story with no text or video in front of him. Just like that. Impressive.

An energetic fellow wearing glasses, a gleeful countenance and a Scotland Yard cap, Mike pulled a handful of peanut M & Ms out of his knapsack before continuing. He started to explain the computer I'd be working on. "It's a dinosaur of a word processor," he said, motioning at the Legend 386SX. "They could call it a Jurassic Park." CCTV had just purchased the system and wasn't about to get rid of it. Certainly none of the functions resembled the little mouse runs on my Mac Classic. I wrote down everything he told me: a dozen or more commands.

Next Mike showed me how to write headlines and lead-ins. We also had to edit the eight national news stories Chinese journalists had written. I could see it would be easy enough to correct faulty grammar. The editorializing was another matter. "Every time you get one of these," Mike said, pointing to a story about nuclear testing filled with lofty assertions about the righteous Chinese position, "you have to use attribution. If someone is editorializing, stick in attribution throughout." The combination of a new word-processing

77

system, plus news editing, which I hadn't done for a quarter-century, had my head throbbing.

Of my first night on my own as a polisher two things can be said. I arrived, and I survived. Barely. The CCTV driver, a friendly guy who was big pals with Mike, didn't speak English, except to say, "My English, no, your Chinese, no." We didn't chat much. I was, as usual, embarrassed by my utter failure at the language.

He accompanied me toward the bowels of the building. First, though, we reached the front door, and the guard had no inkling of who I was or what my function was. Same thing with the guy in the office. After some minutes of pleading by my driver, I was allowed to go upstairs. The door to the studio was locked. Funny how fast Kafka came to mind. Finally, someone opened it.

The viewing of foreign-news stories went all right. Not much in the way of choices. Fang's selections: Gen. Aidid proposes cease-fire, Spanish Prime Minister Gonzalez reviews troops in Bosnia, finance ministers meet in Belgium, UN peacekeepers arrive in Haiti amid new violence. I wasn't sure about the focus of at least two of them. Fortunately, I had the good sense to ask Fang.

I sat down at the computer to write the four international news headlines, armed with a printout of directions Mike had been thoughtful enough to pass on to his subs (his wife, by the way, had a sterling baby boy). I typed them up—"Spain: Bosnia/WTN/Intro (space) Joe Smith ABC"—with only a few computer glitches. Happily, someone was on hand when I needed help. Where were the M & M's?

Then came the text, short and snappy, as lead-ins for the individual footage. "Spain's Prime Minister Gonzalez, reviewing his peacekeeping troops in Bosnia, warned that he would reconsider his country's commitment if the sides don't move faster toward an agreement. ABC's Joe Smith has the story."

Once I finished these lead-ins, the eight national news stories began arriving for my edits. I don't know which bothered me more, the writers' understandably flawed stabs at English or the total non-newsiness of the stories. I understood that Western news agencies were adversaries to the government, while the Chinese media were publicists. Think of it: grain harvest down, but not as far as predicted; export of machinery and technology products increased; a government minister argues for more macro-economic reform in some standardized speech. The best story was about 11 men being arrested for using forged credit cards. At least it involved real people and real news. There were always two national and two international teasers at the top of the show, and I used that as one of them.

Imagine a force-fed diet of these stories day after day. It could wear a citizen down. Heaven knows, the people I was working with were nice enough, but how committed could anyone be to this drivel? Whenever I had a question about a choice, the answer was, "Whatever. Anything." Dinner was more important. Nobody cared. Maybe they just figured it was my job to decide.

I finished my writing at 6:52 p.m., eight minutes before the semi-official deadline. You didn't dwell on excellence in a situation like that: it was strictly survival journalism. I watched the male anchor apply hairspray. We walked upstairs to the studio with the female anchor, who still had curlers in her hair, and some technicians. The anchors were reading my lead-ins aloud as they climbed the stairs. I wondered how they could do a flawless-sounding 15-minute show every night.

They didn't have to. With the camera rolling, they delivered their lead-ins separately, sometimes needing several takes. Then they took off. It was up to a technician to splice the words together with the footage. Live and learn.

When I arrived home at 8 p.m. both exhausted and tense, dinner was waiting. "Hey, you did it," said bottom-line Brooksie. "You got through your first night as a polisher. Congratulations."

On the second day at CCTV, I had a talk with a young writer-performer-producer (I liked the idea that they tripled up—I suspect that eliminated any possibility of a star system). He said the stories, such as they were, got sent in from hundreds of affiliates around the country. The station "leaders," sometimes with help from national "leaders," reviewed them and decided what ran; they didn't particularly care if someone like me decided what went at the top of the news. "It's a very strict form of propaganda control," he said.

On one of my nights they wouldn't use a tape of a tattooing convention or a concert in honor of the Pope's 15th anniversary. Tattooing was considered too graphic for Chinese viewers. The producer just smiled when I mentioned the papal concert as a story possibility—China allows a Catholic church, but not one affiliated with the Vatican. At least not officially.

On my last night of polishing at CCTV, my editor was a woman whose only interest was getting home early. We piled through the copy so quickly that I left out an occasional "an" or "the" or some other article, like some of the Chinese writers I was supposed to correct.

At this point I was going to write a piece of satire about Chinese broadcasting, but it's clear to me that truth in this case was much weirder than fiction. What could I possibly say to top the nightly diet of meetings with foreign leaders to promote "bilateral interests," stories on reform that never mentioned change, puff pieces for companies starting to export or a tourist area building a few hotels, speeches by leaders on inspection tours mouthing platitudes about the socialist market economy?

The day I headed to the China Daily for my interview, with my interested wife in tow, the cab driver didn't have a clue how to get there. We arrived just barely in time for the interview. On the spot, a Mr. Wang offered me a job. I agreed to work two mid-week nights—sometimes it turned out to be Tuesday and Wednesday, other times Wednesday and Thursday—for 80 RMB each (later increased to 100), plus cab fare, with the company having the right to fire me after three nights if it wasn't satisfied.

On dress-rehearsal day, I had lunch with Hal Lipper and another polisher named Paul Ryan. Then work. In a word, shellshock. I entered the three-year-old building, which like most new Chinese structures looked about 50, and took the back stairs to the second floor—the elevator didn't stop there—passed the unvented men's room and found the polishers' room. It was about 15 yards long and seven yards wide: you could just about play squash in it.

The computers sat side-by-side on two tables. No need for individual desks with lots of room for notebooks and tape recorders. We were polishers, not reporters.

I arrived, as asked, at 6 p.m. and edited a story. Working on another unfamiliar computer—this one with infinitely more newsroom functions to worry about—I struggled mightily just to keep the story on the screen. At times this grown man was almost reduced to tears. Fortunately, Ryan, the other night polisher, kept rescuing me. The problems were much the same as at the tv station—lousy writing, non-news stories—only this time I had about five times as much material to deal with.

At 6:30 p.m., Ryan and I attended an editorial meeting. One of the editors went over the stories that would run on pages one and eight. Ryan and I had some say about pictures. Then we went out to dinner. This particular night it was the same place where we ate lunch the week before, with nice chicken, pork and vegetable dishes. It took fully an hour and a half. Apparently, executive-length meals were standard.

Back at work we took on pages one and eight. Page one was a print version of CCTV covering the top news stories of the day. Forget about conventional reportage: all Chinese media are standard government issue. A typical (non) news day consisted of: grain harvest down, but not as far down as predicted (wait a minute—didn't I already write this for TV?); a minister on an inspection tour of factories in the provinces argues in favor of more macro-economics for the 10th time in a week (stop the presses!); an official from (fill in any) foreign country poses with a Chinese minister, each praising improved bilateral relations and "mutual co-operation" (give them the Nobel Peace Prize!). Once again, the staff-written stories were problems, except here they were much longer and much more wearisome. Page eight was international news from the wires: not so much work.

We labored, steadily, for a good three hours before the van the paper had been kind enough to provide for me arrived. I staggered into it for the ride home, unsure if I'd ever be able to master the computer or the copy flow.

On opening night as a paid polisher, I left a downtown duplicate-bridge game at 5:30, quickly discovered that I couldn't get a cab in the rain, and that when I did, I should expect to double the time I'd allotted for travel. The little country boy from Northampton had quickly forgotten big-city rules. On top of everything else, I was underdressed for the chill and got a hell of one myself. All in all, I was off to a wonderful start, arriving half an hour late at the paper and walking into the middle of an in-progress editorial meeting.

This time I was doing most of the page one and page eight work myself, since trainer Ryan, who was on hand as back-up, had the staff send the stories to my queue first. At some point during the night I decided I could handle the computer. At no point did I decide I could handle the copy flow. Ryan offered to come again the next night. I told him to arrive with a book, and I would try to do it all alone.

There was another problem I was becoming increasingly aware of. The older I had gotten, the less certain I'd become. What were once eternal truths had turned into debatable questions. Some might have called it a shift toward wisdom. I called it a shift toward fuzziness. My new enlightenment/befuddlement wasn't so bad outside the newsroom, where life was indeed ambiguous. It was lethal inside, where deadlines were not. I was constantly seeing several different ways to write a story. I didn't have time for that stuff. I needed my 20-year-old self back.

With relatively little help from Ryan, who even went home early, I got through my first full night fine, editing fully 15 stories and captions. "On a rough day at The New York Times, I might have edited three," said Ryan, who had worked there in the Sixties.

As the days passed, I realized I'd been a wee bit tough on the China Daily. "I was in China on a visit six years ago," said a Friendship Hotel resident working at *Xinhua*, "and it has improved a great deal. My wife is teaching English, and she says there are some stories good enough to be used in class."

In one October day's paper, there were actually two good stories. One, on *miandi*, the bread-loaf taxis I took all the time, was actually quite good. You not only got a good idea of the taxis themselves, but how long and hard the drivers had to work to make a decent living. A sidebar on the popularity of bikes and rickshaws wasn't bad, either. What I remember from it, perhaps inaccurately, was that public transportation took a back seat to military spending for many years. Both stories made me feel right at home.

One afternoon I had a catered lunch with Chen Hui, the retired managing editor of China Daily, in the company cafeteria. Hal Lipper had alerted Chen, a bridge buff, that I wanted to write columns for the China Daily. Sixty-five when we met, the cherubic and placid Chen helped found the paper in 1981 after a career in public service that included a stint at the World Bank in Washington. The paper had a circulation of 150,000 in 1993, mostly Chinese readers, and was read all over the country. Chen was proudest of the electronic wonders he brought to Beijing, few of which I understood as he described them and none of which I retained. Evidently, I left my entire memory function in my computer. Let's just say the Daily would soon be state-of-the-art.

I don't want to suggest that the job lacked worth or mirth. By mid-October my bridge column was running in Beijing Weekend, the paper's Friday supplement. Still is, in fact, which makes me an internationally syndicated columnist of sorts. In addition, the 6:30 p.m. meeting could actually be quite enjoyable. A suave-looking man in a vest from the editorial board—they alternated in our area every three months—announced the national-news stories. Another guy read off the foreign-news selections likely to be used on the front and back pages. Page-eight news usually occupied half to three-quarters of the back page, with the rest given over to advertising. "No news, no pictures, full-page," the guy announced one especially chortlesome night.

Later another man with what looked like a whistle around his neck gave us the national news, invariably concluding each item with something on the order of, "It's 22 cm long and in 'Jame's' queue (meaning mine)." I asked him why he wore a whistle. "Actually, it's a pen," he said, laughing and pulling the thing apart to disclose an ink-pusher. "It's easier to have it handy when there aren't any available pockets."

Everyone got a laugh out of a a story about a couple of pandas who were being sent on tour to Taiwan. I was always asked my choice of pictures and, at meeting's end, whether I had any questions. That time I said, "Do the pandas have visas?"

One night I felt like Butch and Sundance in the scene where they were so embattled they just spun and fired without looking. In addition to closing my bridge column—a fairly delicate matter including proof-reading the hands very carefully and cutting or adding to space—I had to field one polishing crisis after another. People were bouncing off me with questions. The toughest story was a 44-cm job on a women's conference in Manila. It began with a description of how the women were dressed—can you imagine a men's conference write-up like that?—and degenerated into pure confusion. I scrapped the lead altogether and somehow found a theme.

Some of the writers began sitting with me while I polished their stories. Authors have a right to know what's happened to their copy, but having a writer at your shoulder while you worked was a little harrowing. "In a few days you'll probably understand the gobbledygook we have in the China Daily," one writer, who actually turned in a relatively clean story, told me. "Chinese newspaper writers have a lot more information than they're allowed to report."

There were some small if symbolic victories. Once I summoned up enough chutzpah to confront an editor about the nightly non-news account of a foreign leader and Li or Jiang or someone billing and cooing. "You're right," he said. "I don't like these stories either, but we have no choice about running them."

More often, when I disputed something there were losing battles, resigned defeats. Here were the last three paragraphs of a story:

"During the briefing, [Chinese foreign ministry spokesman] Wu expressed regret over the detention of a Chinese fishing vessel on August 5 and the recent trial of its crew.

"Malaysian authorities detained the Chinese fishing vessel Suiyi 116 on August 5, and its court arbitrarily passed a ruling on the crew.

"He pointed out that it is entirely legitimate and justified for Chinese fishermen to fish in China's traditional fishing grounds."

I lost two battles on this story. First, I suggested to a Chinese editor that it might be nice if the readers knew just what "arbitrary" ruling the Malaysian court passed. Were the fisherman jailed, executed, acquitted? "We don't have that information," he said.

"Isn't it possible to find out?" I asked. "Where does this story come from?"

"*Xinhua.*"

"Maybe we could call over there." He did, but the national news agency hadn't bothered to find out.

"Now about this 'arbitrary' ruling," I said. "Since we don't know what it was, can we really make such a statement? Maybe we could cut it."

"Oh, no, it's part of the story."

"Well, do you mind if I attribute the statement to spokesman Wu?" They let me put that in. Then they removed it. The story ran as you see it above.

Mostly, my editing was pretty straightforward. Here's an example of the writing I polished at the China Daily. The original lead read, "The Chinese Tourism Authorities has embarked on an ambitious programme to improve the country's tourist service by developing a tourist information network across China."

Excedrin Headache # 4,536. In a nutshell, the lead embraced many of the faults I had to fix: incorrect use of articles, poor grammar, repetition, wordiness, opinion masquerading as fact. Probably not much different than the copy I'd have turned out in French, except for unauthorized opinions. The polished copy read: "Chinese tourism officials have developed a nationwide information network."

My salary of 100 RMB—about $12.50 a night, plus 70 RMB for my bridge column in the weekend supplement—was a better daily rate than that for the fulltime polishers, who in turn made more than the younger Chinese staffers. Hardly fair, since I had no illusions about being a great polisher. I hadn't done serious news writing for 25 years or so, and my average yearly output—one book, 52 bridge columns and maybe a half-dozen magazine stories and opinion pieces—didn't exactly prepare me for tight, concise, deadlined, hard-news editing.

The other polishers were pros as far as I was concerned. We had editors from Scotland, Canada, Singapore and the U.S. I was especially friendly with the men who broke me in: the gentlemanly Ryan, a career newspaperman from Cape Cod who had worked for The Boston Globe, The New York Times and The Philadelphia Inquirer, and the gregarious Lipper, the film critic on leave from the St. Petersburg Times. Ryan hoped to write several books about his experiences in the Orient, and Lipper was making friends and absorbing culture at an astonishing rate. Both had wisely taken their jobs more for personal than career advancement. Any experienced journalist who expected an inspiring newspaper experience alone was bound for disappointment.

The full-time polishers all lived in the same apartment building. As foreign experts, they were housed there for free as part of their contract with the newspaper. The building, which had been recently constructed, resembled a rundown, high-rise tenement.

The polishers were constantly throwing parties in the building. At one swinging soirée, I spoke with a Chinese editor about a visit to the United States he took several years earlier. "I like American newspapers," he said. "You have a lot of variety, with everything from tabloids to serious newspapers."

"What," I asked him, "is the biggest difference between U.S. and Chinese papers?"

"We're too serious. You have a lot in your papers about social life. You have whole sections about sports. We're lucky to have a page."

He was nice to open up to me, even about a fairly innocuous topic. Some Chinese journalists had gone to jail for telling too much. I would hate to think that my buddy's good will landed him in the joint. The record should show, in fact, that the Chinese staffers were uniformly friendly and courteous and as professional as their system allowed.

My polishing experience had considerable ups and downs. At times I felt like a punchy fighter refusing to concede: "Go ahead, give me your best shot. I can take it." That was my macho act to take through the night. Then I would walk outside the building—the van service wasn't always available at the time I left—and realize I was in the capital city of China after midnight, in no danger whatsoever, hailing a taxi. I would look up at the stars, raise my arms in the air, and yell into the night sky, "What a wonderful adventure!" If I hadn't watched myself, I might have started sounding like Brooks.

At other times I could have used Hans and Franz to pump me up and get me through the night. It was an exhausting, sometimes depressing job, and my interest waned quickly. Good thing we were in Beijing for only one semester, because I don't think I could have handled another three or four months at the China Daily, much as I liked the people. I still enjoy sending them my bridge column, though.

Look at it this way: working for the China Daily was one hell of a line on my résumé. If only they knew...

15

HERS: THE WORLDS OF CHINESE TV AND FILM

Teaching was not my only work experience in China. In addition to dubbing for a made-for-tv movie, I worked briefly, like Jim, polishing English-language news at CCTV, China's major national television network. As an academic specializing in mass communication, I didn't consider these jobs moonlighting so much as ad-hoc research. I also interviewed several Chinese film professors and directors as part of my own research.

CCTV provided my first venture into the world of Chinese media. It happened through fellow Friendship Hotel resident Mike Connelly, an ebullient American whose full-time job was polishing for CCTV. Mike needed to take several weeks' leave when his wife delivered their third son by Caesarean section in a Chinese hospital. Along with two others, Jim and I filled in for Mike on the 15-minute nightly show, "English News Service."

Started in 1987, the "English News Service" was one of a variety of English-language features CCTV offered in conjunction with what the network called its External Service. English-language programs have been so popular in China that BBC English teacher Kathy Flower, who had a regular show on CCTV, was once called the "best-known Western face after Karl Marx." CCTV's "English News Service" gave a brief summary of the top domestic and international news stories of the day.

I was dazzled by the CCTV building I thought I would be working in. It decorated western Beijing's skyline like a Steven Speilberg sci-fi prop—a needle of an edifice with a doughnut of glass-paned offices somewhere close to the top. Too bad we drove right by it on the way home after my first night of polishing, and I realized I had been working elsewhere. Things were never what they seemed in China.

Polishing turned out to be more stressful—and more fun—than I expected. Having taught tv production and produced a student news show, I found it a little like a busman's holiday. My afternoon's work began with a story conference on international news with Executive Producer Fang Jiqing. Then he disappeared upstairs into his office, and I found myself virtually alone in the newsroom for the first hour or two. My every minor question and uncertainty reverberated against the windowless walls.

Gradually the Chinese journalists began to wander in and out, entering into their computers the day's domestic stories, which I was supposed to polish. They were nightmares of officialese. It took an agonizingly long time to edit them and crank out a few sentences introducing the international stories. Interns from the China Broadcasting Institute wrote much of the domestic news copy. Woefully inexperienced but hungry to learn, they devoured the mini-editing lessons I gave them while still trying to bring my part of the show in under deadline.

Two and a half hours after arriving, I emerged from this pressure-cooker with a finished script. The anchors grabbed it, rehearsed the wording—sometimes with my help but more often without—and ran upstairs to tape the show. After one session, I followed the two anchors through a mind-boggling maze of corridors and stairwells up to the production studio on another floor and watched the taping. The visuals—except for international feeds from the American-run syndicate World Television News—were abominable. It was heigh-ho, swing-right, swing-left, zoom-in-and-out-till-you've-got-a-headache camera work. Despite my best attempts to retrace the route to the news room, I got hopelessly lost in the bowels of the building, stumbling into a hallway full of extras dressed like Genghis Khan before finding my way back.

The best part of the "English News Service" was that each of the writers took turns as anchors. Some spoke with impeccable British accents, others sounded American, others just sounded bad. According to Executive Producer Fang, the rotation prevented personnel turnover. I thought it helped cut down on American-style celebrity obsession.

As polishers, we had small but genuine input into selection of the four international stories used in the show. Political correctness, Chinese style, might dominate the choices, but since most stories—

like one on a typhoon raging in the Pacific—didn't have explicit political ramifications, we had more leeway than might be expected. If Fang wasn't sure about the relevance of an international story, he would ask for the polisher's advice. For instance, on my recommendation a story about Britain's shoot-to-kill policy was bumped by a funny one on Prime Minister John Major that helped the show's flow.

Since polishers wrote the lead-ins to the international stories, we also got to shape the news slant. I had fun trying to jazz up the copy and introduced a story on tourism in Jordan with a line about walls tumbling down from "Joshua and the Battle of Jericho." We also wrote the teasers opening the show. I tended to spotlight crime news, Western style—stories about smuggling of cultural relics, an arrest of a bank official for stealing, or a kidnapping—probably because they seemed more like real news to a me than the celebration of "mutual cooperation" with visiting foreign dignitaries. For all its stress and frustrations, polishing at CCTV provided insights into a side of life in China most people don't get to see.

# # #

China has gained worldwide recognition for its movies in the past 10 years, but not much has been heard in the West about its women directors. I hoped to interview as many of them as possible. Considering the short amount of time we were in China and my lack of fluency in Chinese, I was lucky to end up with any. I talked with several professors from the Beijing Film Academy, however, as well as two women directors from the celebrated Fifth Generation of Chinese filmmakers. The experience offered an inside look into the Chinese film industry.

Elderly, energetic Zhou Chuan Ji listed not only the Beijing Film Academy but the Beijing Broadcasting Institute and Jiling Art Academy on his business card. Zhou's personal history mirrored some of the dramatic changes China has undergone in the past 30 years. He was working at the State Film Bureau during the Cultural Revolution when he was removed and sent to the Beijing Film Academy as a laborer. "I was a rightist," he explained. "When the cultural revolution happened, I was exiled." The term rightist means

90

one of 750,000 so labeled in 1957 for outraging the Party, however mildly, during the Hundred Flowers movement.

He described watching a woman teacher get beaten to death during those years. So that his wife would not suffer from his political disfavor, he urged her to divorce him. Despite such experiences, he called himself lucky, saying that physical labor had been good for him. Eventually Zhou moved into a teaching position at the school. He was one of the very few at the film academy who read foreign languages—both Russian and English. Although officially retired, he continued to lecture all over China.

When I asked him to name the key element in filmmaking, he said, "You start from illusion." He believed Chinese thinking was not analytic, explaining there was nothing scientific about it, but rather an emphasis on the whole. Chinese traditional medicine was the analogy he used, describing Chinese doctors as not good in the scientific sense but good at ministering to the whole body. He did not think Chinese directors were well educated. "They must have training in painting and music," he said, observing that the last three years of Chinese middle school offered no painting or fine arts.

"There is not one Chinese director who knows what illusion is," he claimed. "There's no movement on the screen." He did give Fifth Generation Directors Chen Kaige and Zhang Yimou, both of whom had been his students, credit for some understanding of the concept. It was also important to fight against narration as a means of propaganda, he said. "You have to prove to the students that narrative is of no use."

According to Zhou, the Chinese film industry was in bad shape, and he had told the government so in a voluminous report. He blamed an emphasis on production rather than exhibition, which left theatres dirty and in poor repair. At the same time, he said, the State was still building big theatre palaces in the grand style of Hollywood in the Forties or of the Soviets. He called the administration of film exhibition "very clumsy," requiring many workers to run a theatre. "The Chinese film industry must die once," he said. "Then maybe they will wake up. Maybe the phoenix will rise again."

Zhou also blamed the industry's disarray on the method used to distribute films. Although the Chinese film industry is nationalized, the government "never puts a cent into it," he said. Once a film was made in one of the 16 regional film production studios, the State only paid the studio for one copy. Income from distribution went directly to the government. Admission receipts dropped from $26 billion in 1982 to under $10 billion in 1992. He attributed the decline to tv and its novelty. Chinese films, he said were "the same as tv—just as bad."

Big-screen video theatres in the provinces made a profit, however, because they showed Hong Kong films that were not subject to Chinese censorship and cost only 10 RMB a ticket. Although these rogue theatres were forbidden by the government, Zhou said they were "out of control." When he visited Nanning in Guangxi Province, not one theatre was showing a Chinese film. They all came from Hong Kong or Taiwan. The case was the same at Fuzhou in Fujian Province. Violence and sex in imports attracted illiterate audiences, while Chinese films were not good enough in their own right to build an audience.

Fifth Generation directors acclaimed in the West were not popular inside China and didn't please the government because of their unvarnished views of Chinese life. "In my mind, the Fifth Generation no longer exists," Zhou said. He saw films like Chen's "Farewell, My Concubine" and Zhang's "The Story of Qiu Ju" as having become commercial. Nor did he think a new, sixth generation of filmmakers had emerged. "They're just trying to make commercial films," he explained. "That's the tragedy of filmmaking. You need money." Serious directors had to fight with the government over every project they started. "It's fatiguing," Zhou complained. Exile, however, was not an option. "If you are a director, you must stay in China," he said.

Zhou described Chinese film as a medium for younger people. The expense of film stock was propelling young people into tv, where less costly video could be used. Zhou mentioned tv movies like "Home Far Away from Beijing," about young girls who come to Beijing to work as amahs, or nursemaids, and "Death of a River," a tv documentary banned after the Tiananmen riots in 1989. Even "Beijingers in New York," a highly popular commercial mini-series, won Zhou's grudging approval. "In China the most important thing is to tell the truth," he said. The trend was for young people to circumvent the strictures of the government-run Chinese film industry by shooting independently with video in the cities and producing non-commercial works. "Independent film in China? Impossible," he said. "I have left the film industry. My efforts are in tv."

"Inspired by the power of the recording machine, young people are trying to tell the truth," Zhou said. "Gradually everybody is making pictures." In contrast, he said, "Twenty years ago it was impossible for me to make films for my own class." Now, through what was in effect an "underground" network, the work of new directors could be passed around from circle to circle. "They are very excited with their experience," Zhou said. "If a work is not too controversial, we try to help it pass. They think we have authority aesthetically. So when I say this is good, they have to listen. We know to take it step by step. It's not yet a movement. They are all scattered. It has to be a movement."

Ni Zhen, an associate professor at the Beijing Film Academy, also criticized the Chinese film industry. A screenwriter, he served as Production Supervisor for Chinese-American artist Chen Yifei's documentary "Reverie on Old Shanghai," which we saw when it opened in Beijing. Ni's path to the Beijing Film Academy was circuitous. He had aspired to be a painter but ended up studying scenery design at the Beijing Film Academy instead. After graduation he was sent to a small studio production house for scientific and technical films. Joining the faculty at the Academy, he taught film art first, then moved into film theory and history. He has conducted research on contemporary Chinese movies and analyses of classical Chinese film. He said his criticism of the industry was not popular with the government.

Ni explained the structure of the Chinese film industry in detail. Individual filmmakers were attached to regionally located production centers, like the Beijing or Shanghai film studios. They developed their projects there. Before a script could go into production, though, it had to be approved by a script committee at the studio. The finished product also needed approval at the studio level. Then it passed through censorship at the State level. Each production center reported to the Ministry of Radio, TV and Film, with control also exerted by the Culture and Finance ministries. The ministries in turn reported to the State Council, which reported to the Propaganda Department of the Communist Party's Central Committee. Probably as a result of these elaborate bureaucratic restraints, Ni said censorship rarely occurred beyond the level of the studios. In the interests of efficiency, the studios tried to anticipate and ward off problems at higher levels.

According to Ni, conflicts between the propaganda and entertainment functions of film in China were increasing. From the beginning of Communist regime in 1949 until after the Cultural Revolution, the Chinese film industry existed as a monopoly. In 1977, however, a new wave of films started to flood the country. While the Propaganda Department of the Communist Party's Central Committee continued to think movies should be controlled, the Ministry of Radio, TV and Film began to dispute that approach.

Like Zhou Chuan Ji, Ni described problems with the film distribution system in China. Since films were released both into theatres and for big screen video, it was no longer possible for the government to maintain control in the traditional manner. He speculated that to stave off bankruptcy, the State might concentrate funding in the biggest of the 16 film production centers, instigate mergers to reduce their number or encourage mergers with tv stations. Collaboration held particular promise, since 5,000 to 6,000 serials had been produced for tv, generating a big chunk of money and propaganda for the government. To counteract the influence of "rogue" video, the State had started scheduling older films about the revolution on tv and in theatres. Schoolchildren were then required to write compositions about them.

Censorship remained a dilemma for most Chinese directors, Ni said. One director had recently been given official notice that he was no longer allowed to make or distribute movies. Ni did not think, however, this director would be arrested. Such a move would have generated too much publicity and conflicted with ongoing economic reforms. In another case, a prominent director had finished a script three years earlier that still was not approved for shooting. The climate for filmmaking was more open in Shanghai.

My interest in China's women directors started before we arrived in Beijing and was sparked by a New England Women's Studies conference I had attended in Boston. A panelist there suggested Chinese films by women directors had a distinctive, female perspective. I wanted to see if women directors in China agreed. The evidence was curiously conflicting, with the directors I met denying any feminist sensibility at the same time that their careers and sometimes their conversation suggested otherwise. On occasion they directly contradicted themselves, first denying that their viewpoint was any different than a male director's, then implying the opposite.

Li Shaohong had much to say about her experiences as a Fifth Generation director. The Fifth Generation—the first class of students to enter the Beijing Film Academy after the Cultural Revolution—has won worldwide acclaim for their work. Influenced by their experiences growing up in China during a period of hardship and social upheaval, they entered film school at a crucial time. They were allowed to use film to express personal visions rather than more programmatic statements of revolutionary zeal.

Li's father was an Army officer, her mother a film director whose career was aborted by the Cultural Revolution. When Chinese schools were shut down in the Sixties, Li joined the Army and went to Sichuan province, where she worked as a film projectionist. After returning to live with her parents in Beijing in the Seventies, she decided to apply to the Beijing Film Academy.

Li said the family's extensive collection of film books saved her when she was studying for her entrance exams. Beijing Film Academy professor Ni Zhen, who was a friend of the family, helped her prepare. During her entrance interview, when Li was asked what film books she had read, the interviewer assumed she had simply memorized titles. She convinced the examiners that she hadn't because she knew the authors as well and passed with flying colors.

Entering with the largest number of female students in history—nine—Li took courses in storytelling, acting, sketches, literary analysis. She spent time studying Russian, French and Italian movies, although not American ones. The women in her class did better than the men, she said. They were a select group to start with, since filmmaking was considered too mentally draining and physically exhausting to be compatible with being a woman.

Nonetheless, Li felt women directors tended to be temperamental. They flourished, had "screw-ups" at home, then flourished again. In her view, love and emotions were harder for women to push aside. "Women tend to look at emotions as the whole of life," she said.

When she entered the Beijing Film Academy at 23, it seemed that everybody was devoting half their time to companions of the opposite sex. "You had to decide," she said. "Were you going to devote time to chasing men or do some serious work?" She remembered having her first-ever love affair while in film school. It could have been disastrous, she said but saw she had to choose between "a rich and colorful life and accomplishment." Writers can have their cake and eat it too," she explained. "Filmmaking is too demanding."

Li didn't start dating her husband, a cinematographer, until her last year at the Academy. The experience of seeing her mother's directing dreams dashed by the Cultural Revolution spurred Li to success. Recently that success had become a source of bitterness between the two, making it difficult for Li to visit her mother in Shanghai.

After finishing at the Academy, Li spent the years between 1982 and 1984 as an assistant director. Some of the projects she worked on were Xie Tieli's "The Father and Son of the Bao Family" and "The Clearwater Bay and the Sweetwater Bay"; Jian Weichan's "The Breadwinner"; and Han Xiaolei's "The Practicing Lawyer." After her daughter was born, Li found she couldn't both be a mother and direct. As a result, her first work as a director in her own right was left unfinished.

Recognition came later, first in 1990 with "Bloody Morning" and then in 1992 with "Family Portrait." Li described collaboration as an important component of Fifth Generation work. The first Fifth Generation film, Zhang Junzhao's "One and the Eight," begun while they were students and released in 1983, was "almost a collective effort," she said. She and her classmates would sit together and discuss the project as it moved through different stages. Li credited director Tian Zhuangzhuang for coming up with the idea behind "Family Portrait." Although she has stayed in touch with her classmates in the Fifth Generation, she said she didn't see them regularly any more. "What the critics say we do has nothing to do with what we do," she claimed. "We're still in our prime. It's still too early to say what our impact will be."

Li called herself a rational person and said the distinctive quality of her directing was its rational part. Her first major film, "Bloody Morning," she described as "compact and dynamic, made with a good structure." Her films, she said, "don't look like they've come out of a woman's hand. Women are more likely to be sentimental."

Li found it "very hard to keep in touch when they [the women directors] keep dropping out of sight." She gave as an example one "hilarious case," a woman who supposedly died after giving birth to a baby and divorcing her abusive husband. Li and her colleagues discussed how they might care for the orphaned child. Then they found out the supposedly dead woman was alive and well in Beijing. "It was a rumor," Li said. "We all had goose bumps." In fact, the same woman had had two divorces and before that, a disastrous love affair. With such a tempestuous personal life, she could not direct and had dropped out of sight.

Despite such problems, Li insisted women directors were just like men. "There are no feminist movies in China," she said. "In China the problems women face are different." When a group of French feminists tried to put together a feminist film festival using Chinese films, Li said they came up empty-handed. "What we have

97

experienced is different," she said. "Before 1949, women lived in a feudal society. Then Mao taught that women can hold up half the sky. We have been taught not to see the differences."

Li thought women directors should make more movies about men. "Women look at the world as a man's world," she suggested. In her own movies, all the main characters have been men. The first time she was asked why, she said she found herself speechless. Then she thought about it and decided it was easier for her to explain the opposite sex. "For men directors, women are at least half their lives, so they pay a lot of attention," she said. "For women, men are all their lives. For a woman with a successful career but an unhappy emotional life, success is meaningless."

Li's first major film, "Bloody Morning," was based on a story by Latin American writer Gabriel Marcia Marquez. In the latter part of 1989, she explained, "everybody thought they should do something, but they didn't know what." Li reread the Marquez story—about the murder of a rich peasant—was touched by it and thought it would be interesting to transplant the idea to China. She saw similarities between the two cultures in both the rural setting and the fight over a girl's emotions.

The censors complained that "Bloody Morning" ended with "microscopic scenes of killing that were too bloody, too sharp." Li defended the violence as a necessary part of the content, but she had to yield. Reviewers said "Bloody Morning" was "better than all of Chen Kaige's work," and it received as much acclaim in China as her more recent film "Family Portrait" did abroad.

Li described "Bloody Morning" as a more profound work with greater impact than "Family Portrait," and she thought it had not been exported because it reflected the dark side of life in China. Because "Bloody Morning" was trying to reflect rural society, the government thought it best to pretend it didn't exist, she suggested. In contrast, "Family Portrait" was more psychological and representative of post-modern China. It centered not on a complete plot but on a state of mind.

Li said her next film was about women—two prostitutes who cause the death of a customer. Li explained that relationships to prostitutes in China were more direct than in other cultures. "Prostitutes hide the least, are the least pretentious," she said. Li hoped to find her own financing in order to retain control of the project. We learned that it was completed, and the film premiered in Beijing in December 1993 as "Blush."

My interview with Hu Mei, best known for her 1985 film "Army Nurse," was conducted on the run. Zhang Dan, a publicist who worked for both China Screen Magazine and the China Film Export and Import Corporation, invited me to a press conference introducing a new thriller produced by Hu.

Hu Mei seemed to be bucking the Chinese film establishment more directly than Li Shaohong. Before attending Beijing Film Academy, Hu worked as an actress in the Army during the Cultural Revolution. After graduation, she moved to the August First Film Studio and made "Army Nurse," "Far From War" and "Gunslinger Without a Gun." After leaving the August First Studio in 1989, she worked freelance in video, even producing her own videocassettes. She described it as "like a war." In a society where most aspects of an individual's life were controlled by the work unit, working independently has not even been an option until very recently.

"Fog House," budgeted at $1.2 million, was the first film Hu had worked on as a producer. The setting was a traditional garden with a Qing dynasty house, and Hu said it had been a struggle getting approval to use it. She was the first woman to produce films in China, starting in 1992; there were three in 1993. "Now everyone's smiling at me because I control the money," she said. The quality of production in China was not high, according to Hu. She said her producing style was different from Hollywood's because she had worked as a director.

At the Beijing Film Academy, Hu was taught that the only function of film was to educate the people. "Now it's different," she said. "Ordinary people are not interested in politics. They want entertainment." Commercial films were emphasizing family and how people could improve their lives. By contrast, in the Fifties the Chinese film industry was dominated by the Soviet influence, with directors at the center. The feeling of making studio films was totally different. "Now it's Westernized," she said.

According to Hu, the art-film wave instigated by Fifth Generation directors like her had turned into a commercial film wave. "It's not easy to make a good commercial film," she said. She described living through China's transition from a socialist to a more capitalistic economy. "Suddenly I had to pay for everything for myself. It's cruel," she complained. "You must make money quickly." Hu learned a lot, particularly to insist on her own style. She said the feeling of making studio films was totally different, but she felt lucky to have established herself quickly. Hu's popular tv series "Endless Love" aired in 1992. She said she hoped to work as both a producer and director. She thought she had made "a good beginning."

As a producer, she gave directors complete freedom, only requiring that the film be brought in on time. Hu explained that she knew how hard it was to win freedom as a director. One well-known director she worked with was so appreciative he told her, "Next time you be the director. I'll be the producer and provide everything you need."

Hu said she would work as producer/director on her next project, tentatively titled, "This Story Does Not Belong to the Outside World." The plot was based on the actual case of a film shot years ago about a man wrongly imprisoned for 30 years. The film's woman director befriends the prisoner and uses him to gain fame. The prisoner is cleared and freed at the age of 70.

Hu envisioned herself producing commercial films and directing art films. She said she was still interested in and good at making films about women and films that were frank and open about sex. She did not, however, see "Army Nurse" as a feminist film. "Woman is born to make men happy. You have to follow nature," she said, seeming to contradict the evidence of her own career.

16

TALKING TO THE AMERICAN PRESS

As part of a long-term research project, I interviewed as many American journalists as I could while we were in Beijing. Of the 26 accredited to represent American news organizations there, I talked to 15. They were an interesting and uniformly impressive bunch, accomplished and dedicated. The youngest was 25; the oldest, 56. All were cooperative about being interviewed, and the majority didn't mind being quoted, despite the sensitivity of relations between China and the U.S.

Most came to Beijing not simply because they were assigned there, but because it was the place they wanted to be. They had made it their business to understand China. Many had graduate or undergraduate degrees in Asian or Chinese Studies, but surprisingly few had academic training in journalism. Only two majored in journalism as undergraduates, although another four had graduate journalism degrees. They still had plenty of professional experience, on average working as journalists for 10 years. Defying the stereotypes of the foreign correspondent as white and male, six were women and three were Chinese-American. There was also one Filipino.

Kari Huus, who was working for Newsweek, said she thought China was easier to live in than the Middle East. Women correspondents did not work as frequently in war zones, she said, and Beijing was a safe place to be. Lincoln Kaye, at the Far East Economic Review, had worked all over Asia and said he felt "a sense of duty" about coming to China. The challenge of learning Chinese provided one of the selecting factors. "It's a kind of intelligence test," he suggested. Christian Science Monitor correspondent Sheila Tefft spent five years in India and two in Thailand before coming to China, because "that's where the adventure lay."

After our interview, United Press International superstringer Matthew Forney took me along with him to a weekly government press briefing at the International Club in downtown Beijing. We got there early, but the cavernous room was already full of tv cameramen setting up. Between 50 and 60 members of the international press community came. Three government officials filed in and sat at a table in the front of the room. The wall that provided a backdrop behind them for tv cameras was red, with cranes—a Chinese symbol for longevity—flying across it in an arc over pine trees. I could see the faint outline of characters that had been painted out and wondered what they said.

There were no breaking stories that day, so the mood was relatively quiet. Just good wishes for the new year. Chinese cameramen scanned the audience, training lights on the faces. Forney explained it was because they liked to show foreign reporters listening intently and copying down the pronouncements of the government's officials. After a few announcements, the three officials took questions. Then it was over, and the foreign reporters hijacked the officials for more questions, shoving microphones and tape recorders in their faces as unceremoniously as they would with any American politician.

The American journalists lived in the international apartment complexes that doubled as diplomatic compounds in Beijing. Their living conditions made a statement about the position and treatment of international journalists in China. In a sense, they were privileged prisoners of the Chinese government, which provided them with housing and a support staff that doubled as government agents. The housing provisions meant most of the journalists lived in the same buildings as their offices—although not necessarily in the same apartment—had the perpetual pleasure of each other's company and were under constant surveillance.

Some Chinese support staff members were friendly and sympathetic, while others clearly took their spying duties more seriously. One journalist described arriving in a colleague's office and discovering a member of the support staff looking through files in the computer. Mail was opened routinely, and most people were followed at least intermittently. One journalist described finding the family's ayi, or housekeeper, going through the garbage. Another said he got weird feedback on his stereo when he played Mozart and attributed it to wiretapping.

It was a hermetic world, with some interesting subgroups. Journalists with Taiwanese wives—none had Taiwanese husbands—were considered a brain trust of sorts because their wives could act as their eyes and ears, speed-reading Chinese characters. These couples attracted government attention because they provided a double threat. Most of the journalists from European countries belonged to the Club Lundi, which met regularly to trade ideas. The Asian-American women journalists had their own group, called "Girls with an Attitude."

One of the biggest frustrations for the journalists I talked to was the limitation on travel inside China. Any time members of the international press community wanted to go outside Beijing, they had to request permission 10 days in advance. Granting a permit often seemed highly arbitrary. "If you're doing a story on reform, you get permission," said CNN correspondent Mike Chinoy. "If it's one on the selling of children, no." Certain locales like Tibet were perennially off limits, unless a visiting publisher or network executive provided an excuse for a public relations opportunity.

Covering a breaking story—a flood or a riot, for instance—became nearly impossible because of the travel rule. Many journalists ignored the rule, but they risked being turned back or arrested. "I just take my chances," said Newsweek's Huus. "I just go. If you speak Chinese well enough, you can learn a lot that way." She described one time "I knew permission might be a problem. I applied but went a couple of days earlier and got all the details." The alternative would have been "officials staring at you...two-hour lunches...toasts...and stonewalling."

Even when they got permission to travel, the journalists found themselves paying sometimes exorbitant fees for the privilege. Applications to travel had to go through the foreign affairs office in the area visited. U.S. News and World Report correspondent Susan Lawrence said she had learned to handle the checkbook journalism problem by bargaining on the phone before leaving. European journalists ignored the travel restrictions and got away with it, according to her, because the Chinese government didn't pay as close attention to them. The Christian Science Monitor's Tefft was about to leave for Wuhan when I interviewed her, and she described the battle she was having with a functionary there. "He has to come along with the person already assigned, " she explained. "We have to rent a car. We can't take a taxi. It must be a mini-van costing $70 a day because I'm bringing a photographer."

The ultimate weapon of control employed by the Chinese government was expulsion. Although it hadn't been used much in the years since Tiananmen, it was a potent threat. U.S. News and World Report's Lawrence said everyone was surprised that Washington Post correspondent Lena Sun didn't get thrown out. Accusing her of having "internal," or classified, documents, government agents broke into her office and terrorized her family and staff. "Expulsion is always on our minds," said Time Magazine Bureau Chief Jaime FlorCruz, "when confronted with whether or not a story is worth pursuing, if you think it may displease the Chinese government."

"They like to make examples of people," said Dan Sutherland of the Washington Post. "If you look at 10 journalists expelled over the last 10 years, each one was a little example." David Schlesinger of Reuters told the story of one foreign journalist caught with an internal document after writing about separatists in Inner Mongolia. The toothpaste he had put on the lip of his suitcase to detect searches warned him that he would be arrested. Government agents stopped him in the airport and made a show of finding a document in his luggage.

Covering the news in China was a closed shop. Since foreign journalists had to have special visas and be credentialed by the Chinese government, there was no such thing as independent or freelance journalists from another country. We were exceptions because we had another reason for being in China and didn't have to register as journalists. This requirement also allowed the government to punish individual correspondents or news organizations if it didn't like their coverage. The number of foreign journalists was strictly controlled, with major American news organizations like USA Today and National Public Radio kept waiting for slots.

Journalists couldn't be sure if they could keep their credentials, so those already working in Beijing found it hard to change jobs there. Renewal time sometimes became the occasion for "handlers," as correspondents called the Foreign Affairs Department officers responsible for them, to issue reprimands or warnings about coverage. The government conveyed its displeasure with former New York Times correspondents Nicholas Kristoff and Cheryl WuDunn by refusing to provide their infant son, born in Hong Kong, with a multiple entry visa. They had to travel back to Hong Kong every three months with the baby and reapply.

Los Angeles Times correspondent Rone Tempest explained, "Your predecessor must be in the same room with you. He hands in his credential, and you get yours." The Washington Post's Sutherland, in Beijing covering for Lena Sun while she was on maternity leave, had to wrestle to get the government to let him stay long enough to brief Sun when she returned. He was first told he would have to leave the day she got back. Even though the government relented and agreed to let him stay another two days, it was on the condition that he relinquish his press pass as soon as Sun returned. One result of such limitations was that journalists tended to save their hardest-hitting stories until late in their tour of duty in case of expulsion.

Although the government refused to recognize its existence, the Foreign Correspondents Club of Beijing was active in defending members' rights. It was particularly vehement when ABC cameraman Todd Carroll was beaten while at Tiananmen Square in 1992, suffering permanent injuries. The club protested again when AP photographer Greg Baker and other foreign journalists were arrested another time for being at Tiananmen Square near the anniversary of the 1989 riots. "Photographers are treated differently," said Tempest of the Los Angeles Times. "I don't like to go with tv cameras or photographers. I think it's dangerous."

"You can't walk around with a tv camera and pretend to be a tourist," ABC correspondent Deborah Wang pointed out. She explained that before Carroll was beaten, someone had unfurled a banner in front of him. Carrying a super-8 video camera, Carroll shot the banner and was attacked by plainclothes police who she speculated had training in martial arts. Carroll suffered soft tissue damage that left him limping and from which he might never recover. "One rule is, don't resist," said Time's FlorCruz. "You're dealing with thugs. There's no story worth dying for."

Despite surveillance, attempts to control coverage, threats and violence, the journalists were resourceful at finding ways to do their job. "I don't feel it [surveillance] very much, but it's there," CNN's Chinoy said. "I know we're watched and the phone's tapped. I try to be as open as possible. What amazes me is how little of this there is." U.S. News and World Report's Lawrence said one tactic for getting Chinese interview subjects safely in and out of the journalists' compounds was to put them in a car with a phony registration plate and drive them in past the guards.

"I go on my way and do what I do," said the Christian Science Monitor's Tefft. "It gets to you every once in a while. I've seen tape on the camera in the elevator and shoe prints on the wall. Things have been disturbed on my desk." Schlesinger of Reuters said government interference fluctuated. "In general, people say it's a light period now. No one has come up with any decent document stories in months. That tells me they're concentrating their efforts on scaring the sources, and it works."

IV

FUN & GAMES

"The Li River winds through some of China's greatest landscapes. Their names alone speak of infinite wonders: Pushing Millstones Rock, Crown Cave, Nine Horses Mountain. I scarcely saw one."

17

HIS: BRIDGE OVER TROUBLED WATERS

"Just as the Russians are good at chess, a game of solitude and isolation, the Chinese are naturals for bridge, a game that brings people together" —Kathie Wei-Sender

Playing bridge was the best thing that happened to me in China. At times, it was the only good thing. Oh, hell, go ahead and say it: bridge kept me alive for five months.

The beginning was hardly auspicious. After 10 days of calling around Beijing and telling everyone I met about my interest in bridge, I got a tip that a game was played every Thursday morning at 9:30 at the Lido Club, a joint-venture recreational facility on the road to the airport. I called over. "Yes, bridge," I was told. "Yes, Tuesday, Wednesday, Thursday at 9:30 in the morning."

Brooks and I arrived at 9 a.m. Thursday. The sign in the lobby said bridge at 2 p.m. "All the time I repeat, repeat, repeat," said the exasperated, French-surnamed club manager. "I try to tell the operators that if you don't understand, ask them to say it again. They just say, 'Yes, yes, yes.'"

I wasn't deliberately misled, but victimized by the cultural phenomenon of saving face. The voice on the line preferred to answer me based on a vague notion or make up the times altogether. To admit ignorance of the bridge hours would have been losing face, a matter of great embarrassment in Asia.

I returned that afternoon, and for the first of many Thursdays played with an international cast of women from places like Germany, England, South Korea, Australia and France. Because I was usually the only man and best player in the group, I was treated like royalty. I felt like the Duke of Earl.

Eventually, I was invited to a game at the home of a Lido Club regular and good friend named Rosa Brown, who was born in Vietnam and taught French at Beijing's International School. Her Chinese guests were Hu Yusheng and Jing Jingshen. Hu, a mellow, retired professor of electrical engineering, spoke English fluently. Jing, a young electrician constantly hustling for jobs, spoke animatedly in Chinese. The language barrier was no problem: we played using bidding boxes from which players took cardboard sheets holding a number and a symbol—say, 1♥—describing their bids.

The afternoon's real surprise was the Chinese playing style. When the dummy placed his cards on the table face-up after the bidding, he'd do so in any order—10 K J 4 7—and his partner would automatically rearrange the cards in his mind. After each hand, the Chinese would recapitulate the play at length. Their recall was extraordinary. I guess when you've learned to reproduce several thousand characters—an assignment roughly parallel to memorizing a series of small paintings, and one requiring patience, persistence and pinpoint accuracy, all ideal qualities for a bridge competitor—52 cards is not much of a challenge.

It was just one small step from a social game to a more structured one at a Chinese club. Since their apartments were so small and cramped, players congregated in duplicate clubs and workplaces. Some 50,000, or one in 20, of the country's million active players belonged to the Chinese Bridge Association (CBA), about the same percentage as in the American Contract Bridge League (ACBL)..

Hu Yusheng was kind enough to invite me to his club for the Wednesday afternoon game. I walked into a tree-dotted courtyard outside the Shishahai Sports School, a physical-education facility on the outskirts of downtown Beijing, and tried to ask someone where I could find the bridge room. A young man in tennis gear approached. "What's the matter with you?" he asked in English.

I thought he really meant, "Is anything the matter? Can I help out?"

At that moment Hu cycled up. Thin as a bamboo reed, he fit into the smallest pair of jeans I have ever seen on an adult. His lined face topped by one of the overgrown crewcuts in vogue, he was a road map of China's last half-century. Hu came to Beijing as an electrical-engineering graduate of Shanghai University, drawn to the capital city with the best and brightest young talent during the heady early days of Communism. A professor at the Qua Bei Institute of Electric Power, he was exiled to forced labor in the countryside during the Cultural Revolution but survived without visible physical or mental trauma. Having traveled widely in retirement and seen two of his four kids educated in the United States, he was now marveling at the madcap change in China's socialist market economy. Mr Hu, how do you do?

We made our way into the office, where I was introduced to the friendly staff, and headed immediately to a conference room for an interview with Lu Jiang, the deputy secretary general of the Beijing Bridge League. Lu gave me a Beijing Bridge League pin, and someone else placed a Coke on the table in front of me. *"Bu xie,"* I said. That literally means, "No, thanks," but in Chinese idiom, I discovered, translates to "You're welcome." (The Chinese don't say "Thank you" very often, because they fear it divides people.) I should have said, *"Bu yao,"* or "I don't want." Linguistic deficiency sentenced me to an unwanted caffeine high.

My inquiry into Chinese bridge continued. "Many things are invented by the Chinese: gunpowder, paper," Lu said through Hu's translation, explaining the ease with which her countrypeople have mastered the great game. "Chinese people have wisdom. If you have one table and four people, anyone can play."

In case you're not a bridge player, let me explain the kind of game we played. Duplicate bridge is the game's major competitive form. Unlike rubber bridge, which I usually describe as "Deal 'em, play 'em, score 'em," duplicate minimizes the luck factor. Players take pre-dealt hands from the North, South, East and West slots of a metal or plastic board labeled with the hand number. When you play a trick, you don't throw the cards into a pile, the way you do in rubber bridge. Instead, you place each card in front of you—horizontally if you lost the trick, vertically if you won it. At play's end, each player returns his original 13 cards to the proper board slot. After two or three hands in the most popular form of duplicate, the boards are sent to the next lower table, while East-West players move to the next higher table. Eventually, all East-West teams play the same hands as the other East-West teams, and North-South teams play the same cards as their own compass-point brethren. You're scored relative to the results of identically located pairs; hence, the term duplicate.

This day's duplicate was played in a light and airy room by the school's leafy front courtyard. All players were given free Cokes or hot water to go with the tea leaves they brought in recycled glass containers about the size of a Jiffy peanut butter jar. In fact, the atmosphere was much like that in an American bridge hall, including the "No Smoking" sign—the first I'd seen in China. All in all, somewhat more comfortable than the People's Bridge Hall I had in mind.

Though the game wouldn't start for 15 minutes, the regulars—mostly elderly men sipping tea—were playing practice games like Little Leaguers who won't wait for their coach.

I had been told that the nicest people in China were the elderly, and I wasn't disappointed. Elders are called *lao*, an honorific roughly embracing old, honorable and distinguished. They deserved it. Like countryman Hu, they'd survived the Japanese occupation, World War Two, the 1949 "liberation," the Great Leap Forward, the Anti-Rightist Campaign of 1957 and the Cultural Revolution. Left with neither illusions nor harsh edges, they played bridge with the same equanimity with which they practiced tai chi. At times I couldn't tell if they were playing or meditating.

There was also a fair number of young people, whose absence is notable at afternoon clubs in America. Thanks to the advent of capitalism, many Chinese yuppies owned their businesses and had time for afternoon games. "Ten years ago this never would have happened," said Hu. Nor would Chinese players have been associating so openly with foreigners.

Again, there were no language problems for me. The Chinese accepted that English was the lingua franca of bridge, and everyone knew the basic terms. In any case, words proved to be unnecessary. At some clubs the Chinese played by using the same bidding boxes I found chez Brown. At other clubs, competitors wrote their bids on slips of paper using the universal terms. I much preferred these

112

ethereal auctions to our own houses of babble, and I would love to hear the sound of silence at the Tuesday evening games I play in Vineyard Haven and Northampton, Massachusetts.

After duplicate play began, I was faced with potential embarrassment when I made an illegal bid. In America, people would have been calling for the game's director with visions of penalties. In China, nothing happened. Nothing. There wasn't even a rules interpreter to be called. "This is not competition." said Hu. "As we say in China, friendship first, competition second."

He wasn't just being polite. To the consternation of Chinese bridge officials, club players could be as chatty during the play as they were quiet during the bidding. The feeling seemed to be, why observe monkish silence when results don't matter? When one of the younger players at Shishahai berated his partner for poor play, an elder patted him on the back and murmured a gentle warning. Following the game, players didn't ask their place in the standings: too competitive. They just wanted to know if they'd won more than 50 per cent of the available scoring units.

#   #   #

Chinese bridge was a happy accident waiting to happen. Students picked up the game in Europe during the Twenties and Thirties—China's paramount leader Deng Xiaoping learned while a student in France—and returned home with it. By liberation in 1949, the game was popular in Chinese universities.

Bridge was politically incorrect during the Cultural Revolution. Charged by propagandists with playing the "decadent Western pastime," Even Deng was paraded through the streets in a dunce cap. He was accused of hiring a special railroad car for himself and his bridge cronies, flying them in when he got bored in Manchuria, and using state funds to construct a personal bridge club, interrupting games only to place his "stinking signature," as critics complained, on documents. Said a Red Guard newspaper, with a notable lack of finesse: "This club, with elaborate facilities for eating, drinking and games, became Mr. Deng's hangout where he enlisted capitulationists and renegades and gathered together demons and monsters."

Once the Gang of Four was overthrown in 1976, Chinese bridge took off so quickly that Deng was named 1980 Bridge Personality of the Year by the International Bridge Press Association. His publicized exhibitions with foreigners sparked bridge playing among the Party hierarchy, and teams have gotten sponsorships from businesses.

The ailing Deng's only official title during our visit was honorary chairman of the CBA. Other leaders, like retired National People's Congress chairman Wan Li, who was credited by the International Bridge Press Association with playing the international Hand of the Year in 1984 and finished second in the 1988 Epson worldwide bridge contest, had been more visible bridge ambassadors of late.

"Bridge is especially suitable for Chinese culture," said Tennessee consultant and former world champion Kathie Wei-Sender (née Yang Xiao Yen in Beijing), a bouncy sexagenarian whose devoted work on behalf of Chinese bridge has made her a household name from Tianjin to Tibet. "Just as the Russians are good at chess, a game of solitude and isolation, the Chinese are naturals for bridge, a game that brings people together." Indeed, the Chinese use the literal translation of the word "bridge," *qiao*, because to *da qiao pai* (literally "play bridge cards") connects people the way a suspension bridge links communities.

"Bridge is also suitable for the Chinese character," said Wei-Sender. "Outwardly, they're very gentle and trained to be humble, but inwardly they walk softly and carry a big stick. In bridge you don't have to say you're good. Your performance does that for you." A Chinese student agreed. "We're weak physically," he said, "but we feel we can beat you with our brains. That's why we play intellectual games."

"Just as physical education keeps the body fit, bridge is exercise to keep the mind fit," said CBA Vice President Li Wei, speaking with the solemnity usually reserved for praising Mao's swim in the Yangzi.

China didn't organize a national association until 1980 but landed the 1995 world championships, to be be held in Beijing

114

during the invariably lovely fall season. The women have finished third in their world championships and the men have placed fifth in the open division. China has been challenging our dominance in great leaps forward.

These days people know about *qiao pai* all over China, and top players have such extensive followings that the day of Chinese bridge groupies may not be far removed. In the fall of 1993, Brooks and I saw an exhibition match between the Chinese and British women's teams at a midtown hotel, where a crowd of fans whispered and applauded when the play was relayed from the competition room to a Vugraph screen.

As Chinese play improves—whether because of inborn talent, traditionally tough education in numbers and memorization, a multi-century cult of perfection or all the above—the international aspirations that glint more often and more brightly in official eyes are said to be producing approval in more substantial form than mere encouragement.

Opinions varied about the extent of the encouragement. All national-team members were amateurs holding full-time jobs, Tang Hou Zu, a Chinese women's coach, told me after I'd watched a game with him at the exhibition. His senior player, 38-year-old Sun Ming, a little woman with a page-boy haircut and prominent cheekbones, sat smoking a cheroot. When I asked what she did for a living, she said, "I play bridge." At the time, Sun had a job with China All-Sports, the country's umbrella organization for all forms of recreation, for something over 300 RMB, or about $35, a month. That may not sound like much, but it was more than she made at the key-lock factory where her talents were unearthed. Her job at the sports agency was undoubtedly less time-consuming, leaving Sun with leisure to update her 70 pages of notes on bidding and play regularly. Sun is so dedicated to bridge that she decided not to have children.

Other international competitors "worked" for their regional bridge associations, or for business companies. The top women's pair, Gu Ling and Zhang Yulin, were employed by the Pearl River Development Corporation in Guangzhou, where their primary responsibility, according to Wei-Sender, was to play bridge wearing the company colors.

"In the United States, you have to do something to support your bridge," said Wei-Sender. "In China, more than half the players are professionals." In other words, they're paid to play bridge for a living under whatever euphemistic cover.

The 10% government-financed CBA contributed time-release salaries—vacation pay—when players trained for four to six months a year. Other forms of financing were readily available. Because of Deng's interest, the Party hierarchy and the public have come to equate bridge prowess with political and industrial success.

Chinese bridge also got more than a little help from its foreign friends. In a fine show of hands across the water, Canadian and American experts in particular have taught officials and players everything from how to organize their tournaments properly to how to chest their cards properly. In January of 1994, at the end of our stay, the U.S. brokerage house Bear Stearns (with offices in Shanghai and Beijing), sponsored the second annual "Bear Cup" in Beijing and kicked $25,000 into CBA coffers. Subsequently, Bear Stearns CEO James Cayne, himself a world-class player, paid for two Chinese teams to attend the 1994 Spring North American Bridge Nationals in Cincinnati.

Not content to follow in established bridge lanes, the Chinese were breaking new ground in several areas. One of these was youth bridge. In the United States the average age of an ACBL member is believed to be close to 60, and only a belated if heroic drive by the organization's education department has recruited some 2,000 youth and junior (under 26) players.

Canvassing clubs all over China, bridge officials in all 31 provinces got the word out when a promising youngster was located. Pan Kaijian, then coaching the national "open" team—invariably a bridge euphemism for an all-male squad—told me he recruited 12 cardsharks to play 600 hands over two weeks. After analyzing the subtleties of their play, he selected six for the national team.

The Chinese were equally adventurous in bidding, combining innovative systems of their own with parts of others. They were

116

especially proud of Wei-Sender's late husband, the Shanghai-born C.C. Wei, for inventing the "precision system" that has been adopted in a number of other countries. As the name implies, the precision system relies heavily on complex and precise statistics, duck soup to the Chinese.

It's intriguing to imagine what China will do for bridge. Some experts say that bridge is more an art than a science and the Chinese tend to bid woodenly by the numbers rather than probe for a partnership fit. Columnist and frequent world champion Bobby Wolff, retired president of the World Bridge Federation, vehemently disagreed when I spoke with him shortly after returning to America. "The only thing they lack is experience," he said. "It's even money whether they'll win a world championship by 2000." Eric Kokish, a Canadian expert and columnist who has coached the Chinese teams, hoped the players could learn enough English to keep pace with the game's state-of-the-art literature. "The CBA is thinking big-time," he said, "and that is one reason they may win a world championship within 10 years." Longtime British team member Raymond Brock was even more expansive: "This is a country that can build a road in six weeks. If they're determined, I think China will become for bridge what Russia has been for chess." They're already determined enough to have launched computer analysis and begun teaching bridge as an elective course at middle schools (12-18).

It's even more intriguing to imagine what bridge will do for China. "When I lecture in China, I tell people that bridge is an excellent way to learn capitalist management," said Wei-Sender. "Each hand is a contract. There's an auction, with bidding and negotiating. The Chinese catch on quickly. The game teaches them to speak good English and become more competitive. It winds up being very good for the Chinese and their friendship with other countries."

Wider applications are obvious. China and the United States are struggling to normalize relations. "Friendship first, competition second" is still the official slogan. Shortly before our visit, "bridge ambassador" Wei-Sender took an American women's team to Beijing for a tournament, followed by a match with the Chinese women that was seen on national television. No ping-pong diplomacy this time—we have bridge-building.

#   #   #

Given China's fanatical attachment to international bridge—they have pursued it with the same dedication they've competed in women's swimming and long-distance running—it was no accident that a visiting bridge maven should get caught up at the high levels of the Chinese bridge scene. When Chen Hui, the retired managing editor of the English-language China Daily, heard I was a bridge columnist, the world really opened up for me. Chen invited me to a team game at the home of Song Zhiguang, retired ambassador to Japan, England and East Germany.

We were driven down an alley in a modest-looking section of town and shown through a gate wedged between high walls. There we found Song's secluded home: a courtyard with hand-onion trees laden with the huge vegetables, which resemble apples, and a house with handsomely stained hardwood floors and shelves full of antiques and books. One such volume, I couldn't help notice with amusement, was "You Can Get There from Here" by Shirley MacLaine.

We were playing with the Chinese elite. They wore not tophats and tails, but shirts, sweaters and zipper jackets to fortify them against the October chill. In Beijing, no one's heat went on until November.

There were no high fives, bragging rights or even congratulations when my team of four won. Celebrating individual accomplishment was not the Chinese way. To the contrary, I'd never seen so many stern postmortems over successful hands. When Song made a spectacular grand slam in hearts, his partner Hsieh C.J., a senior engineer, said simply, "Overbid." He was right. If our host hadn't made a finesse and received a two-two break in trumps, Song would have sung blue indeed.

The day had much to recommend it: company, competition, candies. The ambassador and his wife were the most gracious of hosts. We played 32 hands in three and a half hours flat. We had coffee and tea and Japanese cake, a delicious little cranberry-flavored gelatin concoction.

118

On November 7, I played bridge again with Chen and some of his friends, although not Ambassador Song. This time all of us *lao* huddled in the unheated corridor of a sports arena (heat evidently wasn't on everywhere). Greater love hath no gamespeople.

I think the Chinese have their most enjoyable years after retirement. Most people retire at 60, and the average lifespan is 71. For my well-off buddies, I suspect 80 was not too tough a feat. They had 20 or so years to do anything they wanted.

So why play bridge in an unheated corridor? Just one man's opinion, but I think bridge for the elderly is more medication than competition. The Chinese elders play bridge for the same reason old men play bocce in New York's Little Italy: as a hedge against death.

With Chen's encouragement, I began publishing in the China Daily the weekly bridge column I write for the Hampshire and Vineyard Gazettes back home in Massachusetts. I taught a beginner's course to eight foreign women at the Lido Club. More invitations followed. At one point Rosa Brown and I were guests of guests at a tournament in the Great Hall of the People. All I can say about the Great Hall of the People is that it's so large there are great halls inside the Great Hall. Ours was a second-floor ballroom with mirror-covered columns, elaborate wall tiles, plush carpeting and 25-foot-tall curtains.

We passed through a receiving line, with still and TV cameras trained on us. They must have thought we were VIPs. Among the participants was Deng Xiaoping's wheelchair-bound son Deng Pufang, crippled when he jumped out of or was thrown from a fourth-floor window by Red Guards during the Cultural Revolution. Another showcaser was Minister of Health Chen Min Zhang. The event was staged to advertise the sponsor, Qin Xi Silver Star, which manufactured angora wool sweaters, judging from the souvenirs all the players received. I couldn't understand the announcements, but I guessed that the company name was mentioned three thousand times.

We played several hands with each pair, and then new players were rotated to our table. Eventually, Minister Chen and his partner showed up. Chen bid a contract. His partner laid down his dummy suit, then calmly—and illegally—instructed Chen on which cards to play. Rosa and I rolled our eyes. What do you say to a Chinese minister who bends the rules of bridge? "Nicely played, sir."

I thought the minister's indiscretion might be the exception rather than the rule. Then bridge observers told me they greeted the news of Wan Li's "hand of the year" and Epson event success with considerable skepticism. In 1989 students chanted about Deng Xiaoping, "He likes drinking Coca-Cola, but he is still short; he likes playing bridge, but when he is defeated, he doesn't accept it." Apparently, success in bridge is one of the perks of office.

Rosa and I finished third among the eight North-South combos in our division and each of us collected a pair of shoes. I asked for the biggest size possible and got leather-bound, plastic-soled footwear that were too small for my size-nine feet. It goes with the territory.

And our friend, the Minister of Health? "Oh!" he said when the results were announced. "We finished first!"

My number one participant thrill was still to come. A second man, Gilles de Villepoix, showed up at the Thursday Lido Club game and was paired with me. Whenever the impish Frenchman got a good hand, he exclaimed, "Wah-wah-wah-wah!" with the glee of the roadrunner escaping once more from Wile E. Coyote.

Gilles had worked in Beijing as a cultural attaché and French teacher at his embassy. His wife, Catherine Morel, was second in command for an oil company, and Gilles was retired at 48. Definitely my kind of guy.

Gilles and Catherine loved the game so much they held weekly dinner-cum-duplicate bridge parties at their elegant apartment. Brooks and I quickly became enraptured regulars. We met players from the U.S., Denmark, Holland, Pakistan, Germany, France, Taiwan and China. Their bridge gambits weren't bad. Their conversational gambits were even better.

Would I return to China to play bridge or watch the world championships? Wah-wah-wah-wah!

## 18

HERS: HORSING AROUND IN BEIJING

An ardent horseback rider, I started asking about riding the day I arrived in China. It happened that my *waiban* Zhang Haiyan loved horses, too. Not too much time passed before we made plans to go horseback riding in the Fragrant Hills, about an hour northwest of center city by bus, and less by cab.

Our game plan was to head first for a recently renovated section of the hills known as *Badachu* or the Eight Great Sites. Named for the eight temples that dot it, *Badachu* used to be off limits as a military zone. Now you could hike halfway up through it, hire the horses and continue your journey to the top, crossing from one peak to near the top of a second. From there, you rode back down comfortably in a chair lift. It was an altogether wonderful excursion for outdoors lovers and a little-known delight for diehard equestrians. I could hardly wait.

"Why don't you come over to my place around 11?" Haiyan suggested one Sunday morning, so I hopped in a cab, expecting to stop long enough to pick her up, then head straight for the hills. That's not the way things worked in China.

Knowing how Western accents escaped Beijing cabdrivers, I pointed on the map to a small housing complex tucked between a poultry farm and a winter cabbage patch. Miraculously, we arrived at the right spot. Inside the walls of the complex was a long, two-story building, and behind it, the two-year-old units where Haiyan had an apartment.

"*Ni hao* (hello)," I said to everyone I encountered. "*Zai na'er Zhang Haiyan* (Where is Zhang Haiyan)?" They waved me on in the right direction. Haiyan later explained that since she was the only one in the complex to have foreign visitors, her neighbors had gotten used to such inquiries.

For a one-person apartment, Haiyan's was big by Chinese standards. It consisted of a single room—my rough guess is 8 by 12 or 14—as well as closet-sized, cold-water lavatory and kitchen. At a university, six to eight people might be crammed into a space that size, and they wouldn't have a private bathroom.

If Chinese housing standards were lower than those in the U.S., Chinese hospitality was another matter. Until recently, the routine Chinese greeting was not "Hello," but "Have you eaten?" Haiyan offered beer, soda, coffee and tea, as well as peanuts, crackers and a delicious, salted cross between nuts and potato chips called broad beans. "No thanks," I said. I wanted horses. It turned out we were waiting for Haiyan's friend Mike, a recent Stanford graduate studying Chinese in Beijing. After he arrived, we hopped on a bus and rode for half an hour through truck farms full of luscious-looking green vegetables. The "night soil" responsible for their healthy color wreaks havoc on the digestive tracts of Westerners.

The road our bus took to the Fragrant Hills was lined with a variety of young, fast-growing poplars Haiyan said were probably planted in the last 10 or 15 years. Before that, it was obvious every tree in sight had been cut to make way for farming. The uniformity of these roadside arbor rows was a giveaway to how central planning changed.

Once we arrived at the Eight Great Sites, we paid our admission price and wandered through what looked more like an amusement park than the U.S.-style park I was expecting. Afloat on one pond we passed were vividly colored plastic shapes and a fat, jolly monk, also plastic.

Then we started climbing. I hadn't spent much time thinking about how we'd get to our horses. Haiyan said we'd hike, but hiking means different things to different people. In China it means what I call mountain climbing. The Chinese have been hiking for so many thousands of years they've installed steps on their mountains, though, so mountain climbing there had a slightly different flavor. I trudged. Haiyan and Mike scampered.

Stopping at the temples—all eight of them—at least gave me a chance to catch my breath without losing face. I was particularly taken by the Goddess of Mercy in the Temple of a Thousand Sorrows. Since the proper way to pay respect to Buddha—and the Goddess of

Mercy can be one manifestation of Buddha—was by burning incense, I bought some and lit my offering. It made an impressive blaze.

As I watched, the attendant gestured that I should put my hands together in prayer and bow three times to the statue. It seemed an appropriate sign of respect even for this non-Buddhist Western visitor. Rested, I was ready to continue our climb to the horses.

The view of the city was spectacular. The Chinese have built small viewing platforms along the way to give the best vantage points. Because of the pollution in Beijing, a haze hung over the city most days, but it was still an impressive sight to scan from an eagle's perspective the buildings that housed 12 million souls. For a city of that size, the number of skyscrapers was few. Unlike Hong Kong, which unfolds vertically like the mountains that ring it to the northwest, Beijing expands horizontally. It is flat and less than 200 feet above sea level.

I let my impatience to leap on the back of a horse slip away. A leisurely snack, a little hiking, a horseback excursion: maybe they didn't seem to go together in my one-track Western mind, but they did in China. For the time being I had to admit—at least to myself—I was happy to see a drink concession on the stone-paved terrace where we stopped to catch our breaths. Bottled water never tasted so good. You can be sure that when you stop for a rest halfway up a mountain close to Beijing, a vendor will be nearby with water, soda and haw juice (made from the fruit of a Viburnum shrub native to China), and depending on the time of year, persimmons, pears, peanuts or jujubes.

I heard plenty of American tourists complain about the perpetual pitches at sightseeing spots—vendors shouting "Hello, hello" to catch your attention—but to me it was just another victory for free enterprise. That was the way a lot of average Chinese people put extra money in their pockets. Why shouldn't they?

While we relaxed with our mineral water, Haiyan walked off to hire the horses. Tethered near a temple, they were more nag than pedigreed, but colorfully outfitted with bells and ribbons. Farmers from the outlying districts brought in their work animals and earned extra money by hiring them out to tourists. Haiyan haggled with the owners to fix a price, while I looked them over. Three geldings: a big chestnut, a small gray and a bay with black mane and tail. None could be described as overfed.

To an American used to riding English saddle, either hunter/jumper or dressage style, the tack was a sight to behold. Well-worn, much-patched leather saddles held in place with a crupper—a strap running under the horses' tails—as well as a girth; cowboy-style stirrups that appeared to be nonadjustable; breast straps with bells. In place of a pommel there was a metal bar to hang onto. Rope served as the bridle.

"Pick one," Haiyan said. I chose the bay. His owner, a weathered woman in farm clothes, led the line up the trail with the reins to my mount in her hand. I sat back in the saddle, flicked flies off my mount and surveyed the view. We were on a narrow path very high up. The horses had to walk over slate outcrops, so the footing was less than ideal.

"You can take the reins if you want," Haiyan shouted to me. The most experienced rider of the bunch, I hadn't noticed that my companions were steering under their own power. Soon after, I named my horse Luo, Chinese for mule. Like a lot of trail horses, he had a resistant nature. It was clear there was one woman in Luo's life, and it wasn't me. Several embarrassing disagreements on which way to go or whether to go at all necessitated temporary takeovers by Luo's owner. We finally got going at a steady pace once Haiyan charged ahead on her white steed.

Luo seemed to listen to me better when he wasn't heading up the line. He also responded well to a few kicks and a slap of the reins. As a matter of pride I urged him into a trot and the semblance of a canter, but most of the trail was too steep and narrow for anything except a sedate walk. Just right for watching the scenery go by. We moved along the spine of the hills through uninhabited landscapes, with the city on the horizon. Not many scenic spots that close to Beijing were so completely outside the range of crowds.

More than an hour after mounting up, we arrived at a stone wall and climbed off. Luo and I looked at each other in relief. I fed him a few sprigs of grass, and we bade our goodbyes. Not before the owners, arguing we'd overworked their valuable creatures, tried unsuccessfully to hit us up for a few more *RMB* .

A hike up a stone path took us to another peak, where we caught the chair lift to the base of the mountain. The 25-minute ride down gave us an aerial view of the city and, close up, one of Mao's former residences, supposedly still home to Mao's son and grandson. We also got a look at the Fragrant Hills Hotel, a massive white complex where until the Tiananmen Square incident, the sons and daughters of Beijing's political elite could be seen dallying for lunch and dinner, their black Mercedes speeding down the country road that led to the hotel.

As we walked out, I noticed a number of handsome, well-groomed horses prancing in a parking lot and asked Haiyan about them.

"Oh, they're for the tourists. They're real robbers," she said, pointing at their owners.

"They look a lot better fed than ours," I observed, enviously watching one of the horses perform some advanced dressage moves.

"It's fat, not muscle," Haiyan answered. She obviously preferred the more rustic approach to riding. She was right, of course. Our hour-plus ride cost us less than five dollars. Compare that to the U.S., where a half hour's trail ride costs a minimum of $25. I was ready to call it a day, but Haiyan had other plans.

# # #

We needed to round out the day's events with a nice meal. Haiyan had a Moslem restaurant in mind. I had told Jim I'd be home by six o'clock and tried to bow out gracefully.

"No problem," Haiyan insisted. "You can call him from my place. He can meet us there on his bicycle."

"But I didn't bring my bike," I said. "I came in a cab, remember?"

"I'll ride you on the back of mine," she answered. I couldn't quite imagine this slender if athletic woman lugging me—or me balancing on the back wheel of even the best Flying Pigeon—but I relented.

125

First it was time for a pit stop, though, and I couldn't escape that, either. The bathrooms in China were notoriously, seriously non-hygienic. Theory has it the Chinese think that's appropriate. Why keep a place for waste clean? That observation doesn't quite get it right. The most important difference was not the sanitation level—plenty of public rest rooms in the U.S. are less than sanitary. It was the design of Chinese toilets. They were not vented like American ones, so the odor of raw sewage wafted freely through the air. Like their American counterparts they were white porcelain, but they were built close to the floor. You didn't sit; you squatted. A chiropractor once told me that if Americans had to squat in bathrooms like the Chinese, they'd have a lot fewer back problems.

Nevertheless, the Chinese system took getting used to. Toilet paper was not supplied. You had to bring your own. Flushing systems varied. In some cases, toilets had their own individual flushers, but other times, water seemed to run through all the toilets in a public bathroom at the same, magically predetermined time. These were details the guidebooks didn't lay out for you. Since our Friendship Hotel apartment had a Western-style bathroom, we spent as little time as possible in the Chinese models. The rest rooms at the park were trench style, with shoulder-high stalls so you could chat with your neighbors if you were so inclined.

After our pit stop, we walked to the parking lot to wait for a bus back to Haiyan's apartment. I was so busy watching one of the tourist horses galloping spiritedly in a field that I didn't see our bus pull up.

"Come on!" Haiyan shouted. The crowd surrounding us broke into a run and made a beeline for the bus, every man, woman and child for himself—and look out if you're a passenger trying to get off. Once we climbed in, I could understand why. Even though the bus was a Chinese-style giant "caterpillar"—two sections coupled by a black rubber accordion—there weren't enough seats. Buses in a city the size of Beijing never had enough seats, but the price was right. A few *fen*, the equivalent of pennies. Mike and I had seats, while Haiyan stood next to a little girl who looked as if she would soon climb in her mother's lap. She did, and Haiyan expertly cadged the empty seat.

When we reached Haiyan's apartment complex, we stopped at the main gate to phone Jim. Despite China's astonishing economic growth, most ordinary citizens still didn't have their own phones when we were there. Each apartment complex in a big city would have a communal phone instead. Discrepancies as awkward as adolescent growth spurts cropped up. Chinese businessmen sat at lunch chatting on their cellular phones like their U.S. counterparts. We could only reach Haiyan by beeper, since she didn't have her own phone. She was expert at finding one and returning calls. People even carried fake cellular phones and beepers to look important. As foreigners, Jim and I had our own phone at the Friendship Hotel, but it was easier to call the U.S. than it was to phone towns outside of Beijing. Even within Beijing, you could never be sure when you might get a dead line or a perpetual busy signal, meaning the line was out of order.

After I talked to Jim, Mike and Haiyan unlocked their bikes, and we got ready to cycle to the Moslem restaurant where we planned to meet him and have dinner. Mike had a lightweight, conventional American 10-speed, but Haiyan insisted on carrying me on her one-speed. It was illegal to ride double in Beijing, but everyone did it anyway. Most bikes had a rack on the rear wheel that doubled as a back seat.

Because bicycling has always been such a serious business in China, it was far more highly organized than in the U.S. Ad-hoc bicycle repair shops abounded. So did neighborhood bicycle parking lots, complete with attendants who charged a *mao* (1/10 of a fen) fee. If you parked in the wrong place, you were apt to be fined. The Chinese have even developed an ingenious ring lock that sits around the back wheel and snaps into place whenever you want to lock your bike.

Rarely did bicycles have lights for night riding. Fortunately, everyone drove or cycled slowly enough that collisions didn't happen as often as you would think. Even when they did, the Chinese had learned how to leap off without getting hurt. We did hear of one poor foreign expert who rode into an uncovered manhole, causing considerable damage to herself and her bike.

I had no memory of riding double on a bike even as a child, so Haiyan and Mike had to coach me. The driver starts cycling, and with a running leap you hop aboard sidesaddle. I had a much harder time balancing than Haiyan did carrying my weight. Eventually, though, when we reached a slight rise on a bridge and our momentum was approaching zero, I decided I was too much of a burden and jumped off. She turned her bike over to me and hopped on with Mike. Enough macho feats for the time being.

After rendezvousing with Jim, we headed down an alley to find our Moslem restaurant. Alleys were very different in China than in the U.S., where they usually seem to connote backdoors, decay and danger. Although increasingly obscured by new construction and the kind of grand-boulevard, monumental style of Soviet urban planning from the Fifties, they epitomized traditional city life in China. True, they could be dark and narrow, but they were usually bustling with activity—shops, people, bicycles, even cars coming and going. Certainly this one was that busy.

It led us to an open market where the restaurant was located. Dozens of long wooden tables with benches or chairs, set right on the street, were already packed with patrons. In an open shed on the sidewalk behind the tables stood equally long rows of grills for cooking the meat. We found a table and ordered. The specialty was lamb, and we picked a variety of spicy dishes served with noodles, along with a chewy form of pita bread. Tea came in bowls. Asking for beer glasses, we got more bowls. Whenever we thirsted for something cold, we found that Chinese beer, which has a a low alcohol content, was a particularly good choice of beverage.

Waiters shouted orders back and forth to the cooks, creating a constant din of voices combined with smoke from the grills and the luscious odor of food cooking. Pedestrians, bicycles and cars milled in the street. When meat supplies ran low, helpers carried in dressed carcasses, ready to be cut up and put on the fire. It was a reminder of why some people choose to be vegetarian.

By the time we finished eating, it was dark. Mike, Haiyan and Jim collected their bikes, and we walked back up the alley to Baishiqiao Lu, where I could catch a cab. Fortunately for Jim, there was no rack on the back of his bike, so he didn't have to offer to ride me home. Instead he gallantly decided to accompany me in the taxi. I hailed a *miandi*, we crammed in Jim's bike and collapsed inside. If this Sunday was typical, I could see why the Chinese had a reputation for hard work. Even their days off were hard work.

19

HERS: MOVIE MAGIC

Although Beijing had plenty of movie theatres, we didn't go very often while we were there. One of our favorite entertainments is movies, but running out to the movies lacked appeal when you didn't understand the language. Each of the three times we saw a movie was a big event.

When we heard there would be a screening—with English subtitles—of Fifth Generation Director Chen Kaige's epic film, "Farewell, My Concubine," we knew we had to find a way to see it. Fifth Generation is the name given to the first class of students to be graduated from the Beijing Film Academy after the Cultural Revolution. The most successful and best known Fifth Generation director outside of China is probably Chen Kaige, who established the group's reputation with his 1984 film, "Yellow Earth." Winner of the Golden Palm award at the Cannes Film Festival, his "Farewell, My Concubine" initially was banned in China—supposedly for its portrayal of the Communist Party. After some re-editing, the Chinese Ministry of Radio, Film and Television had okayed its release.

The movie industry has a long and illustrious history in China. Beginning in Shanghai during the early part of the century, it became a powerful instrument of propaganda for the Chinese government after 1949. Regional film production centers were built, and filmgoing became one of the few, government-sanctioned forms of entertainment for the Chinese people. By the 1990s, though, the Chinese film industry was in serious decline. Once the general public was no longer required to see movies as part of their political education, the appeal of boy-on-tractor meets girl-at-collective disappeared. The government was no longer willing or able to subsidize expensive film production centers once the move towards socialist capitalism gained momentum, and the industry has been on the ropes ever since. The growth of television and a booming videotape industry didn't help. All this contributed to the fact that the Beijing screening of "Farewell, My Concubine" was a big event in the Chinese film world.

Our *waiban* Zhang Haiyan arranged to have a friend buy tickets for us ahead of time. They cost a mere 15 RMB, less than $2 apiece. Haiyan warned there might be long lines or the possibility of the movie being sold out, although I suspect she was thinking of the old days. The movie market has become heavily oriented towards kung-fu, and I couldn't even find videotape copies of Chen's older films in the local Beijing video store.

The night of the screening, we met a group of Fulbright friends downtown at the Minzu Hotel. It was my first experience of Beijing nightlife. The streets were crowded and the atmosphere was more like New York City than the gladed confines of the Friendship Hotel. We divided up, with one group going to eat in a Chinese dumpling soup take-out restaurant and another heading next door to a Vie de France franchise specializing in croissants and meat pastries. I stood outside munching a Vie-de-France specialty and watching the crowds pass by.

The movie theatre looked no different than one you might find in any American city, with a ticket window on the street. Inside, the auditorium was huge and sloped down toward the screen. Entering at its center, we saw that the seats in the back of the auditorium were standard, individual cushioned ones. The front had sofas big enough to sit two roomily or three squeezed. Like most Chinese furniture—even taxi seats—the sofas were slipcovered. Usually tan in color, these slipcovers usually looked as if they'd never been washed. Black lacquer or formica pedestal tables were bolted in front of each sofa. If there hadn't been so many of them lined up, the sofas would have looked like the seating for a dinner theater or nightclub.

By the time we arrived, every sofa seemed to be occupied. On closer inspection, we could see that one person had staked out territory on each. With a little ingenuity, we fit ourselves—two by two or one by one—into the empty spots. The idea was to get as close to the screen as possible in order to read the subtitles. Much rattling of candy wrappers and bustling back and forth preceded the

131

start of the film. Once the lights dimmed and the feature got underway, it didn't stop either.

The opening trailers weren't for coming attractions as they would be in an American movie theatre. Just like tv commercials, they advertised products: one for American-style t-shirts and another with cowboys and horses for—you guessed it—Marlboro cigarettes. When the main feature began, the titles were in Chinese, and for a few uncomfortable moments we all thought we would be spending the next three hours awash in a blur of incomprehension. It was a false alarm.

Following the lives of its two Peking opera stars, "Farewell, My Concubine" has a majestic sweep. Issues of gender, sexuality, ideology, public vs. private, art vs. life intertwine as the lives of these two men unfold from the 1930s through the Japanese occupation, establishment of the Communist regime, Mao's Great Leap Forward and the Cultural Revolution. Gong Li, probably one of the best-known actresses in the world, plays a prostitute who marries one of the performers, creating a triangle. China's banning of the film may have had as much to do with the nature of the sex scenes, many of which were homosexual, as it did with sensitive political issues. Movie nudity and lovemaking were generally taboo in China, except on the black market. Particularly startling was the film's frank portrayal of the Cultural Revolution. When they weren't rattling their candy wrappers and talking, the audience seemed to eat it up.

Almost three hours later, we emerged from the theater with sore backs and behinds despite our sofa seats. We stumbled out onto the street and went looking for taxis. Haiyan tried to read a map and give directions to one of our Fulbright friends so he could make it home. Before long we were surrounded by pedicab drivers, the modern equivalent of rickshaw boys. The Chinese pedicab looks like a tricycle with a small car seat attached to the back to carry passengers. For some reason, the pedicab drivers decided Haiyan was keeping this bunch of dopey foreigners from engaging their services. Although we couldn't understand the words that were flying back and forth, it was clear they weren't friendly, and we almost had a fight on our hands. The name-calling of the pedicab drivers hit a sore spot at a vulnerable moment for Haiyan. Later on, she explained her father had been called some of the names used in the movie to denounce party traitors during the Cultural Revolution. That's why the pedal taxi drivers made her so angry.

Our second movie "event" was the Beijing premiere of a documentary, "Reverie on Old Shanghai." Made by Chen Yifei, a Chinese painter living in Boston, it follows a young Chinese woman as she wanders through the city. It is full of impressionistic images of 1930s Shanghai and its street life. The most interesting part of the evening was not the movie but the event itself. Zhang Dan, a young friend who worked for the China Film Export and Import Corporation, wangled invitations for us to the opening. Although there wasn't a swarm of newspaper photographers and tv stations with their camcorders outside, you had the feeling that you were where things were happening with the city's cultural set. It was a youngish crowd, with many Western faces mixed in.

Before the screening started, director Chen explained he had always wanted to make movies, but that such a career choice wasn't possible when he was growing up in Shanghai. I couldn't help wondering who had financed his dream. A press conference followed the screening. Zhang Dan introduced me to Chen, and before I knew it, a microphone had been thrust in my face. I stumbled through a few allusions to Bergman and Fellini-esque images. I didn't want to say what I really thought, that the film was derivative and overblown, with a jarring Western soundtrack.

Our third movie in Beijing was an outing arranged by the Friendship Hotel to see a popular *gongfu*, or kung-fu, satire, "The Romance of Scholar Tang." We purchased our tickets from the Foreign Experts Office, and on the night of the screening trooped to an auditorium near our apartment, where practically everyone in the audience was a familiar face, since most of the other Western residents of our little community in the Friendship Hotel had gathered. The murky plot of the movie hinges on the misadventures of a handsome young scholar capable of remarkable feats of kung-fu. In good Buster Keaton tradition, he nonchalantly flies through the air, gets into plenty of hot water, and eventually lives happily ever after. There were pratfalls along the way involving Western-style vomit, nudity, and ugly maidens.

Not many Westerners can say they launched their movie career in Beijing. I did when I was asked by one of the staff at China Central Television to dub the part of journalist Edgar Snow's wife in a made-for-tv movie. With the centennial for Mao's birthday coming up, there was a flurry of media preparations going on, including this movie about the author of "Red Star Over China" and Mao Zedong.

On the first day of dubbing, I abandoned my journalism students to my colleague John Morgan at the Australian Embassy, which we were visiting on a field trip, and rushed over to the Ministry of Radio, Film and Television. The producer had decided to dub all the Chinese voices first, so I ended up sitting in the lobby for three hours, when I could have been learning about Sino-Australian relations.

The movie tells the story of how Edgar Snow made his way to Mao's mountain hideout with the help of Mme. Song Qing-ling, one of three famous, aristocratic Chinese sisters and the wife of Sun Yat-sen. Snow's wife, Nym Wales, was also a journalist, and the movie has her traveling to Shanxi to visit Mao. For a while, the producers considered having me dub Mme. Song's voice, too. I wondered if it was possible to produce English with a Chinese accent and not make a fool of myself.

Reading the script, which was full of translating errors and awkwardnesses, I sometimes found it hard to keep a straight face. At one point Snow calls his wife "my rib," and at another, Nym complains, "Why must I wait behind you?" I tried to do some much-needed editing of the script, but since the words were already being mouthed in the images, not much could be changed. The actor playing Snow was a Frenchman staying in Beijing while his wife taught French at *Beida*, or Beijing University. He looked fine for the part, but his accent was so strong that his English was often indecipherable. He insisted on doing his own dubbing anyway.

That was not the only way production standards were lacking. While waiting for Nym's scenes to come up, I watched a videotape of

134

the movie footage. Towards the end of the story, Snow was shown driving down Changan Jie and passing the McDonald's that didn't exist in the movie's time frame of the 1970s.

"You're not going to keep that in, are you?" I asked.

"No one will notice," one of the production assistants said.

The recording studio used for dubbing didn't look as if it had ever been cleaned, but it was the warmest room in the building. We all huddled inside it whenever possible. The entrance hall—where we watched rough footage from the movie, ate our takeout lunches and waited around until our parts came up—stayed at frigid, outdoor temperatures. I rarely took my down coat off during three days of dubbing at the Ministry.

Once Nym's part started, I quickly discovered there was a real knack to dubbing. You had to watch the mouths of the characters and synchronize your words to theirs. The entire first day and part of the next, I found my eyes glued to the script and unable to watch the faces. After a while I got the hang of it. When I flubbed a line, announcing to Mao, "My husband wrote your autobiography," no one paid a bit of attention. The movie, with great flair titled "Mao Zedong and Edgar Snow," was still in postproduction when we left China, so I never got to see it, hear how it came out or how I sounded as Nym Wales.

V

ALWAYS TRAVEL FIRST CLASS

"According to ancient Chinese philosophy, water represents the pure and noble. It follows its own path. It seeks its own level. Like a wise man, it does only what is natural." Zhang Honghua, Suzhou.

## 20

HIS: SMALL PLEASURES, LARGE TREASURES

Extended travel is an iffy prospect, especially for the middle-aged and partially bald. Your back aches so much from walking around museums that you begin to bend like Winston Churchill in his later years. Your plumbing balks. You get wake-up calls you didn't ask for and can't fall asleep again. In the end, travel's joys aren't large treasures but small pleasures: an unforgettable scrap of conversation, an unexpected visual treat, an insight or two. The best of travel is sort of like tuning in on "Roseanne" by mistake and discovering you like it.

Brooks's Monday and Wednesday teaching schedule left us time for lengthy excursions. On our first overnight trip from Beijing, we chose destinations it would be hard not to like: Xian and its world-famous terra-cotta warriors, Guilin and its epic journey down the Li River. We were accompanied by Julia Jones, a British actress and television writer; Eldon Elder, the Fulbright lecturer in scenic arts at Beijing's Academy of Dramatic Arts; and Bob Slagter, our other local Fulbright friend teaching political science at the College of Foreign Affairs. Julia and Eldon lent stage presence to this tour de force, while great, bearded Bob contributed his love for anecdotes and food. A day-by-day report:

Thursday—CAAC (pronounced "cack"), the national airline, is often referred to as China Air Always Cancels. The start reminded me less of an efficient airline than a French movie I saw years back. A man approaches a woman standing by a fence and says, "*Vous attendez quelqu'un qui n'existe pas.*" You are waiting for someone who does not exist. When I handed a flight attendant my ticket, she told me, "There is no such thing as seat 11J."

After this surrealistic beginning—I was eventually told to grab any old empty seat—the flight really took off. There were eclectic short subjects featuring everything from mountains to a fashion show, but no headphones to hear the sound with. The box lunch was certainly unique: a roll filled with mystery meat, a roll with a mystery sweet, two bite-sized pieces of chicken, cookies, cake, an orange, a package of dried plums and another package with something resembling pine tar that Brooks said was beef jerky.

Upon arriving in Xian, we thought we might die there too, because our assigned guide Ellen seemed as dour as the Brothers Grimm. Fortunately, she warmed up with the weather.

"Look at those festoons of corn," Bob said while we were being driven to town from the airport. Corn hung from houses in bunches, like bananas.

Otherwise everything was green or brown. Xian air is moister than Beijing's, allowing for the first real profusion of green fields we had witnessed. "I'm not used to seeing green," Brooks said. "It's not easy seeing green," I sympathized.

Xian city is so dirty that brown covers everything, the people included. We climbed the 70 steps to the top of the city wall. Some like the city wall for its human scale and history. I liked it because I bought tiger balm on top of it. A tart-smelling substance made of eucalyptus oil, camphor, menthol, wax and a few other substances, it came in little round tins about one inch in diameter. I rubbed some of it on my temples for a mild headache. I don't recall what happened to the headache, but I got one hell of a buzz.

That's all I can tell you about the Xian wall.

We climbed the Big Wild Goose Pagoda for its name alone. I remembered all seven stories. So did my thighs.

We ate dinner at De Fa Chang, reputedly the best dumpling restaurant in China. Bob ate about 64 of them. There ain't no Chinese food like dumplings. Find that in your guidebook.

On the way back to the hotel Julia exclaimed, "Look at that festoon of lights."

"Hey, that's the second time I've heard the word festoon," I said. Truly a day to remember.

Friday—We got the wake-up call we didn't ask for in the middle of the night. For those of us with dry throats, Julia provided a voice lesson. "Put your little finger between your teeth and your tongue on the soft tissue of your upper palate," she said. "Lean forward and hum. You should feel your nose tingle."

Someone mentioned President Clinton's voice problems. "He hasn't been listening to his coaches," Jones said. "I'm starting to think only an actor can be elected president."

"We've had one actor as president already," I said.

"If Reagan had been a good actor, he never would have been president," said Elder. "His ego would have been satisfied. But since his greatest role was straight man to a chimpanzee..."

The terra-cotta warriors were everything we heard they would be, and more. The 7,000 inhabitants of Emperor Qin Shi Huang's funeral vault, they were discovered by workers digging irrigation ditches. They were in pieces. The people who patched them together were as meticulous as monks poring over manuscripts.

I had new information for them. The first warrior was called Terry Cotter, and the others were named after him. Cotter was later reincarnated as a second baseman for the Washington Senators.

On the way to our next stop we passed by hundreds of fox pelts in a marketplace. "I'm for animal rights, but wearing fur doesn't bother me at all," said a member of our party who requested anonymity for reasons of security. "We wear leather shoes, and there's nothing warmer than fur. Besides, plants have feelings, too."

"They've been talking a lot lately," Bob added.

"According to exhaustive interviewing, there's been an incremental liberalization of their attitudes," I said.

"They don't mind being eaten as much," said Bob.

I liked the Ban Po Museum every bit as much as the terra-cotta warriors. The place was erected at the site of the "cradle of Chinese civilization," a village built some 6,700 years ago. I don't mean a re-creation of the village; I mean the very place. The site comes marked with successive layers of culture: early huts facing south, later ones with windows covered by animal skins, and so on.

I made a fantastic discovery. Next to fire and the wheel, the most important early invention may have been rope. How else were they going to connect wood and stone to make axes? How else were they going to make hoes? "How else were they going to make baseballs?" said Bob.

We saw ethnic music and dancing at night. Some people commented on the lovely white-linen dance. Others noticed that the Chinese audience hardly cheered and there was no curtain call. What I remember was that the guy in front of me must have swallowed a whole bottle of Listerine.

Saturday—The wake-up call we didn't ask for came at 6:30 a.m.

With seven different exhibition areas, the Provincial Museum traced early Chinese history from the Pottery Age to the Bronze Age to the Fresco Age. Or something like that. Guide Ellen, better each day, had some interesting things to say about pots on tripods. "They show a high rank in society. We have an expression: a frog can stand on four feet and a human on two, but it's hard to stand on three."

"I always connected three feet with the riddle about old age—you know, the cane," said Brooks.

What does a man do on two feet, a woman do sitting down, and a dog do on three feet?

Shake hands.

The museum could certainly have used some editing. Some of the enchanting translations I wrote down were "slave trady" and maidens holding "funs."

Back in the city, we wandered through a surprisingly uncrowded bazaar on the way to the Grand Mosque. The city's largest and oldest—1,351 years in age by our visit—it had a series of gardens and courtyards, an Asian twist to a Middle East landmark. We three men took off our shoes—women weren't allow to enter—and were guided through the carpeted interior. We had an eerie sense of 2,000 people praying five times a day; we were in the presence of a great religion.

At night we flew into Guilin, a southern city of 380,000 that variously reminded me of Rio (Elephant Trunk Hill in the downtown harbor), Cortina d'Ampezzo (mountains everywhere), San Antonio (a river runs through it) and Tallahassee (an 800-year-old banyan tree). Our new guide, Ju-li-ya, quoted from the tourist literature: "Stately rocks, green mountains, clean waters, fantastic caves." It was a crime we had to fly out the next night.

Sunday—This was heaven. Railroad whistles sang through our dreams. The wake-up call we asked for this getaway morning actually came on time. Eldon stretched to the sight of a full moon setting while the sun rose. After several days of hearing German spoken by other tourists, we heard the sweet tinkle of French in the dining room. As the American in the credit-card commercial said, *Je mange France!* Not to mention my first cereal in 10 weeks.

The bus caravan to the Li River passed through rice paddies, duck and fish ponds, pigs in the marketplace and water buffalo in the fields. I asked Army vet Bob if the scene reminded him of Vietnam. He nodded. "Lots of water buffalo, lots of water."

We boarded the river boat and headed downstream. Men paddled beside the boat on rafts made of bamboo logs and a cargo we couldn't at first identify. Were they fishing? Doing laundry? They were selling t-shirts.

The Li river winds through some of China's greatest landscapes. Their names alone speak of infinite wonders: Pushing Millstones Rock, Crown Cave, Nine Horses Mountain. I scarcely saw one. Several American women on the boat learned I was a bridge columnist and asked for a lesson. Suddenly, I was falling in love with a new avocation: teaching. You can have your large treasures. I'll take my small pleasures.

21

HERS: WAITING FOR GODOT IN WUHAN

After living in the Beijing area almost two months, we were ready for longer excursions to other parts of China. The trick was to find someone who could make it happen. We asked our *waiban* Haiyan to arrange some trips for us and come along as translator and guide, but she was too busy. We tried talking to travel agents at the *Youyi* and several other big hotels. Wherever we went we got the same answer, "*maio,*" or "impossible." Everything was already booked or cost too much money. Just when despair had settled in, we happened upon a travel agent sitting in the front lobby of the Friendship Hotel.

"Can I help you?" she asked in perfect English, with a bright smile.

"No, I don't think so," I said, looking at the sign next to her that advertised city tours and trips to the Great Wall.

"I can arrange other trips," she said. In 10 minutes she had organized two separate itineraries for us. Her name was Nellie Wang, and we became good friends.

The trip Jim and I wanted most to take before we left China was the voyage by boat through the Three Gorges. The Gorges are the most beautiful section of the 3,000-mile Yangzi River, fifth longest in the world. Since construction of a hydroelectric dam was to lift the water level 150 feet, covering 1,000 historic sites, we wanted to see the Three Gorges before they disappeared. Nellie arranged for us to travel on a Chinese boat rather than one of the expensive luxury liners for foreigners, which filled up many months in advance.

Our Three Gorges trip originated in Chongqing, China's World War II capital. Situated in southwest China, Chongqing overlooks the confluence of the Yangzi and Jialing Rivers. Its streets had the usual Chinese crush of cars and pedestrians. Missing were the bicycles, and one look at the San Francisco-style hills told us why.

"You're lucky. It's working today," said the guide who delivered us to the boat. "Otherwise you would have many, many steps down to the dock." We saw what she meant when we clambered aboard the cogwheel tramway for a precipitous descent to the boat. From a distance our home for the next three days looked sleek enough. Then we went inside.

First class didn't exist—except when heads of state were visiting. Then the staff—none of whom spoke English—cleaned the mysterious, off-limits upstairs quarters, giving new meaning to the term "spit and polish." Our second-class, inside stateroom on the main deck was a claustrophobic's nightmare: narrow bunk beds with dingy sheets—no wonder Nellie had warned us to bring our own. Each bunk was supplied with a lumpy quilt and a rough wool blanket propped fan-like against the wall. Gumdrop-green acetate curtains hung from a ceiling track around each bunk. A battered desk was wedged between the bunks. It was a long way from the Love Boat.

The toilets down the hall really caught our attention, especially Jim's. Three in a row—one of which remained locked for the entire trip—served 24 two-person staterooms. These facilities consisted of a raised tile trench, partitioned, with water periodically gushing through. To straddle the trench, you stepped first onto a wooden pallet, necessitated by sloshing water, then vaulted into position. Whatever you deposited upstream made its way downstream. Toilet paper was supply-your-own. The smell was so strong it clung to your clothes. Portside on the same hallway were three dimly lit, dirty showers. At least our toilets and showers had real doors. That was not the case for third and fourth class, where we could see double-decker bunk beds accommodating 12 and 16 to a stateroom. Their toilets were strictly open-air stalls.

As the trip progressed, we came to appreciate what we had. More passengers, with no sleeping quarters, piled on board at each stop, until the hallways were crammed. People lay on mats, squatted in corners and repaired bicycles in the hallways. Every day more debris piled up—peanut shells, orange peels, glassine wrappers, cigarette butts. After each wave of short-term travelers disembarked, the staff cleaned up. We stuck to our quarters in the front of the boat, shared with two dozen Germans touring China in 21 days. The river stretched out in front of us, and we waited for *Sanxia*, Chinese for the Three Gorges.

One of the best parts of the trip was the way it destroyed the illusion that only destinations count. Time slowed down as we floated peacefully along the river's waters. Jim devoured two books and, after scouring the boat, came up with enough bridge players to put together a game. At night we heard the rattle and hum of the boat, our tea mugs jiggling in their holders over the sink and the clothes brushes banging rhythmically against the wall. During the day I people-watched and took photos or video of the passing scenery. Jim complained bitterly about our accommodations; I played the stoic.

Early the second day, we reached the most scenic part of the trip. I missed five-mile long Qutang Gorge after staying up all night with a violent stomach upset. Digging my chopsticks into an unidentifiable entrée the night before, I emerged with the jaws of a fish. I dropped them fast, but I'm convinced the fish was what destroyed my stomach. That morning I dragged myself out of bed for the other two gorges, Wuxia and Badong. The power of the scenery must have inspired my recovery. The river took our boat through breathtaking outcrops of rock and tree-covered hills that looked virtually uninhabited. For a few hours, the gorges, mist-covered and haunting, were there. Then they were gone, and we moved into the locks that lowered us with three other boats through Gezhouba Dam. In less than a half hour the giant boats dropped 75 feet.

Midafternoon of the third day we disembarked at Wuhan, where the Yangzi, Han and Xunshi Rivers converge. Never had a shower felt so good as at the Qingchuan Hotel. Pleasantly full from the best meal we'd had in days, we sat in our eleventh-floor, luxurious-by-Chinese-standards room overlooking the harbor and watched the twinkling lights below. Destination Beijing the next day. At least, so we thought.

The next morning after several pleasant hours of sightseeing, our guide deposited us at the airport. The "dly" (delay) announcement in chalk on the flight board jangled our nerves. We waited. And waited. Plane after plane disgorged passengers into the waiting room until people were sitting on their luggage, standing in corners and leaning against the walls. The slap of playing cards on suitcases turned into tables for the Chinese game of "Push the Pig" rose irritatingly over the din. Finally a loudspeaker announcement generated commotion. A Chinese businessman who spoke English took pity on our ignorance and explained that all flights had been cancelled due to bad weather in Beijing. We were stranded in Wuhan for the night.

The airline, however, was going to put us up. "Follow me," our Chinese acquaintance said, leading us to a military-style facility nearby. We surveyed the three bunks covered with horsehair mats, checked out the dormitory-style bathroom stalls and weighed our options. The Qingchuan Hotel was too far to go back to. A hotel within walking distance beckoned. It actually had its own, Western-style—if nonfunctional—bathroom. We unpacked our sheets and crawled into bed under a cloud of cold-resistant mosquitoes. I enclosed my head like a turtle in the neck of a t-shirt for protection. The "Regulations on Hotel Accommodations for Passengers" provided our bedtime reading.

They warned us, and I quote,

Guns or weapons carried about in need of work must be registered accurately which can be left with the owner or put under the charge of the local public security organ.

Fatally poisonous, inflammable, explosible or radioactive articles are strictly forbidden to be taken into the hotel.

Excessive drinking and loud confused noise are not allowed so as not to interfere others.

Passengers are forbidden to harbor and dispose stolen goods or harbor criminals and are require to accuse and expose criminals and suspects promptly.

Passengers who violated the regulations should be punished by public security organs according to the regulations concerned, if constituted a crime he/she should be found out criminal responsibility according to the law by submitting to judicial office.

147

The next day we headed back to the airport, enlightened by Chinese hotel regulations and revived by a breakfast of hot dumplings and tea.

Once you start waiting in earnest, it becomes a full-time project. You go to the counter to ask if there's new information. You make trips to the bathroom. You eat. You look at souvenirs. You talk to the few other stranded Western travelers. You try to make phone calls to Beijing. You look at your watch. You review the lost chances in your life.

Eventually a cheer rose in the jam-packed waiting room. A plane had been cleared to leave for Beijing. Since two days' planes were backed up, we didn't take chances. We grabbed our luggage and pressed toward the gate with a mass of travelers. Once the door opened, I was swept through in the crush. Wrong plane. I huddled outside until I could re-enter the terminal. My hands shook for five minutes afterwards from the experience of near-death by trampling.

Twenty-seven hours after our plane was scheduled to depart for Beijing, we finally left. As if that interminable delay wasn't lesson enough about the absurdity of waiting, the plane landed in Taiyuan, a Shanxi Province city, to wait another three hours before we took off for Beijing. Waiting, after all, is a state of mind. A suspended state of mind.

#   #   #

Nellie also arranged a trip to Xian, home of the famous terracotta warriors, and Guilin in southern China, where we saw the magnificent mountains that have inspired so much Chinese landscape painting. The first stop was Xian. The home of China's oldest cultures, Xian is northeast China's largest city and was its first capital. Several other Fulbrighters took advantage of Nellie's travel expertise and joined us. We went first to Xian's city wall, a soot-covered promontory that circuited the inner city for seven miles. It was cold. Not enough of us tourists around even to stir the souvenir vendors out of their housefly torpor.

The Big Blue Goose Pavilion followed, and we warmed ourselves up by climbing all seven stories to survey the city: north, south, east and west. The temple is devoted to the founder of

Buddhism, with one buddha each for past, present and future lives. I paid tribute by burning a candle and shooting some video. That night we had dinner at De Fa Chang, reputed to be China's most famous dumpling restaurant. It was a large, open and noisy place, and we sat together at a big table, eating more varieties of *jiaozi* (dumplings) than any of us could name.

The terra-cotta warriors were housed with some of their equine mounts in a hangar at least half an hour from the city. Considered one of the greatest archaeological treasures in the world, they were discovered in the funeral vault of Emperor Qin Shi Huang in 1974. Seven thousand strong, they are slightly larger than life-sized figures created to protect their master in the afterlife. Each slightly idealized figure is unique, fashioned after what must have been real infantrymen, cavalrymen and servants. Roman Imperial sculpture shrinks besides the grandeur of this sculpted army, lined up as if ready to march into battle.

Photos were not allowed. We walked around the perimeter, which was the size of a football field, trying to conceive of the power and ego responsible for such an undertaking. Seeing the some of the figures that were undergoing restoration helped create perspective. The statues were hollow, and their heads pulled off like marionettes. Next came various related exhibits, including one that contained two bronze funerary chariots, complete with driver, four horses and harnesses trimmed with gold and silver. At half size they were still impressive.

In the afternoon we visited Huaqing Hot Springs, where Xian emperors wintered and Chiang Kai-shek was arrested after fleeing his villa hideout, leaving behind one slipper and his dentures. Another stop was Ban Po Village, a neolithic site once again housed in a giant hangar built on the spot where the remains of these early civilizations were found. The exhibit included four levels of neolithic society constructed in the period from 6080 to 5600 B.C. We learned about the three basic types of buildings early humans here built—half-sunk, round and square forms—and wandered through several museum buildings displaying weapons, pottery and ornaments. The strangest exhibit of all was a building full of photographs of other primitive peoples, mostly from Africa and South America.

That night we dined at a small, very new-looking restaurant where the owner prepared special dishes not usually given to tourists. Two snakes were coiled up in a wire cage by the door, ready to be skinned and fried up. We had tripe, duck with lotus root, two kinds of tofu and other, unidentified substances. A performance of Tang dances and music introduced us to the White Linen dance, in which young women in gauzy white gowns spun their floppy sleeves around.

We arrived at Guilin the next night by plane, and it was easy to tell how different a place we were in. It was warmer. It was rural, and the terrain was mountainous. Like Saturday night in a county seat, the town was jumping. People spilled off the sidewalks and into the streets as busily as in Beijing. Our guide took us to see what was called Elephant Trunk Hill along the Li River, which twists and bends its way through the city. A tree-lined walkway overlooked the giant limestone formation, and below it you could watch boats in the river shuttling back and forth. The hill was lit, so we could see it clearly, as well as the people climbing on steps cut into its precipitous face.

Our main purpose in visiting Guilin was to take a cruise along the Li River. When we left at 8:30 the next morning, the road to Zhujiang Pier was already jammed with tour buses. This was southern China, so we passed rice paddies and water buffalo along the narrow road to the launching point. Our boat, lined up next to half a dozen others, was a double-decker ferry, with tables for eight below and a viewing deck on top.

The scenery was breathtaking. Jagged rocks thrust themselves skyward like sawteeth. They took as many shapes as the mind could invent: "Dragons Playing in Water," "Five Tigers Catch a Goat," "Five Fingers," "Nine Horses," "Dragon Head." I was happy to have the company of other Fulbrighters, since Jim spent most of the trip below deck playing bridge!

We disembarked at Yangshuo, a little, tourist-driven town 50 miles south of Guilin, with a crush of vendors on the walk up from the dock. Jim and I wandered through town on a mission to find tarot root. One of our Friendship Hotel friends, who had a yen for this mysterious vegetable, commissioned us to bring back 15 pounds of it. None was to be found, probably because it was the wrong season, although our pronunciation of the Chinese word for tarot root and complete ignorance of what it looked like may have had something to do with it.

Once we returned to Guilin, we visited Huanzhutong, the Cave of the Returned Pearl. Our guide explained the story behind the name. The interior of the cave was illuminated by a magnificent pearl until a fisherman stole it. Shame eventually got the best of him, and he returned the pearl, giving the cave its picturesque name.

When we got back to Beijing after our trip to see Xian's imposing warriors and mountain-rimmed Guilin, we realized that we had stopped being tourists. We were home.

22

HIS: YIN AND YANG ON THE YANGZI

I complained all the way down the Yangzi River.

A day-by-day description of the journey would be too grim to read, too grim to recount. Let me merely say this: Travel first class in China. We didn't.

Before leaving Chongqing for the trip down to Wuhan, we had a hotel breakfast of hot water, 10-second toast and juice from a rare, acid-producing tree. Our guide Tan said it was orange juice, but I've never seen transparent orange juice. "Radioactive," said Brooks. "Fission juice," said fellow traveler Bob Slagter.

The van taking us to the river passed a lot of men carrying two buckets hanging from poles on their shoulders. We took a short cable-car ride down the steep slope to the river and walked through a gauntlet of souvenir hawkers to the boat. I kept my head down, not because I didn't want to look at them, but because I was afraid of slipping on the muddy steps.

We climbed on board the Chinese boat. "This is going to be a great trip," I told Brooks. "You can't eat, sleep or perform any other natural body functions." No joke, as it turned out. I mean, my idea of comfort was not squatting over a trench.

"It's an adventure," Brooks actually said. "Life's an adventure."

Ah, but there was more. We found about 12 feet of deck space on which to stand at the bow and stern, and I repaired to the forward lounge, the boat's only comfortable room with tables, chairs, a panoramic view and a guide addressing the passengers in German. Some people don't like German tourists because they're loud and boisterous, but these ones danced to the loudspeaker music and were happy to try out their English. We also met a Chinese-Canadian couple and played a few precious hands of bridge with them.

"I can see what constitutes 'all right' to you," my high school and college chum Jeff Koplan said when we dined in Beijing a couple of months later. "The Germans were loud, obnoxious and unruly, but they spoke English, so they're all right. The Chinese couple was

152

nothing but a pair of philanderers, but they spoke English, so they're all right."

A few comments about the view. We saw every variety of Chinese junk, and a Chinese wedding or funeral with people walking along a road carrying what looked from a distance like paper dragons and chanting to the sound of cymbals and drums.

Yes, the gorges: sheer bluffs rising out of the river. Just beautiful. No better, said Mr. Grouch, than what I saw from the Li River during the 75 seconds when I wasn't playing bridge.

I sustained myself by reading "Goat Brothers" by Larry Colton, the lives of five frat brothers from a Berkeley jock house that was well worth the 500-page effort, and "After You're Gone," a collection of Alice Adams short stories that wasn't.

There were a few light moments. At the institutional dining room with institutional food, Bob sat down and broke a chair leg. "It's even an adventure to sit," he said. I did get a kick out of taking some photos with Brooks's camera. I guess it's impressive to find a part of China so uninhabited that the nearest airport to the tourist site is one and a half days away by boat. Also, I coined my first pun abroad. What do you call three beautiful women in China? The Three Gorgeous.

None of which compensated for the constant physical incapacitation. "It shouldn't be 'White Men Can't Jump,'" Koplan said, howling over my description of the bathrooms. "It's 'White Men Can't Squat.'" I want swimming, duplicate bridge, fine food, and, oh, yes, a private bathroom on *my* boats.

## 23

HIS: THE BIGGEST LITTLE HICK TOWN

A few days after Thanksgiving we set out for more travel adventure. Our goal: Tianjin, China's third largest city, the largest hick town in the world.

The Beijing train station was adventure enough. In a side room we stumbled into, about 30 people were squatting and facing the wall, guarded by a soldier with a billy club. They may have been trying to enter Beijing without proper papers. Or we may have been watching a police state in action. The sight was sufficiently chilling that even the Chinese were craning their heads to watch from the waiting room.

Ah, the waiting room. It was about the size of a football field. Like rugby players in a scrum, people were leaning against each other in a line that snaked around the room. We waited in one of the shorter lines, until the woman at the window told us that foreigners bought tickets in another part of the station. After squeezing around the longer queue, we found the foreigners' room. At the first window, you got an application and a registration and paid six RMB for the processing fee. Then you advanced to the ticket-buying window. We didn't get that far. The 11 a.m. train was sold out, and there wasn't another one leaving until 3:30 p.m. No good: our friend Marilyn Goldstein was due to meet us in Tianjin around 1:30 p.m.

Then another American in the foreign devils' room told us we could still get a bus outside. After shadow-boxing with drivers, we found one leaving at 11:30 a.m. There were 12 rows of four seats apiece, with a fifth seat folding into the aisle. The bus was packed by 11:25 and left. The only question was whether to open a window and freeze, or suffocate from the cigarette smoke.

During the trip, an entrepreneur climbed over each row and fleeced the passengers by playing three-card monte. You may have seen the game in Times Square. A man puts three cards on a box, then turns them face-up. One is red and two are black; an alternative method is one ace and two kings. Next he turns them face down and begins moving them around, like a shell game. He stops: you must point to the red card or ace or whatever is unique. He may let you win a few bets; then the sleight-of-hand begins. In the U.S. the pro has some lookouts to warn of cops. They may also hold you up if you happen to win. No such problem on this bus, just a guy stopping beside each row of seats with a briefcase and three cards. I couldn't believe how much money the passengers were spending, since Chinese usually don't have much money. Nice to know some things are universal, like gambling your life away.

We did get to Tianjin on time. Marilyn met us and took us around her university, where she taught art history. Lots of ponds, parks and playgrounds on the premises—the best sight in town. The highlight of the day was, or was supposed to be, going to the famous dumpling restaurant downtown where Richard Nixon hung out. We got there at 8:22 p.m., and it had closed. We found another place called the Hong Kong Restaurant. Their dumpling cook had the night off. Kind of reminded me of the 1984 Saturday night in Cleveland when some other sportswriters and I couldn't find a single downtown restaurant open and had to order pizza.

"We just picked a bad night," said Brooks. Yeah, Saturday night. I don't think they rolled up the sidewalks at 8 p.m. I don't think they ever rolled them *down* . O.K., there was a Chinese section that stayed open later. Some consolation for us outlanders.

The trip was worth it, though. On Sunday we had a great swim in the hotel pool, followed by an outasight Western buffet (no more guilt about seeking out things non-Asian). The lobby orchestra was playing Elvis songs like "Please Surrender" and "It's Now or Never" and making them sound ethereal; I could have sworn the piano was a harp.

Before leaving Tianjin, we went shopping on the lively ancient-culture street and bought two kites, a deck of playing cards, a little fake-jade horse, a fake-jade pig, some wrapping paper and a Mao button. Of considerably more importance, we got insight after insight from Marilyn, a warm and gregarious person who was amazingly close to her students and colleagues.

155

There still wasn't much freedom of choice in professions. Marilyn told us about one history professor who was trained in Russian. One day they gave him a choice of teaching British or American history. He chose American because there's less of it.

Marilyn said a lot of her students complained of stomach aches or couldn't sleep. They were being trained to be educators, but the profession had become so ill-paid and disrespected they felt they had no choice but to go into business. Trouble was, they had no idea what kind of work or how to get it.

One couple, separated by many miles, wanted to get married. In China, you had to get permission from the *danwei*, or work unit. Knowing the students would change locations to be together, both *danwei* turned thumbs-down. Another couple dared to have premarital sex, which was officially banned but increasingly practiced. Their parents were jailed for doing such a poor job of raising them.

"People have tremendous pride in being Chinese," Marilyn said, "coupled with tremendous difficulty in living here."

Who wouldn't in the world's largest hick town?

24

HERS: SHANGRI-LA IN SHANGHAI AND SUZHOU

Most of the time Jim and I were in China we saw things very differently, but we agreed that our last trip was our favorite. We spent Christmas in Shanghai and Suzhou. Jim's son Matthew was visiting from the U.S., and we wanted to celebrate his Christmas-Eve birthday by giving him a taste of travel in China.

The difference between elegant, European-influenced Shanghai and Beijing was evident the minute we arrived at the Shanghai airport. The road from the airport curved, something unheard of in the straight and narrow capital. The light was different, too. Brighter, more southern, it bathed everything in a warm glow. We stopped for lunch at a hotel with gardens and watched, fascinated, as a pair of mandarin ducks swam busily through the ponds ringing the hotel buildings. They were heading to their own little floating house. The drake clambered on board and disappeared, tail up, into a metal feed pot chained to his houseboat.

We stayed in a giant, new four-star hotel on the outskirts of the city in a room with a double bed, a first on our travels. Our guide Tony took us down Nanjing Street, the narrow, occasionally tree-lined and curving thoroughfare that heads directly into the center of town. In contrast to up-front Beijing, many of the buildings on this street were set at angles. Some were round. Many were European in style. We passed People's Park, a race track in the pre-Communist days, and children's "palaces," day care centers or schools, which used to be the homes of the wealthy. I wondered if one of them was Aunt Annie's, where my cousin Malcolm married Fredonia in 1923.

Downtown, an overhead walkway snaked gracefully from one side of the street across and around to the other. In austere, Soviet-inspired Beijing, walkways were underground. By the time we reached the Bund, Shanghai's famous promenade along the Huangpu River, it was dark. We couldn't see much, but we got out and walked anyway. The stately sycamores that had rimmed the Bund for 70 years were gone, felled by road improvement. We looked at the buildings fronting the Bund, and they reminded me of a modest version of Central Park South in New York. Close by was the Peace Hotel, a dignified building where we listened that night to a big-band jazz group that has played there since before the Republic's founding.

Since Shanghai was the cradle of the Chinese film industry, a tour of the Shanghai Film Studio was a must. A 50-year veteran of the studio, Professor Huang Tian Min, escorted us. The professor served as a consultant and translator for the studio. After retiring in the Sixties for 10 years, he returned because no one could do English-language contracts after the Cultural Revolution. Almost an entire generation lost to illiteracy.

Professor Huang told us how the studio produced 20 feature films a year. The film industry in China was united after establishment of the People's Republic. Shanghai was the biggest studio, and as a member of its staff, he had helped establish provincial studios as part of the regionalization of the industry.

We wandered through one studio after another, including a set under construction for a Canton-style *gongfu*, or kung-fu, movie. A joint venture with a Hong Kong company, the movie was due to go into production the next week. The young assistant accompanying Professor Huang got paint on her fingers—the set was still wet. From a distance the people swarming over this make-believe town appeared to American tourists, or at least Westerners. In fact, it was the Hong Kong production staff, looking as different from their mainland confreres as clothes and style can make possible.

We tried to take the professor out to lunch, but he declined. The restaurant of choice at the Yu Yuan Bazaar in the northeastern section of Shanghai's Old Town, may have been too far away, considering the city's oppressive traffic and his short lunch hour.

The Yu Yuan Bazaar was a crowded Chinese version of an American shopping mall. Small shops, stalls and restaurants were crammed next to and into the buildings on either side of a large open area. People milled everywhere. After lunch, we wandered through the shops and throngs of people along a zigzag walkway past the ancient tea house Wu Xing Ting. Set in the middle of a lake, the tea house was a Shanghai landmark. This kaleidoscope of sights was just

158

a prelude to Yu Yuan. Also known as Yu the Mandarin's Garden, it was an especially beautiful spot, secluded in the midst of so much hubbub. Inside the garden wall, rocks, water and buildings were arranged to create a sense of peace and tranquility. In one spot, a stream flowed under the archway of a bridge, giving the illusion that it never ended. In another, a building was constructed to jut out over the water, establishing the appearance of greater depth. One part of the garden wall was topped by a dragon, its body undulating along the wall's length, with the head providing the capstone. Doorways framed gardens and rock sculptures. Archways took as many different shapes as entertained the eye.

From Yu Yuan, we went to the Temple of the Jade Buddha, another big tourist attraction. The temple actually had two buddhas, each made from single gigantic pieces of stone. The larger one was on the temple's second floor. We removed our shoes to enter the main chamber and were transfixed by the chants of monks. The mysterious sounds they uttered seemed to come from another world. Downstairs in a second chamber, there was more chanting. People crowded into the temple to attend the service of a relative who had died. I got in line and prayed, bowing deeply three times while Jim and Matthew watched in disbelief. It was Christmas Eve, after all, and praying in this Buddhist temple seemed a proper celebration.

A group of elegantly dressed women emerged from a side chamber with bright red bags full of paper money. One by one, the funeral party filed outside and tossed their bags into a fire in a brass urn tended by a monk. A pile of red paper boxes also went. Even the smallest members of the family, three little girls, participated. Their elders helped them clasp their palms in prayer and bow three times. This ceremony and the sound of the monks chanting was as wonderful a gift as Christmas carols or spirituals.

Before dinner we wandered through the city's crowded downtown streets, looking for a bar. Bars were not the norm, even in sophisticated Shanghai, so we kept walking. The downtown streets of Shanghai had a completely different feel than Beijing's. There was a compactness and warmth in Shanghai, with its glamorous women, colorful neon and digital screen signs. Different than New York, but

159

more like it than Beijing because of the sense of enclosure by tall buildings. At one point a crowd of gawkers, watching a fight progress between two cyclists, blocked our way. One of the two must have been cut off and suffered a loss of face. A fight was the only way out. First the shouting began, followed by shoves, then fisticuffs. No one in the crowd made a move to intervene.

It was celebration, though, that capped our evening. In the entrance to our restaurant, we came upon the lights and hoopla of a bride and groom being videotaped by a local tv station. Which local celebrity, we wondered? Back at our hotel, after sneaking into the gift shop to buy Matthew a few presents, we had cake and drinks in honor of his birthday.

Early Christmas morning, we boarded a train to Suzhou, 50 miles west of Shanghai in Jiangsu Province. Suzhou's gardens were another unexpected holiday gift. Dating from the 10th century, they were distinctive for their beauty and the limestone rock formations—half natural and half created—that characterized them. Our guide Zhang Honghua was especially good. A man in his forties, he could not get an education until after the Cultural Revolution, when he was already trying to raise a family. His speeches were stilted and rehearsed, but he knew and cared a great deal about his subject.

Suzhou is known as the Venice of China because of its many canals. They feed into the Grand Canal, believed to be the longest inland waterway in the world, stretching from Suzhou to Beijing. Our first stop was a bridge where we could observe the life of the canals. The slower, more relaxed pace was immediately evident. People sat outside in the sunshine, chatting, knitting, working, relaxed and happy to smile at passing foreigners. In turn, as we walked alongside the canal, we could peer down the *hutungs*, or alleys, and guess what people's lives were like. Plants sat on window sills, and laundry dried on poles stuck out of windows. Zhang explained that the neat row of large pots we saw lined up in one alley took the place of toilets and were brought down in the morning to be emptied.

We visited three of Suzhou's gardens. The first was called the Liu, or Remaining Garden. Its name comes from the fact that it was not razed during the Taiping rebellion in the mid-19th century, when

600 Chinese cities were destroyed and 20 million people killed. One of China's most famous gardens, it was constructed in the 14th century during the Ming Dynasty. Zhang taught us that Chinese gardens consist of a harmonious arrangement of rocks, water, buildings and plants. The designers were often artists. He explained that gardens began as holes in the ground and unfolded over years as the creator re-examined the position for each rock or pool, building or plant.

It's hard to explain the feeling such a place creates. It was subtle, with the garden exposing itself gradually. You might walk through a building, follow a path to a bridge across water, pass through a courtyard with rock sculptures, climb an artificial hill. You began to understand how every aspect of what you saw had been considered, from the view when you looked through the courtyard, to the direction the path turned you in as you walked. Choices and viewpoints seemed endless. Each season was accounted for. Winter was the time for plum blossoms, delicately scented.

From the Liu Garden we went to Yu Yin, the Fisherman's Retreat or the Marshall of the Fishnets Garden. Originally built in the 12th century and restored in the 18th century, it was was smaller than the Remaining Garden, but for me more captivating. The full impact of the gardens' beauty may have taken time to accumulate or I may have liked this one's smaller scale. We had to climb over the entryway, which signified the home of a high official, into the ancient equivalent of a parking garage for rickshaws. Then there were the characteristic open buildings, courtyards, walkways, ponds, gardens and rock sculptures unfolding into a magical kingdom.

Suzhou is famous for its silk, and after lunch we visited the city's silk museum. The museum was new and illustrated all the stages in the growth of the silkworm. That series of exhibits was followed by ones showing the process of making a variety of silks. At least a dozen staffers demonstrated the step—as if to us personally—since we were among the museum's only visitors at the time.

Zhang took us last to the Garden of the Humble Administrator. A censor in the 16th century, this administrator must have taken one too many bribes because he was thrown out of office and retired to his garden. When I stepped over a small fence to take a video shot, the garden police materialized, ready to fine me. Zhang talked them out of it, but not without a few fierce looks thrown my way.

This garden was large and very different in feeling than the others we visited. Because it was late in the day, the light was low in the sky as we walked again along waterways, through buildings, across pavilions. Its reddish glow animated the buildings and the grounds. Like the Summer Palace in Beijing, the Garden of the Humble Administrator had a waterside building constructed to look like a stone boat. Zhang said the stone-boat building had four different types of rooms: a hall, a pavilion, a terrace and a tower. If stone could float, why not a different celebration going on in each of the building's rooms?

On our last stop of the day, we leaned over a bridge on the Grand Canal, watching the steady traffic of boats and barges. The pilot's wives, who sat on the fronts of their barges with flags to signal traffic coming the other way, waved at us, and we waved back.

On one of our stops, a lithograph of Suzhou rooftops for sale in a gallery caught my fancy. It was stark black, on a background of muted blue with yellow accents. Its traditional pagoda roof lines and bare tree tops loomed at the viewer from a photographic angle, combining a traditional subject with a modern perspective. I bargained hard for it, but when we arrived back in Shanghai discovered to my dismay I had left it on the train. Our guide Tony rushed back with me. We searched for the empty train, located it and climbed aboard our car, too late. It had been cleaned out.

My disappointment had little to do with the price of the lithograph. It was the need to carry away from our visit to Suzhou a tangible piece of its beauty. Tony guided me to the guard's booth in the train station and negotiated in Chinese, trying to learn who might have taken the lithograph, rolled up in its oblong green box. It was clearly a hopeless cause, but Tony promised to come back the next day. I resigned myself to the loss. Two weeks later the lithograph arrived by mail in Beijing, a much cherished momento of our trip to Shanghai and Suzhou.

162

HIS: QUOTATIONS FROM CHAIRMAN ZHANG

Stilted? Rehearsed? Listen, the best thing about Suzhou was Zhang Honghua's commentary. I'm a sound man, Brooks is a sight woman. I like dialogue, she likes *mis-en-scène.* That's why my favorite movie is "Casablanca." That's why hers is probably "Legends of the Fall."

While the van took us on a city tour, Zhang acquainted us with the place: 700,000 strong, 119 square kilometers, "water country, mild, humid, the land of fish and rice." Perfect description. Who needs to see the place?

We stopped first at a small bridge over a canal. "There are 34 kilometers of canals and 168 bridges," Zhang said. "Our sister cities are Victoria, B.C., Portland, Oregon, and Venice, Italy."

You won't hear this from Brooks, but the canal was a regular sewer. Nonetheless, the balconies overhanging the water had nice bonzai—miniature landscapes with pine, cypress and elm roots. "The canals are dredged twice a year," Zhang explained. "No more is possible, because it would affect the foundations of the buildings."

We passed a bathhouse, and Zhang delivered his first one-liner. "In the morning, the body is full of water. In the evening, the water is full of bodies." A man after my own heart.

We stopped at Liu Garden, which Zhang described as "nature in a nutshell. It's like a dumpling—the more you taste it, the better it tastes." That comment made my mouth water.

A tea house really set Zhang off: "Chrysanthemum tea cures cankers, jasmine warms your blood, and bilouchem, which Chou Enlai gave Kissinger, helps digestion, reduces fat and helps people enjoy life. Our oldest ruler, who lived to be 89, liked tea."

Brooks asked Zhang how the locals survived winter. "They eat mutton in winter, and when you drink ginseng tea, you don't need more clothes."

The spectacular garden features reminded us that Chinese esthetics existed long before Communism and, judging by the care they still get, will long outlive that flawed philosophy. Nothing beautiful escaped Zhang:

- The pebbles arranged on a walk? "Bats represent good luck, cranes longevity, goldfish wealth, lotus beauty, sheep kindness."
- The rocks in a lake? "Limestone rocks are chipped, then thrown in. They are eventually pulled out, pocked with holes. It's a 60-year process. The grandson often pulls them out."
- The importance of lotus? "Students are taught from the 800-year-old article 'Loving Lotus.' Its first lesson is to be honest."
- The rock formations? "The owner felt, 'We live in a city, but we want to feel that we live on a high mountain.'"
- A zig-zagging bridge? "It keeps away evil, slows down your feet and re-directs your gaze."
- A conveniently located mirror? "This is what we call a 'borrowed view.' It captures the moon during the Autumn Festival. You see it three times: once on the water, once in the sky and once in the mirror."
- China's favorite reed? "Bamboo never breaks in a storm. It represents a man of integrity."
- The furniture in garden homes? "There are four elements in gardens—water, rocks, buildings and plants. A garden without furniture is like a person without learning."
- Water? "According to ancient Chinese philosophy, water represents the pure and noble. It follows its own path. It seeks its own level. Like a wise man, it does only what is natural."

Every time we passed from one viewing post to another, Zhang had a verbal delight in store. "Do you know what your national flower is?" he said. "The rose. You decided that in the 1980s. But we think of America as a land of carnations, because you are a nation of cars."

Details began to blur in my mind. Not so the quotations of Chairman Zhang. In the end, I was able to append each of his comments to photos we had taken. The result was the most spectacular—and only—slide presentation I have ever given. Thank you, Zhang.

164

VI

TO EAT WELL IS GLORIOUS

"Dumplings come in two major varieties. You can get big, mysterious ones from vendors on the street as well as at restaurants....Or you can get dim sum, which more or less means little delicacies."

26

HERS: HOME COOKING, CHINESE STYLE

From our first day in China, when we woke up jet-lagged, hungry and unable to find a place to eat, food played an important role in our lives. Both Jim and I loved Chinese food, but we were unprepared for how different the native version would be from the American-style take-out we were used to. Don't look for our Chinese culinary expertise in the pages of Gourmet Magazine. When Pizza Hut opened a franchise in our neighborhood, we waited in line outside for a half hour to devour a pizza deluxe.

After the first, banquet-filled week in Beijing, we were ready for home cooking. The sumptuous banquets provided by the U.S. Embassy, the Chinese government, *Xinhua* and the China School of Journalism were a mixed blessing. Like a Swedish smorgasbord, there was always more food than any gourmand could down in one sitting, but half the time we couldn't be sure what we were eating. Our Chinese hosts considered exotic forms of aquatic food, like sea slugs or eels, the greatest delicacies. We merely found them inedible.

A regular diet of the institutional cuisine at the Foreign Experts' Dining Room was not for us, either. Mongolian hot pot and the fancy restaurants in the Friendship Hotel, delicious as they might be, were too rich for our pocketbooks on a regular basis. The market across the street from the main entrance to the Friendship Hotel beckoned. My language skills were not up to the energetic bargaining necessary in the local market, though, and my teaching schedule kept me too busy to negotiate the individual stalls or shops in the neighborhood for meat, vegetables, fruits, bread and other staples. Asking Jim to do the shopping and cooking did not offer a viable alternative, unless we wanted to starve.

Our salvation arrived in the form of Yin Shuqin, who became our *ayi*, Chinese for "auntie" or factotum. The wife of a retired Friendship Hotel employee, 52-year-old Shuqin had already cooked for another American family. We arranged for her to come to our apartment from 4 to 6 p.m., Monday through Friday and fix dinner for the outrageous sum of $12 a week. That was the going rate. She bought the necessary ingredients at the Friendship Hotel shops and brought them with her.

Every weekday afternoon, she arrived promptly at four, kicking off her shoes inside the front door and sliding into the slippers waiting there for her. Then she opened up her shopping bag to show me proudly what she had bought that day. "Okay" was about the only word of English she knew. Our Chinese was hardly better, and in five months it never advanced to the point where we could carry on anything but a labored conversation.

Usually by the time Shuqin arrived, I was sitting at my computer, too drained from the effort of teaching or making my way through the alien world of Beijing to feel like subjecting Shuqin to my pidgin Chinese. She understood. I often heard her quietly singing in the kitchen as she worked. She would be cutting up spring onions and green peppers or slivering potatoes into paper-thin slices with the orange-handled chopper she had requested that we buy. It looked like a meat cleaver, and once I learned how to wield it myself, I became a devoted user, shipping it home at the end of our stay.

Occasionally, Shuqin came into the living room to ask me a question about what time to serve dinner or how we would like a particular dish prepared. I struggled to understand what she was saying and grabbed for my little red "bible." Not Mao's sayings, but the Oxford Concise English-Chinese, Chinese-English Dictionary. When I pointed to the word I was mangling, she would look at me with her merry eyes, shake her head firmly and say "*bu*," or "no." After a while I understood. The type was too small for her to read. A few minutes later, I realized that her question, *"Shenme xihuan chi fan?"* meant, "What do you want to eat?" I had practiced it with Haiyan earlier that day during my Chinese lesson.

When Jim played bridge in the afternoon, it was sometimes after six before he arrived back home. Busy at my writing, I would suddenly realize that no sounds were coming from the kitchen. Then I would hear a faint rustling in the hall and understand that Shuqin had finished preparations for dinner, but was waiting for Jim to get home before starting to cook.

168

"*Qing ni pengtiao*," I would tell her: "Please cook," not wanting her to keep her own family waiting for their dinner. I could never decipher the Chinese that followed, but it was easy to figure out that she thought it better to wait for Jim.

With my Chinese exhausted by then, I would gesture for her please to come into the living room. Shuqin would sit down in one of our two overstuffed chairs, smoothing her cotton overblouse into her lap, and I sat opposite her. She would talk in Chinese. I tried Chinese, then gave up and spoke English. In time we managed to learn a little about each other. She had a son. I told her I had two sons and a daughter. Sometimes Haiyan would arrive in the afternoon to give me my Chinese lesson and stay for dinner afterwards. She and Shuqin chattered away in the kitchen, leaving me tongue-tied and miserable in the living room.

Shuqin cooked traditional northern Chinese food. Most of her meals were planned around pork, with a variety of vegetables like bean sprouts, potatoes, carrots, onions, peppers, cabbage—and eggplant when it was available. She always served rice, but occasionally we had noodles, too. *Jiaozi*, or dumplings, quickly became one of our favorites. Rather than buying ready-made pastry for them, Shuqin made it herself from scratch and minced the pork and vegetable stuffing so finely it turned into a pungent paste. Lamb with peppers and onions was another favorite, along with shredded potatoes and carrots spiced with hot peppers.

Our kitchen had no oven, so Shuqin stir-fried virtually all our food in a wok. The stove consisted of two gas burners on legs, attached by a rubber tube to a propane gas tank. Lighting it was always an adventure. Industrial-grade peanut oil was a staple in the Chinese diet, particularly stir fry, but my stomach rebelled. Before long, we had to conduct delicate negotiations through Haiyan to get Shuqin first to reduce the amount of peanut oil she used and then to substitute vegetable or olive oil that I bought at the international supermarket downtown. It was important to us not to make her think we didn't like her food.

The truth of the matter was that we didn't like a lot of it. Much as we started out liking Chinese food, we weren't used to such a

169

steady diet of it. When we asked Shuqin to substitute chicken or beef for the ubiquitous pork, it usually tasted strange. Different taste buds, we decided, for different cultures. We craved fresh fruit and salads, taboo for foreigners for sanitation reasons. Although I ate fish regularly in the U.S., Chinese fish made me violently sick. Since my Chinese wasn't good enough to try teaching Shuqin American recipes, we toughed it out.

"*Chi bao le*," we told her every night, "I'm full." In China that is even more of a compliment than "*Chi hao le*," "I ate well." We lost weight.

For breakfast we relied on the bakery in the Friendship Hotel, which carried french pastry. Our favorite was a plain model with a miniscule dollop of chocolate inside. For lunch we tried our luck at the Foreign Experts' Dining Room, where we always met interesting people and had good conversation, no matter how bad the food or service was. The alternatives were to warm up leftovers, make peanut-butter sandwiches or eat in a neighborhood restaurant.

The next good meal was always around the corner. The catch was that you could not be sure how well you might feel afterwards. Hygiene standards were not high at the little neighborhood restaurants with the best prices and food. I learned that from observation when I sent back a dirty glass, watched the waiter swish a little cold water in it from a laundry tub spigot and bring it right back. Everyone had different theories about how to cope with the hygiene problem. Drink beer with every meal "to kill the germs." Drink nothing but boiling hot tea, sloshing around the first portion and slopping it on the floor to sterilize the cup. Carry your own chopsticks. Wipe off silverware and dishes with a clean napkin. I tried them all and still got sick regularly.

We often took the coward's way out and patronized Western restaurants. The Shangri-la Hotel not far from our apartment had an Italian bistro downstairs and a buffet upstairs with roast beef and baked potatoes. I never thought I could be so happy to consume a baked potato. The Yanshan Hotel became a regular haunt for us because we could bicycle there in less than 10 minutes. We would order soup and sandwiches for lunch, have the buffet at night or the

Sunday brunch, if we could manage to make it there before 10:30 a.m. Haiyan tipped us off to the fact that when you ordered eggs at the Yanshan, they were supposed to come with home fries. Since the home fries never appeared, you could demand a rebate on the already rock-bottom price.

A trip downtown for dinner, which meant a 40-minute cab ride, became our preferred weekend entertainment. Soon after we arrived in Beijing we stumbled into Maxim's at the China World Hotel. It was very French, very expensive. Luckily, it was lunch. When the glass of wine I ordered tasted vinegary, I mumbled to the waiter, "*Je suis desolée, mais le vin, il ne me plaît pas.*" He actually understood what I was saying, even if he did answer me in English. We ordered a tiny plate of steamed vegetables and some rolls. The presentation was superb, and the bill came to $40.

We were relieved to discover that some of the other Fulbrighters shared our furtive longings for the taste of Western food. Together we made a beeline for the overpriced Italian restaurant in the luxury Palace Hotel the first week we arrived. Run-of-the-mill Italian cuisine never tasted so good. Even after someone on the Embassy staff told us all the booths in the restaurant were bugged, we went back for reunions. Early in our stay, Justine's Restaurant in the Jianguo Hotel on Changan Ji was the scene of an explosion between Jim and me. I had agreed to meet him downtown for dinner after his bridge game. He waited inside the restaurant for 45 minutes, while I waited outside in the hotel lobby. It took a nice Italian meal and a lot of soothing harp music to cool our tempers.

Our Thanksgiving celebration gave us a new appreciation of that season's cuisine. One of Jim's American colleagues at the China Daily, Paul Ryan, served up real turkey, ordered specially from the Lido Hotel, plus a cornucopia of other American treats: baked ham, mashed potatoes, peas and carrots. After we indulged ourselves at Paul's apartment, Jim left for his polishing job, and I went on to a party at the Hilton Hotel put on by the American Club of Beijing. Each table there had its own turkey and designated carver. The menu expanded to include sweet potatoes, salad, broccoli, cranberry sauce, gravy, stuffing and pumpkin pie. I gobbled up everything and took home leftover turkey.

One night after a trip to the Peking opera, we reached nirvana, our culinary home away from home. A member of the USIS staff in the American embassy had told us about a restaurant downtown, north of Silk Alley and across from the Worker's Stadium where embassy staff took their kids for hamburgers. It was a tourist trap called Frank's Place, the quintessential American bar transplanted to Beijing. American football played on the video screen. American rock music punctured your ear drums. The handsome wood bar was as welcoming as a fireplace, and a dart board hung in one corner.

Early in the evening, you were more apt to find a father sitting at the bar with his two young children than a pair of rowdy drunks. The menu was the magnet. Hamburgers and french fries, lettuce and tomato salads, chili.   Jim and I had pretty much given up hamburgers years before, but the call of a red-blooded American hamburger was too much. The bartender asked what we wanted to drink, but we couldn't make up our minds.

"What about the Memory of You Tonight?" he suggested. How could anyone refuse a drink with a name like that? It was a tropical concoction of rum, liqueurs, coconut and pineapple juices almost as heavenly as its name. We quickly became Frank's Place habitués.

Entertaining while we were in China had its harrowing moments. True, our pizza and beer parties were successes, as long as the cab driver that ferried one of us to Pizza Hut could be persuaded to wait while we went in for the pizzas we'd ordered. Other times we enlisted Shuqin's skills. She met the challenge heroically, preparing and serving so much food that we dined off the leftovers for days afterwards.

One time, though, she wasn't able to help. No problem, I thought. I planned to buy a couple of the eight-flavors rotisserie chickens we had discovered in the market across the street on Baishiqiao Lu. The herbs stuffed into the chicken's cavity permeated the meat, flavoring it deliciously. Jim and I spent the day shopping. First we rode our bicycles to the slightly larger supermarket on the Third Ring Road. Bringing our own bags, we finished one round of

172

foraging, filled the baskets on the front of our bikes and a knapsack, then teetered home. A second excursion was necessary for beer, which came in quart bottles and cost pennies, about a third or a quarter of what you paid for an equivalent bottle of Coke or Sprite. Imagine trying to balance on a bicycle loaded up with beer bottles.

I spent the afternoon preparing a cucumber-and-onion salad—safe for foreigners to eat because the vegetables could be peeled—stir-fried broccoli and garlic potatoes. At 4:30 p.m., Jim went off on his bike to buy the chickens. Plenty of time, since our five guests weren't arriving until 6 p.m. Then it got later and later, but no Jim. He finally threw open the apartment door at 5:30. Haggard, he announced he had looked everywhere, but the rotisserie chicken stand was gone.

In total panic, I raced to the little supermarket across the street on my bicycle, nearly getting knocked over by a *miandi* when I crossed Baishiqiao Lu in rush-hour traffic. I bought three kilos of fresh chicken, mushrooms and scallions. Dinner wasn't served to our patient and well-oiled guests until after 8:30, but they proclaimed my chicken surprise worth waiting for.

The week before our nearly disastrous dinner party, Shuqin had simply not shown up one afternoon. Arriving home at the apartment late, I worried that she had knocked and found no one there. How to reach her was a mystery. I knew there was a telephone for the apartment complex where she lived, but I didn't have the number. Haiyan did, and I tried paging her. When Jim arrived home an hour later and we still hadn't heard from either Shuqin or Haiyan, we gave up and went out to dinner. It was a surprise to discover how fragile the fabric of our daily routine was. One small disruption had made us see how much we depended on it.

When I reached Haiyan the next day, she explained that Shuqin's brother was sick. Shuqin hadn't been able to reach me and let me know. Even if she could have, I doubt I would have understood what she said. When she didn't appear the following week, we found out that Shuqin's brother had died and she had been injured in an automobile accident coming back from his house. What could we do to help, I asked Haiyan. Could we visit her and bring some flowers? Haiyan quickly made it clear that such a visit would have made Shuqin uncomfortable. We felt trapped between the ways we knew how to express our affection and concern and the customs of a culture that was alien to us. Fortunately, her wounds were minor. In another week she was back cooking us *jiaozi* for a farewell dinner, sturdy, smiling and showing off her bruises. The last time I saw her she was walking down the driveway at the Friendship Hotel pushing her shiny, three-wheeled bicycle, as sure a sign of status, Chinese-style, as any.

## 27

HIS: YOU CAN'T BEAT DUMPLINGS

I'll say this about Chinese food: I lost 10 pounds. The absence of pre-dinner rolls and sweets took a nice toll. So did rice, the universal, virtually fat-free staple.

I'll say *this* for Chinese food: except for the ritual runs that struck several times, I had no stomach aches until I ate Western food.

But say this, too, for Chinese food: most of the time you could get a better meal at your local Hunan Garden. It was not just the cooking oil Brooks has detailed; the beef had the consistency of a dog's chew toy.

Not that all the food we ate was awful. I developed such a craving for dumplings that they're virtually all I order even in an American Chinese restaurant. I'm not alone. The kid narrator in the movie "The Blue Kite" said his favorite food was dumplings, the most celebratory meal ordinary people can get in China. So there.

Dumplings come in two major varieties. You can get big, mysterious ones from vendors on the street as well as at restaurants. Some people say the best thing about them is that you can't see what's inside. When it's pork, there's no dining experience in China to match it.

Or you can get *dim sum*, which more or less means little delicacies. We had a brunch of *dim sum* one Beijing Sunday at a Swedish-built apartment complex for foreigners. There was one course of little dumplings after another: pork, shrimp, vegetable, as well as other little entrées of duck, spare ribs and cabbage. Hard to beat, especially when our hosts insisted on paying.

Unfortunately, we couldn't eat dumplings alone. Too many lunches were spent at the *Youyi*'s Foreign Experts Dining Room, that wonderful place where waitresses expected you to order as soon as you got the menu and postage-stamp paper napkins were cut in half, presumably to economize. Virtually everything was awful; I'm not sure they had dumplings and I was so turned off by the place I wouldn't have dared taste them if they did. Eventually, I ordered what I considered the only safe dish on the menu: mashed potatoes.

We complained about getting served dinner by *ayi* every night at 5:30. "They do that because they eat lunch at 12," a Bulgarian friend, Kalil, told us. "In fact, earlier. I know of a professor who used to lecture until noon, but the students were packing up and leaving at 11:45, so he began stopping early. They told him all the food would be gone at noon." Well, we forgave *ayi* when she served dumplings.

One night we had dinner with fellow *Youyi* dwellers Keith and Joyce Clemenger and their one-year-old son. Keith was the Beijing-office director of the Committee on Scholarly Communication with China, an organization that arranges exchanges of China scholars. Joyce was a can-do Midwesterner: the 440, the state choir, that kind of thing. Very nice, cheery people who showed us the ropes. We ate at a state-run restaurant across the street from the *Youyi* and had our first Peking duck—hardly fat-free—in Beijing. Dipped in onion-and-plum sauce, the duck really seemed more American than Chinese. No dumplings, they.

I asked Keith to describe the difference between Chinese food in China and in the States. "We're mainly used to Cantonese food, which is sweeter and oilier than we get here. We have rice with the main dishes, the northern Chinese like it afterwards." Our Shanghai guide Tony told us much the same thing. The food in southern China is clean, fresh, and multi-ingredient, he said, not as spicy and a little sweeter than the Beijing variety. Another major difference, according to Keith: "When the [northern] Chinese go to America, they wind up cooking for themselves."

Naturally, we longed for Western food from time to time. We were eating dinner at an Italian restaurant in the Shangri-la Hotel when we witnessed what I consider a universal truth. There were half a dozen Europeans at the next table. Suddenly, one of the men shouted, "Shit!" so loudly it could be heard all through the restaurant. A waiter had spilled wine on him. The owner came over and—I thought with great restraint—repeated "It was a mistake, sir," several times while the guy raved on.

176

I was glad that the offending guest was not American. When we were on a cruise in the Galápagos Islands in 1992, I couldn't help noticing that of all the tourists abroad—Americans, Germans, English, Japanese and Ecuadorians—the best behaved were Americans. "The Ugly American" must have produced a generation of sensitive, enlightened travelers.

One cold winter day we walked from the *Youyi* to the nearby *Yanshan* Hotel for dinner, tripping and stumbling over frozen sidewalks that hadn't been sanded. Sometimes back home in Massachusetts Brooks had suggested a modest dinner out, and I would say, "Let's make a real meal out of it—you know, candlelight, nice conversation, a little white wine." At the Yanshan we had the full metal jacket—soup, chicken, lamb chops, cherries jubilee, crepe suzettes, candlelight, nice conversation, a little white wine—for about $19. The Yanshan was a better bargain than the downtown restaurants or—how dare I preach such blasphemy?—Frank's Place.

Some edible meals were neither Western nor dumpling. At a downtown restaurant owned by *Xinhua*, we had a banquet for the renewal of John Morgan's contract—any excuse for a banquet would do—featuring everything from relatively fat-free Peking duck to pineapple wrapped in honey. I felt as if we were talking to compatriots, especially during a round of Japan-bashing that made me as uneasy in China as when I heard it in America. "The Japanese are weird," one of the Chinese said. "They spend six days a week at the office, and then talk business on the golf course on Sundays. No family life. Strange people." The memory of the Japanese occupation still intact, the Chinese referred derisively to their neighbors as "our friends the Japanese."

Among our hosts was a young man who actually said, "I can see political reform following economic reform."

What? Was this the scoop of the year? "What do you mean by political reform?" I asked. Brooks gave me a sharp poke in the leg.

There was a brief silence. "Market economy," the guy said.

For most banquets we had the usual quota of 15-20 varieties of vegetables, fruits, seafood and, just for the occasion, edible meat. At the semester-ending banquet the CSJ threw for Brooks, we had a hot-pot meal, in which you cook your own food by holding it in your chopsticks and dunking it in a large copper container filled with boiling water. The school's dean, Liu Binjiang, kept proposing toasts with shot glasses of a throat-rattling grain alcohol called red sorghum, a.k.a. the great white dry.

After many toasts, I proposed one. "The best thing about China is the people," I said. "In the spirit of bilateral relations and mutual co-operation"—that got a big laugh—"I hereby declare that we will return."

For dumplings, we just might.

## 28

HERS: A TRIP TO THE HEALTH CLINIC

Many of our friends warned us that we could expect to get sick while in Beijing. Because most homes are heated by coal, a brown-gray haze clogs the city's skyline in the cold months. Western visitors tend to have respiratory infections as a result. Living as we did in the Friendship Hotel, however, we were on the northwest outskirts of the city where the air was cleaner and didn't have respiratory problems.

Hygiene practices in relation to food were a different matter and led to frequent digestive upsets. Fertilizer for Chinese fruits and vegetables is called "night soil." It was manufactured from human waste, and while Chinese digestive tracts were accustomed to it, Westerners paid the consequences when they ate unpeeled raw fruits and vegetables. Soap and hot water were generally in short supply in restaurants, and we noticed that our Chinese friends routinely wiped off their glasses, plates and utensils with a handkerchief or tissue.

Once after a visit to a neighborhood restaurant, I found myself with a severer than usual stomach ailment. A trip to the Friendship Hotel's medical clinic seemed in order. The clinic was in one of the cluster of buildings just across and down the street from our apartment. Sticking my head inside, I could see a murky intersection of gloomy, aging hallways. Half a dozen white-coated clinicians, mostly women and presumably doctors, were either sitting or standing in a dimly lit reception room to the left, smoking and waiting for patients. There didn't seem to be any but me.

They waved me eagerly to the reception window, where I showed my official *Xinhua* health card, issued by the China School of Journalism. In China, everyone has access to medical care. The question is, are you sure you want it? One brave couple we were friends with had their third child by Caesarean section in a Beijing hospital, but most foreigners headed to Hong Kong or home for any major illness or hospital procedure. Fulbrighters and others living long-term in China paid a substantial premium for evacuation insurance, which covered fees for medical evacuation of as much as $50,000.

The reception clerk processed a sheaf of yellowing papers for me and told me to go to Room #7. "Left and down at the end of the hall," she said when I looked bewildered. The doctors, I noticed, had all disappeared. Time to look busy? I walked into the one open door on the corridor and found a dingy, poorly lit cubicle with a bank of windows on one side and an alcove on the other. Chairs rimmed one wall and a desk was positioned in front of the fourth, with a white-sheeted examining table next to it.

The doctor, a woman, showed up a few minutes later and asked the usual questions about the nature of my symptoms. Nausea? Vomiting? Diarrhea? How much? Watery? Fever? The difference was that since I found it so hard to understand what she was saying, she had to repeat the questions several times. They continued. "How long in China? Good health before?" Her clinical manner was at least as good as the actor in the commercial who intones, "I'm not a doctor, but I play one on tv."

It was time to take my temperature. She told me to lift my shirt and clapped a thermometer into my armpit. We waited about five minutes for the results. Next she took my blood pressure and listened to my breathing with a stethoscope. Then I was asked to lie down on the examining table so she could palpate my innards. The table was as hard as the floor. "Push this up," she said. "It hurts here?" She was right each time. When she asked, "Liver problems before?" I started to get worried, wondering if my liver was enlarged or lumpy or God forbid cancerous. Did I have hepatitis?

"Is there a problem with my liver?" I screwed up the courage to ask.

"Liver okay," she said, writing out prescriptions for me. There were three. Berberin for diarrhea. Belladonna for pain, and yeast for digestion. I was hoping for laudanum next.

"Take these to fallacy," she ordered. Fallacy? The word didn't sound like pharmacy at all, but I figured out what she meant. Back to the window in the reception area for a stamp on the prescriptions,

180

then to another window I hadn't even noticed on the way in. The process was very Chinese. Two or three people to do the work of one—each in their own order. The prescriptions came in three tiny paper envelopes—and they worked. Thanks to the belladonna, I spent the afternoon napping as comfortably as any Victorian lady with the vapors.

The clinic became a favorite hangout for Jim. When he went to have a urinary tract infection treated, he was given a regimen of 20 pills a day. They included what looked like a squash ball packaged inside a ping-pong ball. When he opened up the ping-pong-ball case and tried to follow instructions to cut up the squash ball into pill-sized portions, the knife bounced off it like rubber.

"I didn't know whether to swallow the damn thing or bake it," he complained.

Later when he pulled a calf muscle playing tennis, the clinic doctor prescribed a "Deer-Horn Tiger-Bone Plaster." The plaster patch healed the pull in just two or three days, but the rash it left behind on his leg lasted over a week. "Let's hear it for those tiger bones," Jim said. "How 'bout them cats?" He still carries a stash of Tiger Balm ointment in his travel kit.

VII

BEAUTY IS TRUTH, TRUTH BEAUTY

"Zhang Haiyan, who was to become our most intimate
Chinese friend and associate, was as American as a Valley
girl. Thirty -one, fluent in English and amazingly
articulate, she peppered her conversation with 'hell' and 'in
your dreams, home boy'."

## 29

HERS: THE STORY OF ZHANG HAIYAN

Chinese Communist society is organized around the concept of *danwei*, or work unit. Your work unit is the source of almost everything that matters in your life, from housing to permission for getting married. It is one of the most dramatic ways in which life in China differs from the U.S. For example, at the China School of Journalism unless you were a foreigner like me, work was where you took your shower two or three times a week, where you made most of your phone calls and where you got, among other foodstuffs, your eggs—a gift from the school authorities.

During the tremendous changes that have overtaken China in recent years, the iron grip of the *danwei* has loosened. Once people started go into business for themselves and make money as they have in increasing numbers, they could escape the dictates of the *danwei*. It hasn't changed, though, for most ordinary people—or for foreigners.

My *waiban*, or *danwei* liaison, was assigned to me by the Foreign Affairs Office at the China School of Journalism. As the FAO contact, Haiyan was the person who made sure my needs—not just work-related ones either—were met. If we wanted to travel, she helped make the arrangements. If I wanted to change my teaching schedule at the school, she negotiated with her boss on my behalf. She made sure I got my mail and translated at formal occasions, such as when we were banqueted by school officials. She exercised considerable control over most of my activities. And because she knew the language and customs so infinitely better than I, she was a font of knowledge about everything you might take for granted as an academic from the U.S., such as how to buy a ream of paper, get school stationery, have copies made.

Among Fulbright FAOs, Haiyan seemed exceptional. Thirty-one years old when we met her, she grew up in Lanzhou in the north-central province of Gansu, where during the Cultural Revolution she, her mother, her university-educated father and her three brothers were "thrown back" to work on a pig farm. Haiyan's earliest memory was of standing on a table, clinging to the bars in the window of the house where she'd been locked in while her mother and brothers went to work. Her father had already been "arrested." She couldn't have been older than two or three at the time, and there were rats on the floor.

"It wasn't abuse," she was quick to explain. "My mother didn't have any choice. There was no one to watch me." When she was seven, Haiyan's mother died of liver cancer. Haiyan learned to keep house and cook for her brothers and father, developing considerable inner resources from those hard times early in her life. She very quickly became my closest friend in Beijing. She gave me Chinese lessons twice weekly and ate dinner with us several times a week.

Haiyan's facility with languages was enriched by a gift for mimicry. When she first met Jim and me at the airport, she came across as a mix between a Valley girl and an East Coast intellectual. Not just the idioms and inflections, but the gestures, too. She had them down to a T. Many people she dealt with assumed she was Chinese-American. Born in the States, they thought. When Australian John Morgan, who was teaching Western journalism with me at the China School of Journalism, arrived, I could hear her accent shift to accommodate his. She could do a British accent, too.

With a round face, glasses, long black hair and a lean, athletic body, Haiyan was both articulate and intelligent. A top student for seven years, she was headed for a job teaching English at Lanzhou University. In China then, you couldn't just pick up and move to another region of the country when you felt like it. There were ways to do it through the back door, working deals through connections, but it wasn't easy. Haiyan wanted more than an obscure teaching career in a backwater province.

In the mid-Eighties, she saw a notice in the newspaper about how China's news agency *Xinhua* was forming the China School of Journalism. She wrote to the school, sending a résumé and a tape showing off her English language skills. Impressed, they hired her. Arguing they had invested too much to let her go, her provincial

186

university fought to keep Haiyan, but as part of *Xinhua*, the new China School of Journalism had more clout.

After teaching English to journalism students for a few years, Haiyan won a grant to study journalism herself. The next step in her career was assignment as a foreign correspondent. She competed against 200 men, coming out on top in the required test. Posted to Cairo, she became the first single woman to serve as a foreign correspondent for *Xinhua*. Also called the New China News Agency, it is the government-run equivalent of the U.S.'s Associated Press. Sending a woman abroad was very unusual. Only one other had ever been given such an assignment. After managing to get her husband out of the country, that woman went to New York with her two children and disappeared. It was a mark of great confidence that *Xinhua* gave her the Cairo assignment.

Why had *Xinhua* taken such a risk with Haiyan? It probably was partly due to reforms going on at the time, partly because of her considerable talents, and partly because, impatient with the progress of her career, Haiyan had threatened to quit. She was gutsy and ambitious, and the school knew it might lose her otherwise.

At an early age Haiyan had decided that she would never marry. "It just didn't seem to be what I wanted," she said. She cherished her autonomy, despite the fact that at the time she was getting close to 30, the age at which Chinese women turn into old maids. "For my father it meant a great loss of face," she said. "He told me, 'You're by far the best looking in the village. You're the most successful, and you make the most money, so why?' He didn't understand."

Haiyan found her tour of duty in Cairo, the base of *Xinhua*'s Middle East operations and one of its biggest bureaus, a harrowing experience. Independent of spirit, she was confined to a dormitory that seemed prison-like, living in close contact with the rest of the bureau staff and subject to constant supervision. She described sneaking out into the desert at night for moonlit horseback riding and camping excursions. In the meantime her male superiors were warning her not to fraternize with foreigners, who they said would only want to exploit her sexually. When she scooped the other correspondents, she found her stories getting spiked, newspaper lingo for news stuck on a paper spike instead of being published. In China she had always been able to create for herself an island of freedom, and her confinement in Cairo was suffocating.

Then Haiyan was sent to Kuwait to cover the Gulf War. While there, the unimaginable happened. She met and fell in love with Canadian tv cameraman Mike Parsons. The romance blossomed. After her two-year stint in the Cairo bureau, she was rotated back to China and returned to the China School of Journalism. She and her Canadian cameraman decided to get married, so Haiyan applied for permission to emigrate to Canada. *Xinhua* was not very happy about losing one of its best teacher-correspondents, but as Haiyan said, "they could give me a better salary, they could find me better housing, but they couldn't find me a husband."

When we arrived in Beijing in the fall of 1993, Haiyan expected to be in Canada within another month. When we left at the end of January, she was still waiting. Apparently the Chinese government wasn't holding up her emigration; it was the Canadians.

"They have to investigate me and be sure that I have never been arrested everywhere I've been," she told me again and again when I asked why nothing was happening during the months we were in China. "They also have to get the Egyptian government to certify that I wasn't involved in any criminal activity the entire time I was over there." She said getting married in China wouldn't have helped. It simply would have meant that she lost her housing and her job while she waited for the excruciatingly sluggish wheels of the Canadian bureaucracy to turn. Periodically we would hear of how she had talked to this or that friend of a friend, who reported that the consular officer working on her application had gone to Hong Kong on sick leave, that her paperwork was in the computer, that approval was imminent.

The month before we left China, I saw much less of Haiyan. Her father became seriously ill, and she agonized over whether to make the long trip by train to Lanzhou for a visit. If she did she might miss her visa interview with the Canadian Embassy. Her brothers called with the news that her father was deteriorating and was asking for his only daughter. The morning she completed the 30-hour train ride to Lanzhou he died—before she could reach him. During the return trip, she found an abandoned baby on the train. She and a couple she had befriended on the train took care of the little girl, who they discovered had been born without an anus. It was Christmastime when she arrived back in Beijing. She left the baby girl with the couple she had met on the train while she went to met her fiancé, who was arriving in Beijing to visit. Together they were going to try to speed up the emigration process. The infant died before medical attention could be arranged.

Haiyan and I had been so close in the previous months that I felt the loss of her companionship acutely, even resented it. I wasn't ready to have us go our separate ways, just as I wasn't ready to leave China. Once we were several continents apart, though, I could better appreciate her suffering and her stoicism. My friendship with Haiyan remains one of the most deeply felt and treasured parts of my experience living in China.

In time, the school decided that if Haiyan was going to marry a foreigner, she would have to leave the China School of Journalism. She took a public relations job with the U.S./Hong Kong joint venture firm Grey China. For more than a year she did not respond to our letters or to our anxious phone calls to her fiancé in Canada. Then just before publication of this book, she called. She had arrived in Ottawa.

"I didn't write because I didn't have anything to report," she explained. The couple's plan had been to wait until after Haiyan was safely out of China to marry. They finally went ahead with the ceremony, and the Canadian government quickly approved Haiyan's visa. She left China, at last, to launch her new life.

189

30

HIS: THE BEAUTIFUL PEOPLE

There were times in Beijing when I would see a Chinese woman walking down the street so beautiful that, had she been a redhead, I would have thrown away my life for her. The next woman would be twice as attractive. Then I would see a third woman so unearthly and fetching that I immediately forgot the last two.

Was there a modeling convention in town? No. Just three Chinese women walking down the street.

After you've been in China for a month, you never want to see another Caucasian face.

Let's stop right here for a politically correct gut check. Some 95% of all Chinese have Han ancestry, so it's perfectly fine to make wild generalizations about their appearance. They are a beautiful people.

Oh, that sweet face—to paraphrase George Frazier on Ted Williams's swing—that sweet, sweet face, anointing the afternoon. What did I love about the Chinese face? The yellow-ivory skin color? The high-plateau cheekbones? The teardrop eyes? The delicacy of the features? Whatever, I looked at the unattractive people twice. They were the rarity.

Beauty is only skin-deep, but it runs deeper still in the Chinese character. One morning I was race-walking around the *Youyi* grounds when a Chinese man fell in step with me. We started talking. I braced for some request, the kind various literature had warned us about. The blameless fellow, a teacher at a primary school, just wanted to talk, test out his English, make a foreign friend.

The Chinese may have mouthed clichés about foreign devils and big-noses, but they rarely practiced them in personal contact. Once you got past the cab drivers, peddlers and young hustlers on the make, the Chinese couldn't have been nicer. I know this is said about a lot of foreign cultures; this time it's true. No one at the newspaper or bridge club rubbed me the wrong way: not one person.

I think the Chinese just practice what they preach: "Friendship first, competition second."

History has a lot to do with Chinese character. When my old friend David Lebedoff visited China in the early Seventies, he was struck by how few questions the Chinese asked him. He was in China during the Cultural revolution, and they were looking inward if at all. By our arrival in 1993 they were fascinated about the West and none too shy to ask questions. If Brooks's students were any indication when we accompanied them on a tour of *Xinhua*, China's national news agency, the Chinese young have become perky, pleasant and provocative. We handled their rapid-fire questions as deftly as Ozzie Smith taking batting-practice grounders. "Are there scholarships for Asians at Western journalism schools?" Yes, but there's probably a cutback in favor of Americans. "Are blacks encouraged to play basketball in the United States?" Yes. They're also exploited. "How do you become a sportswriter?" Start on the news side and learn real journalism first. "What skills are important for a journalist?" Curiosity, interest in people, respect for the language. They had follow-up questions, too.

At other times their questions were more personal. One day I addressed the combined population of Brooks's and John Morgan's classes at the China School of Journalism. For about an hour I went on about getting a job, interviewing and writing. Some students took copious notes. Others were concentrating so hard they had to close their eyes and bury their faces in their arms on the desk.

Afterward, the students had many questions, though not the ones I expected. "What do you think of women's emancipation?" I got a laugh when I said I was a dependent spouse. "You've been very busy—do you want to retire to something quieter?" Yeah, pinballs.

We found curiosity among older people, too. One of our guides, Bob, shot questions at my son Matthew while he was visiting China: "How much do you pay for your apartment? How big is it? Two bedrooms? A bathroom? A TV? A car? You've got it made!" Pointing to our noses and foreheads: "You look just like your father!"

Turning to me without even taking a breath, he continued: "Why did you get divorced?...How do you make a living as a freelancer?"

Understand that what may seem nosy to Americans shows genuine interest among Chinese. To them, it's a form of closeness.

Even more than decency, it was steadfastness that amazed me about the Chinese. The old men at the bridge club were the most extreme example, but few Chinese seem ground down by their rough history. I asked a Chinese professor labeled a "rightist" how he found out the truth. "Somehow," he replied. That comment struck me as a metaphor for China. The truth will out—somehow—and so will the human spirit. Am I getting too misty-eyed? Our friend spent seven years doing heavy farm labor during the Cultural Revolution. "They thought they could take away my mind," he said. "You can never take a man's mind."

One night I rode the China Daily van home with two of my editors, *lao* Liu (*lao* means elder or honorable, remember) and Huang Qing, the highest-ranking woman on the paper. *Lao* Liu lived with one daughter, while his wife and other daughter remained at their south China home in a city on the Yangzi River. Liu and his wife weren't divorced; she just didn't want to leave her elderly father. The couple lived some 1,000 kilometers apart and saw each other twice a year. Huang came to Beijing from Shanghai, where she was teaching English when the unborn Daily was undergoing its final preparations in 1980. She passed interviews and tests to be hired despite no background in journalism—quite an honor. Her real interest, however, was not the paper as much as joining her husband, who was working in Beijing. I got the impression from such matter-of-fact accounts that spousal separations were commonplace in China. Evidence of stoic, unavoidable hardship—individuals subsumed by the State? Until recently, people hadn't had much choice about professions or locales.

One young Chinese reporter told me about her own living quarters, which the paper provided not far from the *Youyi*. She, her husband and infant daughter had a bedroom and living room to themselves. They shared the kitchen and bathroom with another three-person family. She took the China Daily van to work when she could. Because reporters' hours were irregular, she sometimes missed the van and had to bike half an hour to the office or travel by bus. The Chinese at the paper got no compensation for cabs. Her husband, an engineer, had a one-hour bike trip or took two buses and one subway to his job. Understandably, he wanted work closer to home.

Character also seemed to be molded by language. At one of our parties, Rachel Connelly, an economist from Bowdoin teaching at a Beijing graduate school, held forth on the subject.

"I have an eight-year-old son attending Chinese school," she said. "When I ask him about his homework, he says, 'I have three lines.' He means he has to copy three lines of Chinese characters. There's a great deal of memorization and neat handwriting required, and you have to be very quiet and orderly. I think the process contributes to learning science and math, but not the more creative aspects of literature and writing."

I asked a lot of people about the Chinese character. The Confucian ethic, training in politeness and respect for elders were cited. Struggle? It's a liberal myth that struggle always ennobles; sometimes it just erodes. When I asked our *waiban* Zhang Haiyan about stoicism, she couldn't quite put her finger on an explanation. "Something about the culture," she said.

Not surprisingly, our friend David Jenkins, the multi-degreed *Xinhua* polisher, had some deep thoughts on the subject. This essay he penned at my request may shed some light on the Chinese character:

#   #   #

DA JIA

As history teaches us, it is a dangerous practice to base broad generalizations about a people on isolated words and phrases plucked at random from the warp and woof of their language. The pitfalls are many and various; false etymologies are just so many toadstools. Ezra Pound made a hobby of retooling Chinese to suit his poetic sensibilities. The linguistic executive Benjamin Lee Whorf

193

based his dubious linguistic theories about covert and overt categories on some pretty shaky assumptions about Hopi word formation. And the Soviet linguist Marr industriously reduced the workings of language to the grist for Stalinist propaganda mills, decreeing guilt by word association to all those who didn't toe the Party line. During the Cultural Revolution in China, language became a few sayings in Mao's little red book, and people who played fast and loose with those words did so at their own peril.

Still, words have histories and associations, and the meanings of words and phrases are often rooted very deeply in a people's world view and sometimes suggest insights about the people who use them. They are just the tips of icebergs. Take the Chinese expression for the word " da jia." It is both word and expression, as a matter of morphological fact. The first of these two words, "da," means "big," "large." The second word by itself can mean "family" or the place where the family lives, their home. Put the two together, and what do you get? "Large family?" "Big house?" No, you get "everybody," as in "Is everybody here?"—"Da jia zai bu zai?" So a logical assumption is that the Chinese think of "everybody" as a large family. In English, we are likely to ask, "Is everyone here?" That standard English formulation obviously emphasizes the "one," the individual, and not the family.

To extend this speculation: the Chinese speak of a country as a "guo jia," where"guo" is country and "jia" again is family; the country is seen as a family (and incidentally, for the Chinese, China is the motherland, not the fatherland). Leaders are often referred to affectionately as "grandpa" or "uncle" or even "father," as in "Grandpa Mao." Americans talk of Washington as the father of the country, but parents don't teach their children to look up to "Grandpa Nixon" or "Uncle Lyndon" or "Papa Clinton." "Papa Hemingway" yes; "Papa Clinton," not hardly. American nicknames are as likely to dismiss their leaders as embrace them, as in "Tricky Dick." Or we think of presidents in terms of their policies: "Reaganomics." The Chinese certainly have their share of slogans," such as "the Four Olds," or "the Hundred Flowers Campaign," or "the Four Modernizations." The slogans may be short and simplistic, and they may be metaphorical and allusive. But when it comes time to refer directly to a leader, whether with words or pictures, they are seen as elders, respected family members, smiling in the midst of adoring young children. Of course, after Orwell we are suspicious of such unthinking admiration. We know that big brother is not our friend and provider. And Papa Stalin was a monster. But even after the excesses and failings of his regime have been admitted, the image of Grandpa Mao, Uncle Mao persists. He is laughing among school children (members of his extended family, each and every one.)

Let's consider two corollaries to this thesis. First, no matter how much one Chinese suffers at the hands of another, they remain in many ways, inescapably, members of the same large family, tied by the ties that bind. Facial features. Genetic heritage. Thousands upon thousands of years of history, tradition, belief. China the Middle Kingdom, the center of the civilized world. And at the center of the center, in the deep heart's core, the son of heaven, the emperor. It is fitting and proper that Mao founded the modern Chinese Communist state from the balustrade above the wall that separates the Forbidden City from Tiananmen Square. That's where the emperor used to walk. Mao was father to his people, the father of new China, but he also knew the symbolic importance of his role. He was also the new son of heaven, and he lives on, on the hundredth anniversary of his birth [1993]. Grotesquely, perhaps, his body may endure for ten thousand years in its marble mausoleum; wax-effigy father, preserved for the ages in formaldehyde, cyronic, still smiling. Ten-year-old children retrace his footsteps, from the forums at Yanan to the Long March. They are led by their teachers, their elder brothers and sisters, on summer excursions, winter excursions, fall excursions, spring excursions....Many of those same teachers suffered terribly during the Cultural Revolution days, but they are dutiful, and they are still part of the Da Jia. So they smile and tell stories about Grandpa Mao, balanced by stories about Xiao Ping. (Deng Xiaoping; '"Xiao" means little, perhaps Mao's little brother?) Little brother Deng, under house arrest during the Cultural Revolution...In this most familial of all possible worlds, even the neighborhood police officer becomes "Auntie Policewoman."

195

Corollary number two. All of those not part of the "da jia" are profoundly on the outside looking in, or potential invaders and usurpers, or as a matter of historical fact invaders and usurpers. As all space cadets know, the only human construction visible from the moon is the Great Wall, built to keep the Mongols out. During the Cultural Revolution, anything foreign was considered evil, and foreign was defined not only in terms of race and place, but in terms of time and tradition. The family was Mao's family. Even today, amidst all the trumpeting of China's new openness, xenophobia remains integral to China's world view. You are either a member of the inner circle, the large family, or you aren't. If you aren't, you are a "big nose," a "foreign devil," or simply a "waiguoren"—a person from a country on the outside. You will always be on the outside looking in.

#   #   #

Couldn't have said it better myself.

HERS: LEARNING TO SEE THROUGH CHINESE EYES

One advantage of living in another culture was that you saw things from a native's point of view. China consisted of more than Communist ideology. Its cultural traditions reached back a thousand-plus years to long before the advent of Communism. While intellectual fashion may dictate that culture *is* ideology, everyday life is not always a matter of intellect. Living in China helped take us past our assumptions about its politics.

As an American committed to democracy, I never dreamed I might celebrate the birthday of the Chinese Communist regime and enjoy it. But October 1, 1993, found me in Beijing observing National Day, the Chinese equivalent for July Fourth, along with millions of Beijingers.

China's National Day is celebrated like Fourth of July with bands, military parades, firecrackers. It comes in fall rather than summer, though, and that makes a difference. September and October are the most beautiful months in Beijing. The weather is temperate—60s and 70s—sunny, and not too windy. Parks like Beihai, Purple Bamboo, and Badachu fill. Beijingers savor fall the way they respect old age. National Day in July, when it's hot and rainy, would not be the same. Jim and I spent the afternoon in Purple Bamboo Park, people-watching and being stared at—and photographed, since park-strolling foreigners were an oddity. We stared back, watching middle-aged couples basking in the sun on park benches and children hopscotching across rocks in one of the lily ponds.

Certainly the holiday reflected underlying political tensions in China. The government has been leery of large gatherings since the Tiananmen tragedy in 1989—everyone in China considered it a tragedy—so on National Day a few subdued military exercises were the only formal commemoration. Plus a lot of extra flowers. Flowers in pots—especially roses and chrysanthemums—filled the city from the time we arrived in August until the frost came in November.

They were part of Beijing's enthusiastic but unsuccessful bid that year for the 2000 Olympics. They softened the urban drabness and added spots of color along boulevards, in front of public buildings and at entrances to parks like Purple Bamboo.

In 1993 National Day was a particularly big event because it coincided with the Mooncake Festival. The combination was especially Chinese, since the Mooncake Festival is one of the traditional holidays that predate Communism by hundreds if not thousands of years.

Also called the Mid-Autumn Festival, it began in the 16th century when a Qing emperor built a temple honoring the gods of the moon outside Beijing. *Qiufen*, the holiday chosen to pay tribute to these moon gods, comes on the fifteenth day of the eighth lunar month—the fall equinox. It's a family-oriented time when everyone gets mooncake confections from employers, friends and others and enjoys the fall weather.

For days before the event, we saw people carrying home tins of mooncakes tied on the racks of their bicycles. Newspapers were full of grumblings about the inflation-ridden prices for mooncakes that year—rising as high as several hundred dollars. Our mooncakes came in a big, brightly colored tin box from *Xinhua*. Filled with sweet potato and date paste, they were built to last, like Christmas fruitcakes. We traded stories with other Foreign Experts, like kids comparing loot on Halloween night, about what kinds of mooncakes—and how many—we got.

Tradition has it that mooncakes were instrumental in helping the Chinese peasants in revolt against a despotic emperor. A message giving the date for the uprising supposedly was baked into the cakes as a way to spread the word. Makes you wonder if that's how fortune cookies got their start. The confluence of National Day and the Mooncake Festival won't happen again until 2012.

For most Beijingers, the biggest part of the long weekend caused by National Day and the Mooncake Festival was the chance to take time off from work, but we Foreign Experts were treated to a special evening's entertainment. If ever an event was manufactured, it was the performance by the Central Folk Song and Dance Ensemble and the Chinese Acrobatic Troups. It did at least provide insights into how the Chinese think of themselves.

Planned by the State Bureau of Foreign Experts to honor the 44th anniversary of modern China's founding, our variety show still had one foot back in the dinosaur days before tv and other media took over. We were bused to the China Grand Theatre, a large "cultural palace," where the evening's entertainment was reminiscent of the old Ed Sullivan Show with singing, dancing and acrobatics. Instead of lockjawed Sullivan, though, an Asian glamour puss in slinky black velvet introduced the acts—for those foreign experts who understood—in Chinese.

The dancing was energetic, athletic and colorful, with an emphasis on ethnic costumes, including the Uygur and Miao numbers. No skimpy outfits peddled skin the way we're used to in the States, and the difference was notable. Female allure was still the main message, but sex wasn't the whole mix. Eroticism was not just female body parts the way it has become in the States. It had more to do with movement and physical coordination.

One double-jointed performer twisted her body into pretzel forms that were alternately fascinating and repulsive. Another performed a "Willow Dance" in shadow silhouette, waving her hands and wiggling her slender body with impressive control. It was hard to figure out how she managed to make her hands look so much like tree branches.

The acrobats were all children. One boy and girl balanced on rolling cylinders. A couple of others juggled each other with their feet. Still more balanced porcelain bowls on their heads and body parts. The end of each routine involved prancing around like mechanical dolls to elicit applause and create vaudeville-style transitions. The children were presented as prodigies—or miniature adults—not much different than the way Americans treat children on tv sitcoms.

The grand finale for the evening was a Tibetan dance called "Reiba on the Grassland." Featuring men and women dancers in Tibetan costume, it was an earnest nod toward a particularly Chinese form of multi-culturalism. Tibet is far from the only autonomous—

the word is a Chinese euphemism for ethnically distinct—region in China. To say that the Chinese are genuinely concerned about Tibet and other autonomous regions was not necessarily to support their policies of oppression there. We all dutifully applauded at this sugarcoated effort to idealize one of China's autonomous peoples.

Celebrating National Day, eating mooncakes and attending the variety show were all part of learning to see through Chinese eyes. We might not have agreed politically with the Chinese, but we could still appreciate a culture vastly different from our own.

3 2

HIS: POLITICS AND PEOPLE

I am not professing to give you the final word on China. As we painstakingly alerted you at the start of this venture, that should be left to China experts and correspondents. Don't begrudge me, though, a couple of viewpoints and some interesting observations made by friends.

First, this message. If there was one thing I was sure of when we landed in Beijing, it was that China had no business getting either the 2000 Olympics or renewal of its Most Favored Nation status. Within six weeks I had changed my mind on both subjects.

Like many Westerners, I originally resented the nerve of a country with China's human-rights record even applying for the world's most-watched event. My mind wasn't changed by China's leaders. The argument "we need law and order to feed 1.17 billion people" hardly justifies shooting dissidents in the back of the head or operating slave-labor camps filled with political prisoners. I reversed myself based on the arguments of Western visitors and ordinary citizens.

A Chinese woman who was no friend of the leadership put it this way. "There's a power struggle going on between hard-line Communists and reformers. Losing the Olympics could strengthen the hand of the hard-liners. Now they'll say, 'You see—we never could trust the West.'"

Two days before the Olympic vote, which went narrowly to Sydney, Australia, I approached an Australian woman at a bridge club. "You must be pulling hard for Sydney to get the Olympics," I said.

"On the contrary. It will be very good for human rights if China wins. Under the scrutiny they'd get, the leadership will have to improve its record."

Another Australian—a man who will rent his Sydney apartment for a small fortune in 2000—said the West was more than a little hypocritical in opposing China's bid. "If you're prepared to trade with China, it's a bit off to say, 'You can't have the Olympics because you've been naughty boys on human rights.' I didn't want Beijing the get the Olympics for the Communists, but for the people of China."

The more China is isolated, the worse its leaders behave. Just look at the Cultural Revolution. There was no turning back when television covered Deng Xiaoping's visit to the United States in 1979. When Chinese viewers saw America's vast wealth, they knew they had never had it so bad. Suddenly, they developed an irreversible craving for our soft drinks and blue jeans and cars. Economic reform became inevitable.

The Chinese were proud of having the world's fastest growing economy at the time we lived there and eager to show it off. But does economic pluralism create political pluralism? China is a schizoid society, a Western correspondent told me. It rushes madcap toward a "socialist market economy" even as it rounds up another herd of dissidents for show trials and possible execution.

Would landing the 2000 Olympics have changed that dichotomy? We'll never know. During the Olympic campaign, the Chinese made at least token gestures toward political reform: a prisoner released early, a greater willingness to allow criticism. A temporary lull to be sure, but the Chinese would certainly have had to deliver on their Olympian promise to reduce Beijing's pollution and increase its open space.

All over Beijing, a slogan enthusiastically if ungrammatically promoted..."A more open China awaits 2000 Olympics." An even more open China might well have have conducted them.

As for MFN, we had lunch with a senior diplomat who had longstanding ties to China. "You know what Most Favored Nation means?" he said. "That no other country will get better treatment, not that you have special treatment yourself. About 145 countries have MFN, including Yugoslavia and Iraq when I last checked.

"It's a big mistake to attach MFN to human rights, a non-market issue. In any case, human rights are something we achieved over hundreds of years with great effort. Now we want it done immediately, our way—the same old problem about imposing our values on other societies. So we put a June deadline on a country that has been around thousands of years. I'm not opposed to pushing human rights; you can bring them up many other ways, that's all."

My own feeling was that China would never make significant human-rights advances as long as the current crop of old men were in power. Might as well give them MFN, keep them associating with foreigners and hope for incremental improvements. Actually, the optimum scenario has little to do with democracy. By the time we arrived, the democracy movement was already in tatters. Americans got a different idea, because they were constantly hearing references to Tiananmen Square or quotes from expatriate Chinese who were there. If significant change is to occur, it will come from workers aroused over their conditions, not students waving the American flag.

The most conservative correspondent we met surprised me by saying that, for its first five years under Communism, China was ruled by "altruists." Whether or not one agrees, it's indisputable that the country began reforms that resulted in quadrupling the literacy rate from 20% to 80% (although most Chinese still know only 1,000 characters) and doubling the life expectancy from 35 to 71.

A friend who was in China in 1949 said that Mao was neither inaccessible nor out of touch in the early years. Soon afterward, however, he began secluding himself, issuing wrong-headed decrees and assuming total power. In the words of Lord Acton, "Power tends to corrupt, and absolute power corrupts absolutely."

The minister of health and other officials, active and retired, that I met were uniformly cordial in social situations. I labored to convince myself that I could tolerate political differences if they were honestly grounded in culture. My problem was that the leadership wasn't honest. Let the experts debate major issues; my insights came from direct experience with lesser figures and understanding of minor but meaningful issues. It confounded me that the cadres would dissemble about such matters as their bridge players being professionals and their athletes ingesting illegal substances. American politicians lie too, friends told me. One major difference: our leaders are held accountable.

Back at the lunch with the diplomat, we talked about communication in China. The embassy had no interest in film except as it pertained to political matters. They found tv more interesting, since it was harder for the Chinese to control tv programming even though they could pretape. Our friend gave an example of how the censors missed things on many fronts. An item appeared in a factory managers' newspaper calling for democratic reforms and was passed around, making quite a stir.

One effect of economic reform was that reactionaries in the government were farmed out to cultural affairs, so our embassy friend predicted a less open period for Chinese film. He felt that since people in general were less fearful—good guys and bad guys— the bad guys weren't afraid to commit crimes like abductions of women, kidnappings of children, train robberies.

We heard his perspective on what had happened at Tiananmen Square. He said there were no killings in the square itself. The army was not happy about being called in and sent unarmed soldiers first, without proper equipment. No face shields, no body shields, no water hoses for riot control. The soldiers weren't properly trained, and some were dragged out of their vehicles and killed. Because the army had no intermediate position, it followed up with automatic weapons, killing many. A Harvard study of the news coverage concluded that 50% of it was accurate. This embassy official thought that was a good rate.

I asked the diplomat to name the biggest change he had seen in China. "The openness. Twenty years ago people were afraid to speak their minds; now they do it all the time. I assembled a bunch of prominent Chinese women, some of whom didn't know each other, for a lunch with an American politician. One of the women said, 'We will get more freedom, but it will be a long, hard struggle.' She didn't care who was listening."

During the lunch break in the tour we took with Brooks's journalism students of *Xinhua*, the national news agency—fully three hours from 11:15 a.m. to our next obligation at 2:15 p.m.—we headed down to the cafeteria. We needed a lot of help in getting meal tickets, figuring how much they were for, and ordering food in the helter-skelter tray line. After gulping down some surprisingly tasty chicken cutlets with bean sprouts, cucumber salad and beer, we sat down in a dark lounge and spoke with some of Brooks's students. Actually we interviewed them too, because this was nothing if not an opportunity to learn facts free from government censorship.

I asked a youth to tell me about his background. "I was born in 1966," he said. "My name is Wen Ge. It means Cultural Revolution."

That practice of ideologically correct names was not uncommon, said Haiyan, who was seated nearby. Depending on their birthdates, other kids had been named Jiefang (liberation), Yuan Chao (support the North Koreans) or He Ping (peace). "In America," Brooks responded, "people name their kids according to what soap opera star is popular."

I asked the students about changes in the economy and recent Chinese history. Ten years earlier people got food on ration cards controlled by the government: some 70% for rice or flour and 30% for corn flour, corn and sorghum. You might get one quarter of a kilo for cooking oil and half a kilo for meat. Per month. No wonder most Chinese were running out of steam at 11:30 a.m. every day. To move was to risk losing those coupons and any little thing that came with them.

The workplace was every bit as dreary. China's "Iron Rice Bowl"—a cradle-to-grave security/control system that laid out your life for you, no questions asked, while sapping incentive, the will to work, social mobility and creativity—left little to the imagination or the inspiration. In the early 1980s Deng Xiaoping returned the land to the peasants, who had to give some of their earnings to the government but got to keep the rest. As a result, production soared. Fruits and vegetables were suddenly available in vast quantities.

Privatization begun in the mid-Eighties and the transition to the "socialist market economy" was in full swing by 1992. The *danwei*, or work unit, system declined. People felt they could make more money privately. In the two years preceding our visit, the

205

number of private companies had doubled and foreign investment tripled.

The change wasn't problem-free. When Beijing gave money to local banks to pass on to the peasants, some bankers handed out IOUs while investing the money in real estate. There was little regulation: you got the impression anyone with a two-seater biplane could proclaim himself an airline. In short, corruption was rampant. What a great opportunity for business.

On the way home from a trip to the Ming Tombs, we visited a farmers' village and met a couple who lived in a two-room house: concrete floors, sleeping mats laid out over a *kang*, or raised concrete platform, pinups on the wall (a sign of how much things have changed, to be sure). "Farmers village" was actually a misnomer because the land was not fertile enough. At the time China had 22% of the world's population and 6% of its arable land: so much for "The Good Earth." No, this was an industrial park, more or less. The industries included a mineral-water factory and a trinkets plant. The couple made about 3,000 RMB a year and collected another 200 from us for an old scale and a jade piece that we bought. The old fellow said he liked the market economy because farmers and factory workers were getting bonuses. At 63, he was retired but kept busy patrolling the nearby mountain as a security guard to keep people from smoking and starting fires in the dry season.

On another occasion we had dinner at our favorite Italian restaurant in the Palace Hotel, with Marilyn Goldstein of our Fulbright class, a Chinese student, Fulbrighter Bob Slagter and his *waiban*. I made a point of sitting with the Chinese women. I introduced the student to Italian food, recommending lasagna. It was sort of like teaching someone someone chess or "Prufrock." They should be grateful for life.

"There's an old Chinese saying," said Bob's *waiban*. "If you see two young people eating many dishes, they've just started going out. The man is trying to impress the woman with his generosity. If you see two young people eating just a few dishes, they've been together a long time. The woman has ordered, and she's trying to save money."

Marilyn's student's father, an editor, was imprisoned 10 months during the Cultural Revolution. Seemed he made two terrible mistakes. First, he sided with a man who was fighting his wife's divorce proceedings. She went to the authorities with wild accusations, and both the student's father and his male friend got pulled in. Second, he wrote a poem about a bridge that had been built over a river in his south China province. The bridge would "join the two sides together," he penned innocently enough. When the authorities interpreted that as a plea for reconciliation with Taiwan, he was denounced as a counter-revolutionary and jailed.

Marilyn's student was troubled by some aspects of the new market economy. Education used to be truly public, i.e., paid for by the State. Now students had to pay for incidentals. There were nine years of compulsory education, but in a lot of poor rural areas it was compulsory in name only because most people couldn't afford to educate their children. A charity called the Hope Project was raising money to guarantee every child an education—20 RMB would finance a kid for a year—but Marilyn's student was disturbed that the government's priorities were tilted so heavily toward the Olympic project that charity had become necessary. Meanwhile, teachers were still underpaid. They used to do tutoring after class for free. Now they were charging. The student emphasized that the move to a free-market economy was still transitional.

A foreign journalist we knew wasn't ecstatic about the socialist market economy's effect on greed and academic standards. In one economic zone in 1992, he said, not a single kid advanced from primary to middle school. They were more interested in turning a profit moving produce. A big problem in China, he went on, was its failure to allow gradual change. Someone started to inch across the street. Someone joined him. Suddenly, there was a huge crowd crossing the street—and a reaction. Jail them or shoot them? The authorities typically overreacted. Beijing was working pretty well because the Party has told people, "Get on with it," he said. The rural areas were not working so well, because the local bosses, pretty much autonomous, were kicking people around—sometimes literally by whipping them with electric cattle prods.

Rachel Connelly, the economics professor on leave from Bowdoin to teach in China, had some further thoughts on the subject. People were unquestionably better off, she said. A few years earlier, when the Connellys first arrived in China, there was just about no food available. Cabbage was stale, because there was no place to freeze it. Now you could buy everything. With restraints off, the towns around Beijing were pouring produce into the capital city and making out like legal bandits.

Here's the "but." Echoing the *Xinhua* students, Rachel said that the Chinese were actually trying to practice unfettered capitalism more than a socialist market economy. They didn't realize that even the most capitalistic country in the world had child labor laws and a minimum wage, with a little common sense sprinkled in. The Party apparently thought reform meant supply-and-demand, sink-or-swim social Darwinism across the board, same as the 19th-century robber barons felt. The cadres were even demanding that universities make a profit. Never mind that we Americans have schools with hundreds of years' worth of endowments. Never mind that we don't expect our philosophy departments to finish in the black.

The result was an amazing situation in which universities had sideline industries—say, a shoe factory—to help them break even. As a result, the emphasis shifted to how the shoe factory was doing, not whether the students were being educated and the professors properly trained and promoted.

Before cabbing to the airport to pick up my son Matthew, who was visiting during Christmas break at Stanford's graduate school of engineering, we headed to an open house at the apartment of our friend, China Daily polisher Hal Lipper. We met a nice Chinese-American couple from L.A. Sherman left the mainland in 1986. Betty left Taiwan about the same time, and they met at school in the States. Brooks asked Sherman what difference he noticed in China since returning. He said people are not wedded to the "idea," which I took to mean a combination of the party and nation-building. Now they wanted to make money.

We found some similar themes elsewhere in the country. In Shanghai, which means "above sea"—several meters above the water, actually—our guide Tony took us to the Peace Hotel to hear the famous Old Jazz Band, a six-piece orchestra of septuagenarians. They played a wide-ranging variety of tunes, including some jazzed-up Christmas carols. "Why don't you ask for a song?" Tony said. "We wrote down "In the Mood" and "St. Louis Blues." Tony took the requests to the bandstand. He returned ashen. "It costs 30 FEC per tune," he said. "This is terrible. Shanghai has changed."

One afternoon I travelled over to the Sheraton Great Wall Hotel and had lunch with a physical-education professor known to one and all as Sunny, a short, athletic woman in her early 50's with glasses, an unmarked face (no surprise in China) and a ready smile (no surprise at all given her name). We shadowboxed about where to eat and settled on a Cantonese restaurant on the second floor of the hotel. When I saw the white tablecloths and the hovering waiters, I had a vision about Maxim's de Paris. *Deja vu* all over again, as Yogi Berra is supposed to have said.

Sure enough, the prices were astronomical and they added on a 15% tip. We had a fish described to me as "pomfret" and a vegetable dish consisting of baby corn, mushrooms and something else. I was lucky to escape with a $30 bill.

When the first dish arrived, Sunny tapped on the table twice with the middle and index fingers of her hand. "There's a story about this," she said. "An emperor during the last dynasty decided to go about the country unnoticed. He served his assistants food. Since they couldn't kowtow to him, they showed they liked the service by tapping on the table."

The conversation—two hours of it—made the afternoon worthwhile. Sunny came from heavy-duty academic/intellectual stock. I lost track of the doctors, chemical engineers and sculptors in her family. Sunny knew her strengths early on. "People told me I could use 10% of my brain in science and get 100% results, 50% in social sciences and get 50% results, and 100% in athletics to get 10%. I love physics!" Naturally she was forced to play softball for the regional team and study physical education at the university level.

This was all before the Cultural Revolution. I asked her how she fared during those 10 years. "Fine," she said. "My students liked me. Other teachers didn't fare so well. "They were no better or worse than I was—their students just didn't like them."

A lot of self-criticism? She nodded.

Sunny's career path was carved in stone. Physical education was taught for the first three years of college. It seemed to vary between subjects like martial arts and basketball and covered a great gamut of skills. Sunny herself was a big tai chi fan and tried to sell me on its virtues. She said if you felt tired it was possible to spend no more than five minutes on the discipline, standing up straight. You had to work toward longer, bent-legged sessions. "We Chinese have a saying," she said. "The stronger your legs are, the longer you will live."

Happily, science's loss was sport's gain. A dozen or so years ago Sunny figured she was using about 10% of her brain and taught herself English from books, tapes and the Voice of America. The combination of her bilingual skills and sports orientation made her a natural translator at various international sporting events. She became friends with Amherst College baseball coach Bill Thurston when his team visited China.

A young woman assistant at a Shanghai movie studio had a more wrenching story to tell. Premium apartment space in Shanghai being as costly and scarce as it was, she commuted two hours by bus each way. She had a degree in nuclear physics; naturally she was ordered to the studio because she spoke English. She really wanted to teach kindergarten.

On our creep through traffic to the next destination, I asked Tony why so few Chinese women were seen smoking. "Well," he said, drawing a long lung-scorcher out of his own noxious weed, "for a lady to smoke on the street, people must think she's very loose." The idea that, maybe, you know, no one should smoke was absolutely unthinkable. The huge government tax on cigarettes might have been a wee bit of a factor.

Back in Beijing, we had Brooks's students over for a pizza party. I took a *miandi* with one student to pick up the pizza. He said he lived in a unheated room with three other students in the school's only dorm. (men and women slept on separate floors). *Xinhua* hired the best students after graduation; the only way to go to work elsewhere was if your company paid Xinhua 20,000 RMB.

At American parties we eat, drink and talk. Chinese party goers played games and danced. This being an American party, the Chinese students compromised by talking, watching TV (there was none in the dorm) and playing a game on Brooks's computer.

These young people were interesting, interested, high-spirited, funny, charming and other good things generally. The women seemed especially concerned with how they were going to manage both a career and a home. We tried to tell them that men and women could share responsibility and, besides, women could always put off marrying. Which only brought up the popular Chinese stereotype that a woman who doesn't marry by age 30 will never marry.

China is very image-conscious. When fellow Fulbrighter Marilyn Goldstein was in Hangzhou, her car got caught in a huge traffic jam because two trucks tried to cross a narrow bridge in opposite directions and caught bumpers. She jumped out and started taking pictures. A policeman came rushing up to Marilyn's guide. "How dare you let her take pictures!" he shouted. "People will see the traffic jam and think bad thoughts about China!"

One night we had dinner with my old friend Jeff Koplan, a doctor and official then at the Centers for Disease Control and Prevention, along with his son Adam and a friend of Adam's. They were in town on a work/vacation tour of China.

Before dinner at the Beijing Grand Hotel, I had a drink with Jeff and a Taiwan-born colleague named Ray. According to Ray, the much-ballyhooed low statistics on infant mortality and other medical factors could be misleading. "If a child dies at birth, they may not report it," he said. Similarly, what constituted starvation and homelessness were equally misleading. "Some of the homes simply can't withstand the cold. There are seasons where there just isn't enough food in some areas."

For his part, Jeff added his own uncertainty about the socialist market economy. "There used to be a kind of social-services net: people taking care of people," he said. "Now it's just a matter of economics. When we visited an area, the 'barefoot doctor,' who is now called the village doctor, would only consult with us if we paid him. We almost had to pay him to enter the room and again to leave it. It may reach the point in China where services are available only to those who can afford them. The profit motive can be especially dangerous in areas of public security. If the police could make money by holding you up..."

Are there any conclusions I can make from these disparate experiences? Let me put it to you thusly. A month before our trip to China, I felt I knew a lot about the place. After all, we'd been briefed, we'd taken Chinese lessons, and we'd read books galore. A month after our arrival, I felt I really knew China. I mean, now we were living there. The day we departed I turned to Brooks. "You know," I said, "I'm just starting to get a bead on this place."

Therefore, I leave the summation to the redoubtable Marilyn Goldstein. "Poor China. They're committed to Confucianism, Communism and capitalism at the same time."

## 33

HERS: FRIENDS FAR FROM HOME

China was a country where it was hard to make friends with natives. The language created a close to insurmountable barrier, along with the natural reticence of the Chinese toward *waiguoren.* Family and friends seemed far away not just because of the geographic and cultural distance between Beijing and the U.S. The 13-hour time difference meant our day was still the night before for them. Phone connections were erratic and expensive, regular mail was slow and e-mail was still inaccessible. Our first friendships blossomed quite naturally among the other Fulbrighters, who were undergoing many of the same experiences we were having.

When we traveled, we often were accompanied by our colleagues, and the trips deepened our friendships. Bob Slagter was a political scientist from Birmingham-Southern College in Alabama, teaching at the Foreign Policy Institute in Beijing. A Vietnam veteran, he was a stocky man of medium height who walked with a sailor's roll and had thick, curly brown hair and a graying beard. Like a true academic, Bob loved to hold forth on the subjects that interested him—Chinese history, world politics, the ins and outs of academic life.

He hid his keen intelligence behind a deceptively who-gives-a-damn, good-ole-Southern boy affability. In addition to having served in Vietnam, he visited friends in Thailand regularly and clearly enjoyed life in the Far East. A conscientious objector, Bob had fulfilled his military service as a medic. He told us, however, he had started carrying a gun while in Vietnam. Of course we wanted to know why. He reluctantly explained that he needed it for protection after stopping American soldiers from raping Vietnamese women brought in for medical treatment.

Eldon Elder, a set designer with impressive and lengthy theatre credentials who called Manhattan home, was teaching in Beijing at the Academy of Dramatic Arts. Between his idiosyncratic outlook on life and an acerbic wit, he often had us in stitches. I remember one topsy-turvy exchange we had in Xian while looking at three-legged urns in a museum display case.

"She looks like a fat lady, doesn't she?" Eldon said, referring to one large urn.

"Why a fat lady?" I asked, puzzled.

"Oh, of course she does," he insisted.

"I suppose you mean those are hips?" I asked, referring to the sides of the urn.

"She looks like a fat lady, and I wonder when she is going to sing," Eldon pronounced, before moving on to the next case of artifacts.

Eldon served as our arbiter of taste. After I raved about a theatrical performance of "The Joy Luck Club," he quietly explained that the production was lacking in imagination, both because of hastily done set design and undramatic staging.

Marilyn Goldstein, a pre-Columbian specialist teaching art history at Nankai University in Tianjin, served as honorary Jewish mother to us all. Her natural warmth and enthusiasm smoothed out whatever frictions developed among us and belied her recent loss of husband and son.

People and adventure gravitated to Marilyn. After we spent Christmas together in Shanghai, she continued on to Hangzhou, where she had been invited to lecture. She described how her hosts had taken her for a picnic in the park, getting her up early in the morning to watch Peking Opera on the grass. Everyone had to stand, but Marilyn's hosts dragged a park bench over especially for her.

She was eager to follow the old Silk Route through northwest China, and a group of historians visiting Nankai University were scheduled to go. Marilyn requested permission to accompany them, but University officials wouldn't let her miss classes. When they relented at the last minute, she scrambled to catch up with the group, traveling by plane, train, truck and mule. The cave paintings she saw outside Urumqi made every bit of the uncomfortable journey worth it, she said.

In Shanghai at the end of a long, intimate talk about family, work and life, I said to Marilyn, "I wish I had time to write about it

214

all."

"You will," she said. "Life is longer than you expect."

We also developed friendships among the other foreigners living with us at the Friendship Hotel. Although some of them seemed like misfits or refugees from their native country, they always had interesting stories. And some were exceptional people. When my colleague John Morgan found out Jim was a bridge player, he introduced us to an American polisher for *Xinhua*, who lived in his building. We became fast friends with David Jenkins and his stylish Bulgarian wife Cecilia.

David's restless, brilliant and scholarly mind was a wonder to behold, but he could hardly be confined to the stereotype of an academic. An avid tennis and darts player and an amateur musician, he was on his second stay in China, and he was much happier about it than Cecilia. In an effort to mollify her, David brought home a parakeet named Mimi. After talking to it regularly, Cecilia concluded that the poor frightened bird spoke only Chinese. To help Mimi feel more at home, she arranged visits with another parakeet. Next David bought Cecilia two baby rabbits. They grew rapidly, noisily chewing on large quantities of Chinese cabbage in the kitchen and threatening to reproduce there.

Cecilia was not Cecilia's real name. The Bulgarian version sounded more like the tsetse in tsetse fly, according to David. Cecilia had met and married David in Bulgaria, while he was teaching there on a Fulbright. After a first marriage to a rock musician with a peripatetic lifestyle, Cecilia had settled comfortably into life with David in the U.S. China did not suit her. Through Cecilia, however, we got to know members of the Bulgarian community in Beijing and even learned a little about the influence of the Turkish-Ottoman Empire on the Balkans. Cecilia's Bulgarian friends included Kalil, a young hotel manager; his mother Radka, who worked as a polisher for Radio Beijing, and Ivoil, the first Bulgarian to receive a Ph.D. in China. His degree was in Condensed Matter Physics from the Institute of Semiconductors of the Chinese Academy of Sciences.

One Friday night when Cecilia was at an interview for a joint-venture job with l'Oréal Cosmetics, David, Jim and I went up

215

Baishiqiao Lu to Pizza Hut for dinner. In an almost non-stop rush of words, David condensed his life story into a little over an hour while we ate our pizza.

His father, a Mormon, had owned a drapery business in Salt Lake City, and cancer claimed David's Jewish mother when he was 14. About the same time, his father lost the drapery business and went on the road as a salesman. David acquired several new stepmothers in rapid succession, one of whom was not much older than he.

If not for his talent as a golfer, David might never have gone to college. He started playing competitively in high school and was followed around at one match by a recruiter for the University of Utah. David told us it was the only time in his career as a golfer that he shot two eagles in the same round. The recruiter offered him a scholarship on the spot.

At Utah David ardently pursued a sports career—playing golf in good weather and skiing in winter—and still managed to be Phi Beta Kappa. When it was time to pick a major, he looked over what he'd taken and found he had the most courses in Russian Studies. It made sense. As a child he had been captivated by the sound of spoken Russian.

"We don't control our destinies," he said. Accordingly, he passed a bulletin board advertising a Junior Year Abroad program in Germany. Off he went and ended up living with another man and a six-foot redheaded named Margaret, with whom he fell madly in love.

Returning to the U.S., he arranged to meet Margaret at the airport in New York. In a scene worthy of "Sleepless in Seattle," they missed connections, and David ended up staying with a French woman he had met on the flight back. That ended the relationship with Margaret, who went on to make millions in real estate.

Life at the University of Utah wasn't quite the same after Germany, and David's golf game wasn't as sharp as it had been either. Nevertheless he got his undergraduate degree and continued in a master's program. A vacation to New York during semester break turned into a permanent stay. Settling in Brooklyn, David joined a Born-Again Christian religious group that his sister and her husband belonged to. He was accepted into an MFA program at Columbia University, wrote poetry every day, and turned over his paycheck from working in the school library to the religious sect.

After he tired of subsidizing the drug addicts and homeless people sheltered by the religious collective, David resigned from active Born-Again Christendom. He also stopped writing because it had begun to seem vain and selfish to him. Instead he went back to school, this time enrolling in a doctoral program in Comparative Literature at the University of Texas in Austin. He taught for a year in northern China, then in Bulgaria, where he met Cecilia.

After finishing his Ph.D. at Texas, David took a job with Nova University in Fort Lauderdale, Florida. When his contract wasn't renewed, he returned to the University of Texas to write several textbooks, and Cecilia started a business there. After a winter in upstate New York living with his sister and her family, he had found his way back to China.

Jim's friendship with retired French diplomat Gilles de Villepoix led to a series of memorable social events during our stay in China. Every weekend, Gilles and his wife Catherine, a French oil executive based in Beijing, hosted elegant dinner and bridge parties for their friends. Their huge apartment was filled with Chinese art—scroll paintings of opera masks, an antique wedding basket, blue porcelain, vintage 1930s posters of Chinese beauties—and countless frogs. Their 10-year-old son had his own wing, complete with a playroom filled with plastic knights and warriors arranged in encampments across the floor.

There were as many as 20 people at five tables of bridge—French, Pakistani, Chinese, Taiwanese and Dutch among other nationalities. A sumptuous Western dinner with wine was served first. Then we got down to the business of duplicate bridge. Catherine, who had lived in China since 1975, was the quintessential French hostess, dressed in blue jeans, chain smoking and talking in a husky, Edith Piaff voice. Almost everyone there except us smoked, and I finally had to ask if I could open a window. Eventually I even stuck my head out of it.

Esther Sampson and her husband Lance lived in the Friendship Hotel near David and Cecilia. We went to a party at their apartment to see a movie featuring the British rock group Pink Floyd because Esther's daughter was about to marry a member of the band. Half Chinese and half English, Esther was probably the most fascinating person we met in China. With features that were a strikingly beautiful mix of East and West, she carried herself with regal bearing.

Her parents had met at the British hotel where her Mandarin Chinese father was living while he studied at the London School of Economics. Her Jewish mother was a chambermaid in the hotel. After they married, Esther's parents settled in Shanghai, where she and her siblings were born. When she was 11, the couple separated, and Esther returned to England. Her mother was unable to hold the family together in London, so Esther went to a foster home until her teenage years. Then she rejoined her mother, who was running a rooming house. A Chinese boarder helped Esther track down her now-wealthy father, and he began sending the family monthly checks from Shanghai.

At 17 Esther met and married a dashing Chinese captain who served as one of General Claire Chennault's Flying Tigers and was working at the Chinese Embassy in London. When her new husband was recalled to China by the Nationalist government, the couple got as far as Hong Kong. Esther, whose sympathies stood firmly with the Communists, walked out. In her memoir "Black Country to Red China," she describes how she had to spend that first night on her own in a whorehouse hotel, fending off an American sailor's advances, before stowing aboard a cargo boat headed for north China.

Arriving in Tianjin, Esther joined the Red Army. After many adventures and sorrows, she went to work for the newly formed Radio Peking, helping set up their English-language broadcasting program. She described working to build a reservoir near the Ming Tombs outside Beijing. It was hard to imagine the fierce idealism that spurred Chinese cadres used to office work to do their stint of several weeks' digging.

A Czechoslovakian colleague at the radio station caught Esther's fancy, and they planned to marry. The Chinese government, however, asked the Czech Embassy to forbid him to see her. Its report labeled her the daughter of an American spy and the ex-wife of a Kuomintang airman. In other words, a contemptible revisionist. Disillusioned, Esther returned to England and met her current husband Lance, a newspaper executive. The 1989 riots in Tiananmen Square inspired her to return to China temporarily. Then after Lance retired, they came back again together. Lance had run a string of newspapers in England and was working as a polisher at Xinhua, while Esther did consulting.

Whenever we got together with the Sampsons, the conversation revolved around words. One evening we traced the origins of subliminal slurs like Indian giver and Dutch treat. Our last night in China was spent having dinner with them, and we bequeathed them our dictionary of American slang.

VIII

COMING HOME

"In the end, travel's joys aren't large treasures but small pleasures: an unforgettable scrap of conversation, an unexpected visual treat, an insight or two."

34

HIS: I COULD HAVE KISSED THE GROUND

Anyone can spend five months in a foreign country and emerge changed, enlightened, matured. The trick is to spend five months in a foreign country and get absolutely nothing out of it. I am sorry to say that I did not entirely succeed in this objective.

On the day of our departure, the van arrived 15 minutes late. Poor Haiyan, who had shown up earlier to begin shepherding us through our final stages, pleaded with me not to worry. Are you kidding? I freaked out. Every fear I had of of wiretaps and listening devices overwhelmed me. We were plainly going to be "detained," which of course meant imprisoned and tortured. Until the moment we boarded the plane, I growled and raged. I never even bothered to thank Haiyan for her yeowoman service.

When we were seated on the flight to Hong Kong, I turned to Brooks and said, "No more third-world countries."

Nice guy, eh? If you insist on some analogy, I was like a caricature from "The Ugly American."

Once home, Brooks and I co-authored a magazine piece about our trip, Brooks taking the high road, I taking the trenches. "Is Jim Kaplan really like that?" people asked my friend John Bowman.

"No, no, that's just a comic persona," John said. "He actually loved it over there." John Bowman is a very good friend.

Cut me some slack, though. *You'd* turn sour if you were deprived of a language you could speak, a comfortable bed and "The Simpsons."

I was messed up indeed. One night soon after our return from China Brooks was asleep when I descended to the basement on some forgotten task. Heading back to the first floor, I discovered that I had locked myself out.

Panic! I pounded the door and yelled for Brooks. No dice: she slept like the dead. I wandered back down to the cellar and surveyed the evening ahead. Fortunately, our cellar is more like a second first floor; it comes complete with a phone, a desk, two couches, a wet bar and our cat. It also comes *un*equipped with a bathroom. I looked at the sink.

Thank heaven for Typical American Ingenuity. Swiftly, I called information for the police, then explained my problem to an amused desk sergeant. "You see, officer, it's like this. I went down to the basement and found the door locked from the outside when I came up. I couldn't wake my wife. So here's what I'd like you to do. Call my number. I won't pick up. When my wife answers, you can explain my problem to her."

The phone rang four times, and the answering machine turned on. The message: "Mrs. Kaplan, this is the Northampton Police Department. Your husband is locked in the basement. Could you please go downstairs and let him in?" That finally awakened Sister Sleep.

I blame it all on China.

That's not all. Because we couldn't get CNN or ESPN on our *Youyi* tv and the International Herald Tribune's news was always a day late, I stopped following baseball. In fact, I was sitting at a tennis tournament in Beijing when someone told me, "You know the Jays won it, don't you?" I didn't.

Now, I discover, I've almost completely lost interest in following sports—no small setback for a lifetime sportswriter. Not even my four-ply attack on bridge (reading, writing, teaching, playing) has filled the void.

O.K., the experience wasn't all bad. In addition to keeping those 10 pounds off, I've found to my amazement that I haven't finished a single caffeinated soft drink since returning. No Coke, no Pepsi. I sometimes even get the requisite five fruits and vegetables a day. All of which makes me healthy, which makes me sick.

Like many Americans abroad, I became fanatically patriotic. Now my plans for travel consist of visiting the nine states I haven't seen—Alabama, Mississippi, New Mexico, Colorado, South Dakota, Montana, Idaho, Oregon and Alaska, in case you're interested. That should supply my travel needs for the next five years. I also fell in love with that distant childhood treat, mashed potatoes, thanks to *Youyi* cooking.

We actually appreciated aspects of Chinese culture like respect for elders, especially since we've both turned 50. We loved the simple life: Ayi preparing our dinner, the International Herald Tribune supplying our daily (non-sports) news fix, even the fewer choices available. In fact, the only daily uncertainty was what time I would start yelling at my cab driver. All in all, a pretty basic life. There's a lot to be said for tyranny.

As a result, we decided to simplify our lives back home. We sold the apartment we owned in New York City. We purchased bicycles—not only sturdy hybrids but a stationary bike. You find me an easier way to get a workout on a cold winter's day. I've also found—at least in part from my China Daily experience—that the best way to beat the blues is to stay busy.

You can only simplify so much, though. Because we no longer get the Herald Tribune, we're once again swamped by media. Brooks still insists on taking fool trips to third-world countries. Our latest jaunt was to Peru, where we enjoyed every possible form of traveler's sickness along with Machu Picchu.

I certainly see my own land with dramatically different eyes. The one thing foreigners can't understand about America is the number of guns on the street combined with the prominence of violent crime. After reading reports from afar about the Long Island Railroad massacre and other daily fare, I now keep the doors locked day and night as I always should have. I no longer beep at other drivers unless we're about to collide, because I know they will pull out a gun, a hatchet or a crossbow and kill me. Instead, I've created a cardboard sign with one word on it. That word is "Sorry."

I've been changed by Deng Xiaoping's simple words to justify capitalism in a Communist country: "Learn truth from facts, not ideology."

Without too much pomposity, I think I can safely say that we need that philosophy in America. Why, just the other night I was reminded of the phrase while watching "Northern Exposure." The scene: Maggie has been elected mayor and convened her first meeting of the city council. The issue: should Cicely, Alaska, acquire a dumpster to spare its garbage-hauling citizens the 6.2-mile trip to

225

an out-of-town site? No! say the council's three free enterprisers. The city action would constitute big government: a veritable welfare state. Yes! say Maggie and the Canadian-born councilor. The government can act in the interests of the people.

An ideological argument over a dumpster: what perfect satire! What an uncanny description of public life in America: platitudes and banalities wrapped around the flag, facts dumped for slogans.

"Learn truth from facts, not ideology!" I yelled at the tv. Alone among all Americans, I put the great phrase to use.

So the Middle Kingdom left me confused, scared, healthy, clear-thinking. Maybe China wasn't all bad.

## 35

HERS: NOTES FROM A BEIJING JOURNAL

How did living in China for five months change me? It isn't easy to get beyond the obvious clichés. Change me it did. I suspect it had to do with the pull of opposites. I also think it had to do with the daily struggle that, as a person whose work is tied up with words, I had communicating in a place where the language, as well as the culture, was so dramatically different. Living in China was humbling... inspiring... exciting... frustrating... challenging... complex. These excerpts from the journal and letters I wrote while I was there may help convey some final sense of my feelings about China.

#   #   #

Culture shock, it seems, comes in waves. We're over the first hump. I know where I am when I go out the back entrance to the Friendship Hotel. I can conduct simple financial transactions at the local shops and stalls without feeling totally ripped off.

The next level of culture shock has more to do with the creeping frustration at still not being able to communicate properly. It's exhausting. Now that the initial strangeness of being here has worn off, I keep expecting myself to operate at some normal level of efficiency, whatever that is. Wrong. Since the novelty of where you are has worn off, the difficulty of translating your still-strange world into familiar terms weighs on you.

#   #   #

It's 6 a.m., and I can hear street noises. People riding by on their bicycles. Conversation bits that could be in any language—taps, squeaks, rattles and clatters that come out of the common vocabulary of human activity. It's early enough that these sounds still compete with the crickets. There is no wind, and except for smog on the horizon, the sky is clear. Last night Jim and I ate an Italian dinner in a Western restaurant. That was a different kind of longing.

#   #   #

Ayi fixed us a delicious stir-fry of slivered potato, onion and carrot; pork and cucumber; rice. We walked up to the coffee shop in

Building #1 for dessert and lemon tea with one of the foreign experts teaching English. The pianist who plays a mix of classical and cocktail music there was joined by a violinist. Our neighbor wandered by with her little boy, who delighted in splashing his hand in the fountain.

\# \# \#

A brief shower last night seems to have cleared the air, because the sky is exceptionally blue. It almost never rains in Beijing outside of the rainy season. We bicycled to the Summer Palace today. It was less than an hour's trip from the Friendship Hotel and strenuous only in that we didn't know exactly where we were going.

\# \# \#

One of the adjustments I'm still making is to life in a big city. The outdoors are so much a part of my life in Northampton, and that's had to change here. What's interesting about it is that I now suspect a good deal of what I appreciate about living in Northampton is the opportunity to slow down the hyper-real pace of life in the U.S. Even if Beijing is a big city, the pace here is slower.

I guess I expected a slower pace to be boring, but it isn't. It's just different, and I find myself experiencing the difference in unexpected ways. For instance, I don't feel I have to entertain my students quite so frenetically. Even when I'm in the classroom five hours straight, I don't experience the kind of burnout I would in the U.S.

\# \# \#

I bicycled to Zhang Haiyan's nearby apartment for a horseback-riding excursion on Saturday. The tire on my bike was flat, though, so first I had to get it fixed. There are bicycle repair shops on every other corner in Beijing. The one I went to said I needed a new tire, but I didn't have time or enough money with me, so we settled for a new inner tube.

After a long, pleasant afternoon on horseback, it was almost dark by the time the bus dropped us off near Haiyan's apartment. I hurried off on my bike as fast as possible. That wasn't very fast since my tire was just about flat again. It was soon clear I wouldn't make it all the way home. Not only that; it grew pitch black, and I was totally lost. I saw a woman and child inspecting their own bike and stopped, asking in my pidgin Chinese if they knew where I might find some air. They quickly produced a pump, sending me on my way with a newly inflated tire and directions on how to get home. In 500 meters the tire was flat again.

What do you do in Beijing when it's dark, you're lost, you don't speak the language and you're pushing a nonfunctional bike? Hail a taxi. I flagged down two before I found one willing to take me with my bike. Miracle of miracles, we were already on Baishiqiao Lu, the boulevard where the Friendship Hotel is located. If I'd just kept walking, I could have gotten home by myself.

#   #   #

We moved into what I've determined is the second phase of Culture Shock. That's when the initial glamor and excitement have worn off, giving you a false sense of confidence. Your eye may not be as sharp for detail in the same way as when you first arrived, but your insights may be more substantial. When I started writing, I thought, ho hum, what can I say about what we've done this week that's interesting. Not much. I'd already forgotten a lot of what we did or else discounted it as routine.

#   #   #

We woke up to snow yesterday, which is unusual for Beijing. How is anyone to ride a bicycle? Bitter cold today. The roads have congealed into ice. Nothing is sanded. Walking, let alone driving, is hazardous. Inconceivably, people still pass by on their bicycles.

#   #   #

Our Fulbright friend Marilyn Goldstein told us a harrowing story about her trip to Xian. As a visiting art historian, she had been invited to view some of the archaeological sites that were not open to tourists. After she arrived, her hosts called to say they were delayed by car trouble. After a while, they picked her up in a borrowed vehicle and took her to visit a tomb site. As they were getting ready to leave, and Marilyn and one of the archaeologists were standing by the car, the brakes failed. The car rolled over the side of an embankment. Good thing they weren't in it. While the hosts went to

229

get help, they left Marilyn standing alone in the dark in the middle of nowhere. After nearly an hour, they returned with a three-wheeled vehicle to cart her home.

When it was time to deliver her to the airport, her hosts found yet a third car. It was raining, and the windshield wipers on this one didn't work, making it almost impossible to see. The driver and another vehicle collided, throwing Marilyn against the front seat so hard she injured her shoulder and leg. The police came and whisked her off to the airport so she wouldn't miss her plane. Chinese hospitality gone astray. Marilyn was more worried about her hosts than her injuries.

#   #   #

The Chinese are an enormously idealistic people. I have begun to see how that enables them to endure terrible hardships. Idealism is sometimes a form of escapism, an excuse for inexcusable behavior.

#   #   #

The Chinese seem to devote considerable energy to construction, and I wonder to what end. It's as if only tangible signs of progress are acceptable. A brick enclosure is going up in the deer park at the *Youyi*. It will confine the animals to a very small area, and I pity the poor deer. Trees are being dug up along the Third Ring Road in anticipation of improvements. The *Youyi* is a perpetual beehive of construction activity—around the new Friendship Palace, on the rotary next to Building #1, near the post office.

#   #   #

An Embassy friend told us a funny story about the Vietnam war. Firmly against it, he said he had voted for Richard Nixon after a friend sent him a scholarly article indicating that Nixon wanted the U.S. to withdraw from Vietnam.

Later he was serving in the military and blowing up enemy pipelines in Cambodia, when his squad was nearly ambushed by an enemy patrol. When they dropped under a bush to catch their breaths, he muttered to one of the enlisted men, "You know, I voted for that guy."

"Who?" a soldier asked.

"President Nixon. He was supposed to get us out of here."

230

"But he did, sir," the soldier answered. "We're in Cambodia."

\# \# \#

Our Fulbright friend Eldon Elder says two of his colleagues spend most their time in south China, where they're building a Disney World-style amusement park. Maybe that's why they wanted a foreigner at the Academy of Dramatic Arts—to teach their courses for them.

\# \# \#

My colleague John Morgan and I took our lunch-hour walk over to the canal west of the school today. This time there was water in it, and the wind wasn't blowing at gale force, the way it did last time we took a walk. A man on a bicycle wagon wheeled by. It was loaded with strings of garlic, and I wished I had bought some. On our way back, we walked past a noodle factory. The noodles were hung out to dry on lines like wet laundry.

\# \# \#

I would love to see spring come to Beijing. I remember how the gingko trees with their fan-shaped leaves turned yellow in October. When we returned from one of our trips, they had all fallen to the ground. I remember the grass in the courtyard of our apartment building that grew so long it looked like a field of scallions. I remember the first and only real snowfall and how pretty the apartment building looked, with its gaily painted arcade and gate. I wonder what memories spring would bring if we were here for it.

\# \# \#

Translation of a Li Bai poem we bought a calligraphy version of in Wuhan:

LEAVING THE WHITE KING CITY IN EARLY MORNING

In the early morning I left White City in colored cloud.
In a thousand miles I returned to Jiaoling in a day.
On both cliffs of the Three Gorges I can see monkeys cry
    ceaselessly
While my light boat passed through 10,000 ranges.

\# \# \#

231

The International Herald Tribune is our connection to the outside world. Compact and well edited, it culls the most important international news from a variety of sources, including the New York Times, the Washington Post, and the Los Angeles Times. We look forward to reading it every day.

One night when I was coming back from buying it at the newsstand in Building #1, I came up behind a man who had lights on his shoes. I didn't believe it at first, but each time his heel hit the ground, a little red light on the back of it glowed.

#   #   #

What did I see today? Blue sky. Beijing's sky is perpetually blue. The weather was warmish for January. I have learned the route most taxis take downtown to Changan Ji, the main east-west drag. Naming the streets is my way of making them familiar. I like the music of the names. Up to Beisanhuan, right turn down Gulouwai to Andingmen and around the rotary at Changan back to Yabaolu. Past Ritan Park.

Going back the sound of the street names makes a different kind of music. Up Andingmen farther to Xitucheng, then left onto Xueyuan and over to Beisanhuan. I remember the landmarks—intersections, buildings, canals, even fences and bushes. Above them all, blue sky.

#   #   #

Here's a potpourri of "Chinglish" sign gems:

The manager has personally passed the water for your protection.

Please take advantage of the maids.

Welcome to the Square where famous leaders and generals are buried every Tuesday and Thursday.

Leave your clothes with us and have a good time.

Because of the impropriety of entertaining members of the opposite sex in your rooms, please do it in the lobby.

Doctors specializing in women and other diseases.

Please leave your valuables on the counter.

Look-see. You might find yourself laughable.

#   #   #

232

When interviewing American journalists based in Beijing, I most often met them in their homes or offices. That humanizing environment provided snapshots of their personalities and lives.

Sandy Hendry, the Glasgow-born correspondent for the Journal of Commerce and at 25 the youngest of those I talked to, lived with his Polish wife in a high-ceilinged, first-floor apartment. Like any young married couple's first home, it was decorated with a few framed posters, a modern desk and a black, beanbag-style vinyl chair.

ABC correspondent Deborah Wang's apartment could have been transported by cargo container directly from New York. It had a big, modern kitchen and ultra-stylish, white furniture in the living room, dining room and study. Deborah had spread her own Afghani rugs over the wall-to-wall carpeting to liven the place up a little.

Time Magazine Bureau Chief Jaime FlorCruz's office was a homey place with lots of bookcases. Two giant oil portraits of Mao hung on the walls, along with a series of framed Time covers on China.

The New York Times office of Patrick Tyler was like another replica of the Big Apple. American magazines decorated one bookshelf, along with the New York Times Book Review. We sat in chic-looking, vaguely Oriental wooden chairs, and by the second hour of the interview, they became distinctly uncomfortable. A humidifier pumped steam into the room in an effort to combat Beijing's dry air.

Christian Science Monitor correspondent Sheila Tefft had a big, sunny office with a solarium that seemed to reflect her friendly, Midwestern background. We sat on a dark blue corduroy sofa opposite her desk. The wall to our right was a solid bank of white bookcases filled with newspapers and the paraphernalia of the working journalist.

#   #   #

BEIJING NIGHT

Slipping into the blackness of a Beijing evening—
Frigid, still—
I find myself at home in so much intimacy
Of sky, moon
Sliced thin and fields of slender, white clouds.

Under nighttime's cozy mask I am free to wander
Where I like,
Impervious to the season's Siberian chill,
Past Asian
Arches, treed Soviet-style blocks.

Musicians jam inside, and Chinese tennis players
Smack icy
Balls through artificial light. Breadloaf taxis cruise past
Seeking fares,
Heedless and too eager for escape.